THE ONE-EYED DRAGON

£2-00

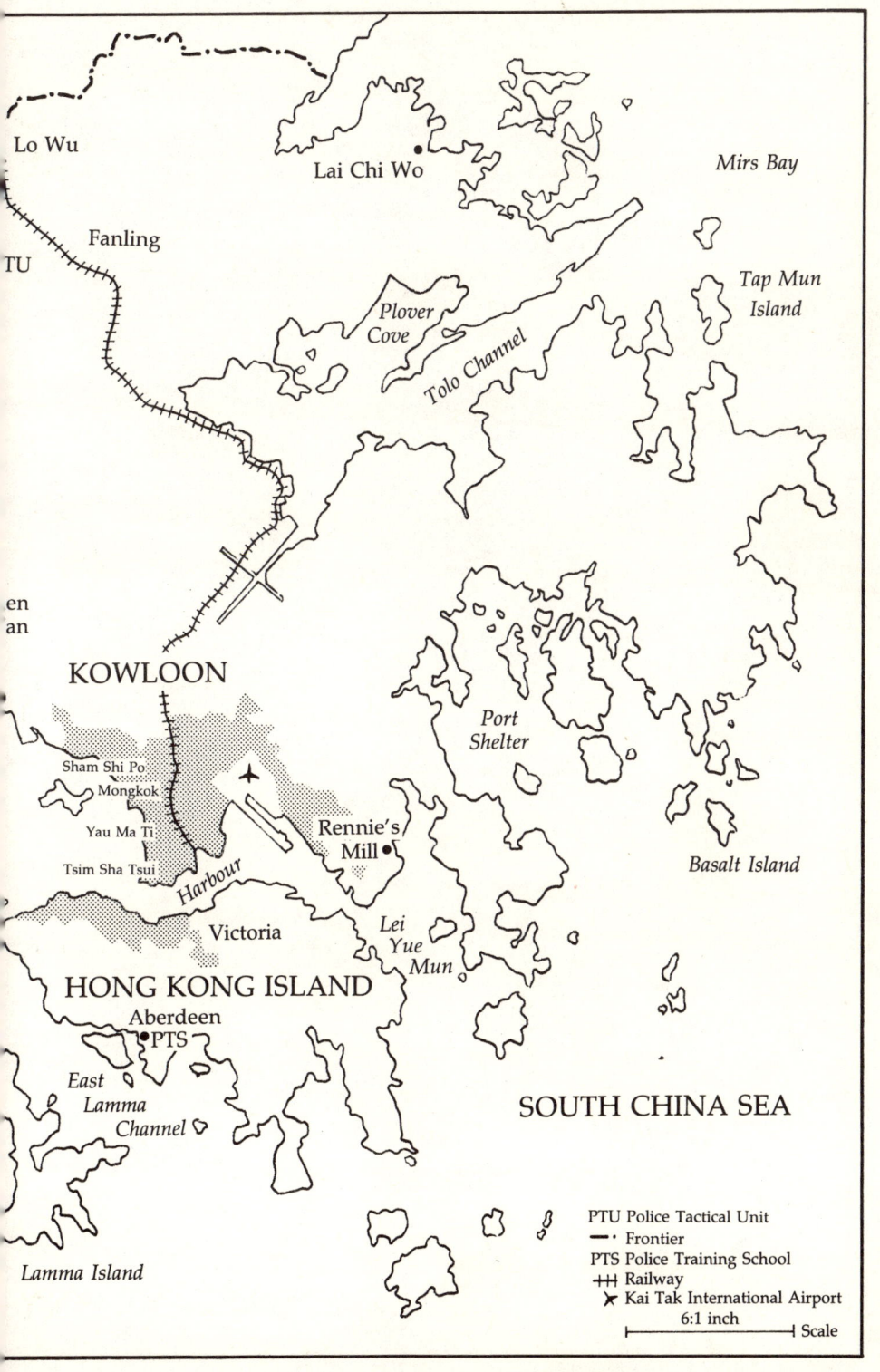

Lo Wu

Mirs Bay

Lai Chi Wo

Fanling

TU

Tap Mun
Island

Plover
Cove

Tolo Channel

en
an

KOWLOON

Port
Shelter

Sham Shi Po
Mongkok

Yau Ma Ti

Rennie's
Mill

Tsim Sha Tsui

Basalt Island

Harbour

Victoria

Lei
Yue
Mun

HONG KONG ISLAND

Aberdeen
PTS

SOUTH CHINA SEA

East
Lamma
Channel

Lamma Island

PTU Police Tactical Unit
—· Frontier
PTS Police Training School
+++ Railway
✗ Kai Tak International Airport
6:1 inch
Scale

THE ONE-EYED DRAGON

THE INSIDE STORY
OF A HONG KONG POLICEMAN

Anthony Annieson

LOCHAR PUBLISHING   MOFFAT · SCOTLAND

© Anthony Annieson, 1989

Published by Lochar Publishing Ltd
No 8, The Holm
MOFFAT DG10 9JU
Tel: 0683 20916

British Library Cataloguing in Publication Data
Annieson, Anthony, 1931–
    The one-eyed dragon: the inside story of a Hong
    Kong policeman.
    1. Hong Kong. Police. Blaze-Gosden, Tony
    Rn: Tony Blaze-Gosden I. Title
    363.2'092'4

    ISBN 0-948403-19-5

Jacket photographs of Hong Kong courtesy of the Hong Kong Tourist Authority.

Front insert photograph, Associated Press.

Typeset in 10 on 12½pt Palatino by Hewer Text, Edinburgh and printed in Great Britain by BPCC Wheaton's Limited, Exeter.

CONTENTS

Dedicated to
Charles NG Chuen-chung
CPM Royal Hong Kong Police Force
and all my splendid Chinese colleagues
with whom I had the honour to work in the RHKP.

ACKNOWLEDGMENTS

This book might not have been written, and certainly could not have been written in time, without the help of my wife Barbara, who not only helped me to structure it, but also filled in the gaps in my eclectic punctuation from her bucket of spare commas!

To Rosie and Rob, many thanks for their moral support through the 'boggy' patches!

Mr Alan Castro, the highly-respected former Editor-in-Chief of the *Hongkong Standard* Newspaper Group, for all his help both now, and in the past.

Mr Mike Parry and Mr John Knight of the Disablement Advisory Service, Department of Employment, Swansea, with my gratitude for the equipment and computer training, by means of which this book was written.

PREFACE

This book is about the British Colony of Hong Kong, once crudely described as an Imperial pimple on an Asian elephant's bum!

From the time it was first occupied by the British, Hong Kong has been a place to wonder at, a place of incredible extremes in everything from the ferocity of its occasional 140 mile per hour typhoons, to the incredible beauty of its women folk, the staggering capacity of its people for hard work, the extreme poverty of many of its refugee population, and its amazing ability to create wealth. A place where truth has always been stranger than fiction and where frequently what was regarded as fiction, even slander, turned out to be the truth! It may be that full justice will only be done to the Hong Kong story, some time in the future, in a work of fiction!

The world at large has long seen Hong Kong as an exotic oriental trading post, full of glamour, intrigue, espionage, shady dealings, sex, drugs, corruption, and money making – with money to the forefront. All this may be true, to some degree, but Hong Kong's greatest enthusiasm is possibly reserved for gossip, preferably over a gambling table, or a mahjong game. Gossip lubricates Hong Kong's social wheels, in all classes of society.

This book contains quite a lot of gossip in addition to many facts, speculation, and much thinking aloud. It has a brief history of China explaining the events that led to the creation of Hong Kong as it is now. This is followed by a condensed record of my own eighteen years of experience as an officer in the Royal Hong Kong Police Force. Much has had to be written from memory, and the memories of friends. The reason for this is that on my retirement from the Hong Kong Police, almost all of my diaries, personal papers, and some photographs, were removed by persons unknown from the sealed Customs container in which my personal effects were being sent home. Nothing else was taken although there were valuables. When the container arrived in the UK the seals were still intact! So basically this is a book of yarns, gossip and true stories, as well as some that should be true. No apology is offered for my obvious respect, admiration and affection for my Chinese colleagues in the police force, especially the remarkable Charles NG Chueng-chung, to whom the book is dedicated. Without his quiet courage in the face of danger I seriously doubt that I would be alive today. It is an old Chinese belief that if you save another person's life you become responsible for them, like a brother. I can think of no finer brother for any man to have, than Charles NG, worthy holder of the Colonial Police Medal.

The concluding chapter contains my personal views on the topic of Hong Kong's possible future following its surrender to Chinese control on the 7 June 1997. The great majority of the Hong Kong Chinese are, in my opinion, the most hard-working, likeable, intelligent, shrewd, entrepreneurial, innovative, boisterous, fun-loving, family-loving, good-food-loving, gambling people in the world. They should be declared a 'major human asset of planet Earth' by the world community, and should be at least as well protected from exploitation and cruelty as pandas, whales, or Birds of Paradise! The Hong Kong Chinese people are the basic magic of Hong Kong with the striking scenery and exotic atmosphere of the Colony just a magnificent backdrop. If you are able to do so, go and meet them now, before 7 June 1997.

This book barely scratches the surface of Hong Kong life, and is just a peep through a crack in the lid of an oriental Pandora's box!

Anthony Annieson
7 June 1989

One

A QUICK TAKE-AWAY HISTORY

Mention China and the Chinese to most modern people and the majority tend to think of three things: Chinese take-aways, Chinese restaurants, and China tea! If pushed, they may mention the Chinese birth-rate, the size of China's population, and the sayings of Confucius as misquoted in fortune cookies. When China's fascinating history is considered, it is amazing how little factual information is known about this hugely important country outside its own frontiers. Historical religious bias, Imperialism, racism, exploitation, even comedians, have all combined in the past in a spontaneous conspiracy to make the Chinese figures of fun or mockery, stereotyped in books and movies as frightened pig-tailed cooks or laundrymen saying 'Me no likee', or as sinister Fu Manchus, or as the homespun American Chinese detective Charlie Chan with his endless regiment of numbered sons. At least, this was so until the Korean War and China's participation in it as an ally of North Korea. It is strange that Europeans, and people of European descent, generally do not seem to respect or take foreigners seriously until they have spilled much blood fighting each other on a battlefield. Everyone has taken the Chinese seriously since Korea, even the Russians! The Russians take them so seriously that they have maintained a minimum of forty three military divisions, approximately 1 000 000 or more men, on their common frontier since the ideological split between Beijing and Moscow in 1961.

The history of China is part of the history of Hong Kong, as the story of Hong Kong is an integral part of the history of China. How strange it is to think that the China of today might not exist if upper class Europeans had not acquired a taste for tea and if the Hong Kong entrepôt had not been created by the entrepreneurial spirit of a pair of Scottish opium-traffickers, Messrs Jardine and Matheson!

For the Chinese take-away school of history, it is almost quirkily appropriate that one of the earliest known man-made objects found by archaeologists is a Chinese chopper made of hornstone; found near Beijing in red clay deposits dating back in time some 500 000 years. The origins of the Chinese people are not certain but it is generally believed that they may have evolved from many different ethnic groups and from many scattered centres of primitive culture. It is believed that the earliest Chinese civilisation, the oldest in the world, began in the region of the Yellow River valley some 2200 years BC, where the almost legendary Sage Kings are credited with the development of agriculture, medicine, and river conservancy. Next came the Shang Dynasty, from about 1766 BC to 1123 BC, during which civilisation spread out from the Yellow River to the north and south. From this time dynasty succeeded dynasty for more than 2800 years with ever-spreading civilisation, centralisation in government, and advances in agriculture and technology. This civilising progression was interrupted only briefly, in the Chinese time scale, by some 300 years of Dark Ages and approximately eighty-eight years of Mongol rule. It may be that it was originally from memories of those times of disruption and chaos that came the Chinese curse 'May your children live in interesting times'!

The event that was most drastically to influence China's future history was the edict issued by the Manchu Emperor Kang Hsi in 1685, opening the ports of China to foreign ships and foreign traders, exposing his previously exclusive Chinese Empire to foreign influences and exploitation, and at the same time laying the foundations of the eventual destruction of his Ching dynasty. The Emperor reigned at the same time as King Charles II of England, Czar Peter the Great of Russia, and King Louis XIV of France, and of the four of them the Emperor was by far the most enlightened in his administrative and social policies. However, in this one foreign and economic policy decision he displayed all the flair and good judgment of the man who paid extra for the last ticket available for the first voyage of the Titanic! Kang Hsi was not to know that thirteen years after issuing his edict on trade, an English trading ship would arrive in China that would start the countdown to the destruction of China's distinctive civilisation and the eventual triumph of European Marxist 'civilisation' in his country.

In 1699 the East India Company ship *Macclesfield* made a voyage to China that proved so immensely profitable it was repeated annually. The *Macclesfield* delivered Chinese silk, tea, porcelain, and bric-à–brac, to a European market that had developed an insatiable demand for these unique Chinese products. It was unfortunate for the Chinese that they had little taste or desire for European goods and they demanded payment in silver for their products. As a result, an adverse balance of payments was soon established in China's favour, the East

Not a job for small boys! The Emergency Unit with a 'model' prisoner.

The Hongkong Standard

Top. Kai Tak main runway in 1956, Hong Kong island in the background.
Above left. Western district waterfront – domain of the dockside coolie.
Above right. A quiet day on Shanghai Street.

India Company and the Indian Government suffering a trade deficit. They were saved financially by a totally unpredictable Chinese taste developed from a curious Dutch East Indies social habit!

Early in the seventeenth century, Dutchmen in the trading areas in Java began taking a pinch of opium in their pipes of tobacco to induce a mild feeling of euphoria as they drank their evening gin after a hard day's trading. This habit was noted and copied by Chinese traders who did not care for Dutch gin. Unexpectedly, the Chinese rapidly developed a need for ever greater quantities of opium. They began progressively reducing the quantity of tobacco in their pipes and increasing the amount of opium, until finally the tobacco was dispensed with and only pure opium was smoked in pipes modified for that purpose. The introduction of opium smoking to China bears a strange similarity to the introduction of cocaine, heroin, and other drugs into modern societies. The Chinese traders were the historical equivalent of the pop and film stars of today, and were similarly regarded with some suspicion by the 'Establishment' of the time in China. They made lots of money, and led lives that were glamorous and interesting in comparison with most of their hard-working, conventional, stay-at-home contemporaries. They were also freed from the normally accepted decencies and social constraints of Chinese civilisation by being abroad in the company of 'foreign devils' and 'barbarians', able to indulge in any new vices and perversions that might catch their attention and, as with their modern counterparts, there were always people available who were ready to sell them whatever they wanted for a profit. The train to Hell always has legions of volunteer ticket sellers!

No one can say with certainty when opium smoking was introduced to China. but what is known is that the habit quickly changed from being an indulgence of the rich and spread widely through the lower and poorer classes to the great joy of the European traders, especially the East India Company as the Company controlled India, where the best opium was grown.

The directors and shareholders of the company plundered China, through the sale of opium, until the British Government wound it up in 1813 – and promptly took over its monopoly in India! Within twenty-four years, by 1837, half of China's total government revenue, $20 000 000, in silver was going to pay for opium, mainly to British traders, and to the profit of the British and British Indian governments. In 1840 it was revealed in the British Parliament that one sixth, 16.7 per cent, of all the public revenues of Britain and

India taken together, came from opium profits and tea tax! The modern equivalent would be approximately £25.5 billion! The glory of the Victorian Empire was founded to a great extent on the bones of Chinese peasants addicted to British opium. It is hardly surprising that the British were prepared to fight two Opium Wars to keep the drug trade going; whereas the Chinese Emperor tried to stop the trade which was bankrupting China, causing civil disorder, mass starvation, and much misery. It was during the first Opium War that Hong Kong became *de facto* British territory when the British Union Flag was hoisted at Possession Point on Hong Kong Island on the 26 January 1841. Possession was legalised by the cession of Hong Kong to the British Crown, which was confirmed by the Treaty of Nanking in 1842. Later, in 1860, the Convention of Peking also ceded Kowloon and Stonecutters Island in Hong Kong harbour, to the British Crown.

It was all rather similar to the situation portrayed in a type of western movie made in Hollywood in 1930s and 1940s, where a heavily-armed squatter gang would take possession of somebody else's range and start exploiting the neighbourhood until brought to justice by a band of good and honest men driven to take up arms to right the wrongs being done. In the case of Hong Kong the script would have to have been altered to show the squatters being presented with the freehold rights to all they had taken plus a licence to exploit at will!

Until it became part of the British Empire, Hong Kong and its more than 200 islands had been nothing but a nest of pirates who preyed on ships making coastal passages, and small villages of farmers and fishermen near the coast. They were infamous for their greed and liking for rape; and only remained at large because the Manchu Emperors had no unified navy to deal with them. It has been claimed that there was, at one time, a woman pirate captain who operated with particular efficiency and discipline from Lantao island achieving much notoriety at the Imperial Court. So much was she admired for her organisational and maritime skills that she was offered an Imperial pardon for her, and her gang, if she would accept the rank of Admiral and the duty to clean up the pirates in the Pearl River Estuary and the islands of Hong Kong. Legend has it that she not only accepted, but also succeeded in driving out the pirates, then followed this up with making a good marriage to a high official by whom she had many healthy children. True or not, it makes a thundering good yarn and boat people were still telling it only twenty years ago!

The pirates were never fully wiped out and many continue with opportunist piracies to this day. There have always been pirates all along China's coast from Hainan island in the south-west to Manchuria in the north-east. They preyed on any vessel that seemed easy pickings, and they were able to hide from retribution almost anywhere along China's thousands of miles of deeply indented coastline. Between piracies they could easily become seemingly innocent fishermen or traders. The British spent many years attempting to suppress piracy in the South China Sea after taking possession of the Colony. Mirs Bay and Bias Bay to the east of Hong Kong were favourite places for pirates to lie in wait for ships, and they attacked merchant ships with ferocious enthusiasm gaining rich prizes. The merchants of Hong Kong were always ready to tolerate Chinese killing, looting, and raping other Chinese, but they would never permit any threat to their profits. As a consequence the Royal Navy began a series of campaigns against pirates that continued intermittently until modern times. In the ten-year period from 1848 to 1858, the Navy sank more than 200 pirate junks, killed hundreds of pirates, and seized thousands of prisoners many of whom were ceremoniously hanged after proper legal, if peremptory, trials. British warships diligently hunted out pirate settlements and made amphibious assaults upon them levelling them to the ground and seizing the inhabitants. It had little effect in the long run: pirates are like Dragons' Teeth, plant a few of them in the ground, by judicial process, and a dozen will spring up for each one buried! Chinese pirates were still actively plundering cargo and passenger ships in the South China Sea in the years between the two World Wars, frequently taking them to Bias Bay to await the arrival of ransoms for the passengers.

The early years of Hong Kong as a British Colony were packed with major events, both natural and man-made. As the Colony became established and developed services for shipping, in addition to its import and export trade, the world came to do business. The very fact that it had a British administration, and matters were dealt with under laws and business practices understood by Europeans, made it more attractive to some than various other ports in China. An added boost came with the discovery of gold in Australia and California. Chinese coolies were cheaper than any other workers and could be taken on as indentured labourers with no rights to protect themselves from exploitation. An added attraction of the coolies, in contrast to workers of European origin, was that when they had finished their job, or had become unfit for further work, they could be ordered out the country.

It says much for the ingenuity of the coolies that so many of them managed to remain in America, send back to China for wives, and establish their own dynasties in their new land, based on sheer hard work and enterprise. Even at its worst, life in America was far better than anything on offer in China. Even today the Chinese colloquial name for The United States is 'Gum Saan', 'Gold Mountain'!

The development of dockyards and high standards of shipbuilding, refitting, and repair brought more and more business into Hong Kong harbour. Associated services, supplying ships with all they required, built up a ships' chandlery market unrivalled anywhere outside Europe or America. The prosperity of the Colony basically depended on the number of ships that used the harbour and the various services on offer, and year after year the tonnage of shipping entering port increased. By 1850 the tonnage of ships using the harbour had increased more than a thousand per cent. Even whalers and seal hunters began to call in transit between hunting grounds.

The energetic efforts of the Scots Jardine and Matheson had a major effect on the prosperity of Hong Kong. The creation of their 'Dai Hong', the 'Great Houses or Businesses', by the 'Taipans', the 'Great Ones', rich and powerful men of trade, and the rapid diversification of their business interests helped materially to establish the credentials of Hong Kong as a growing place to be taken seriously and not just dismissed, as it was in some British circles, as a 'barren rock full of, plague, scandal, or controversy'. The story of these two energetic and imaginative Scotsmen, plus a cast of millions of Chinese, is in effect, the story of Hong Kong.

Hong Kong's 'Dragons of the Apocalypse' have always been typhoons, plague, cholera, fire, and floods of refugees from China whenever rebellion or strife wracked that troubled land. The Tai Ping Rebellion against the Manchus established a pattern in 1850 that has been repeated up to the present day. Thousands of Chinese fled into the Colony to escape the fighting and the savage repression that followed the defeat of the rebels. Many of them stayed behind when things had calmed down and created the beginnings of a permanently resident population who, for 149 years, have preferred British colonial administration, with all its faults, to anything else on offer.

By the end of the nineteenth century the population had grown to more than 150 000 people all crowded together in squalid conditions in an area of approximately forty square miles. For this reason, and also for reasons of defence, on 1 July 1898, the British negotiated a ninety-nine year lease of the New Territories including some 250 nearby islands, increasing the Colony's land area by 365.5 square miles and extending its frontier from Boundary Street in Kowloon to the south bank of the Shum Chun river about twenty-one miles to the north.

It is always a matter of interest, and sometimes ribald mirth, to ordinary people when experts make mistakes. The greater the number of experts involved the greater the public hilarity caused when they slip up. The negotiations for the lease of the New Territories were conducted at a time of great international rivalry between foreign powers seeking concessions and influence in China and involved a cast of thousands in delicate international diplomacy. Queen Victoria and the Crowned Heads of Europe, the Presidents of America and France, and the Emperor of Japan, their courtiers, diplomats, bureau-crats, civil and military advisers, surveyors, engineers, geographers, and scores of unknown experts, considered, pondered, and advised, on the international, political implications of the transfer, to British control, of a bit of southern Kwangdung Province barely half the size of London. After all this, and only after the leasing negotiations had been publicly concluded, did it become apparent that the world's greatest experts in everything had missed a bit. The diplomatic elephant had laboured mightily – and laid an egg!

It was a tiny eight acre scrap of land on the border between Kowloon and the New Territories, later to become infamous as Kowloon Walled City! This eight acres has remained as a legal 'black hole' ever since, owing to doubts about sovereignty and, therefore, a source of much malicious comfort to all laymen subject to haughty condescension from 'experts'.

As the nineteenth century drew to a close, China was still a land of turmoil, and the Boxer Rebellion sent, ever more, refugees flocking over the Hong Kong Frontier. Plague struck and killed 8000 people. Even after the discovery that the rat flea carried the plague and the adoption of public health measures to combat it, other serious diseases remained. Tuberculosis, malaria, and cholera were still tak-ing a dreadful toll in human life up until thirty years ago. Typhoons wreaked havoc. One of the worst on record struck with particular ferocity in September 1906, killing 10 000 or more, Chinese and fifteen Europeans. Fifty-nine merchant ships were severely damaged and over 2500 Chinese vessels were wrecked and sunk.

The history of Imperial China came to an end in 1911, the same year the British government stopped the importation of opium into the country. Revolution ended the Manchus' two centuries of occupation of China after their conquest of the country in the seventeenth century. This revolution came as no great surprise to western observers who had watched China suffer in turmoil under the inept regency of the two and a half year old Emperor Pui-yee, nephew and only male heir of the late Emperor Kuang-hsu who died childless. But like so much else to do with China the successful revolution was different from all other revolutions of the era, it had not started over discontent at lack of constitutional reform, as reforms had begun in 1909. The spark that lit the revolutionary fires seems to have been the Peking government's attempt to make a cheap takeover of a locally owned branch railway line in Szechwan, upon which construction had barely begun. The stockholders were furious at the low price offered and their dissatisfaction erupted into open revolt in September 1911. By coincidence, a mutiny broke out among troops in Wu-chang about ten days later, on 10 October, and this is regarded as the 'formal' beginning of the revolution. The date 10 of October has been China's National Day ever since. Angry stock- and shareholders have brought down incompetent company chairmen and directors on many occasions, but those in the Szechwan Railway Company appear to be the only ones who have brought down an Emperor, an aristocracy, a dynasty and a historically established system of government! This was, however, just the prologue to more long years of suffering and turmoil in China and more problems for Hong Kong.

From 1911 to the communist conquest of the mainland in 1949 Hong Kong's fortunes rose and fell in common with the rest of the world and particularly those of China. The transition to a Republic plunged China into one of the most awful periods of turmoil ever experienced in its llong history. Warlords, little more than uniformed bandits, flourished and claimed powers over great stretches of the country, and backed up their threats with bullets and brutality.

Piracy flourished along the whole oof China's 1200 mile long coastline. One ship was set on fire by pirates causing the deaths of more than 300 passengers. Bands of terrorising brigands roamed at will throughout southern China sometimes making excursions into the New Territories. Refugees poured into the colony in an unending stream. In the whole of China's vast area the rule of law, and true justice, could only be found in tiny Macao and its slightly larger neighbour, Hong Kong. Public works were created by the government in the great depression of the 1930s to help the Colony's people through terrible times.

The Japanese war with China beginning in 1937, sent ever more refugees into the Colony, more than half a million of them, to live in squalid refugee shacks, completely overloading the sanitation system and bringing a smallpox epidemic. The death rate from disease rose and rose, despite the best efforts of the over strained medical services and charities. Still the population rose until it exceeded 1 600 000 people.

The Japanese invaded in December 1941 and by massacre, mass murder, torture, rape followed by bayonetting, deliberate starvation of the people, mass drowning, using people for target practice, and the utmost inhumanity to man, left barely 600 000 gaunt starving survivors to greet Admiral Harcourt as the Royal Navy sailed into liberated Hong Kong on the last day of August 1945. Everyone in the world is constantly reminded of the Nazi genocide in Europe, down to the last detail, nobody seems to be particularly interested in the horrors perpetrated on the Hong Kong Chinese, but of course, they were not white were they? Much the same kind of thinking seems to have polluted the thinking of all parties in the modern British government as 1997 approaches.

Even 'Peace' in 1945 didn't bring Hong Kong much peace. Civil war raged in China between Nationalists and Communists sending ever more refugees into the Colony, and the communist victory brought no peace only more trouble. Nationalist ships fired on a small British trader, in June 1950, killing six passengers and wounding another six. The communists followed suit in August 1950 firing on three British and one American ship – merchant ships. In the middle of August a Royal Navy destroyer gave them a taste of their own medicine by firing on Communist gun batteries. They did not like that; they preferred unarmed merchant ships.

The Chinese Communists tried to create trouble among the thousands of refugees in the colony, and Communist agents fomented riots in the streets ostensibly on behalf of the refugees welfare. Duncan MacIntosh, the Scottish Commissioner of Police, and the best the Colony ever had, arranged with the Governor that every refugee in the Colony should be freely offered their full transportation costs, and ten Hong Kong dollars expenses, for each one of them, without limitation on numbers, who wished to return to China. Of the estimated nearly two million refugees in the Colony at the time, only one accepted the offer, an old man who was nearing death and wished to be buried in China with his ancestors!

This was typical of the canny common sense of Duncan MacIntosh, a man with a down-to-earth distaste for 'flannel'. When great problems were experienced on the frontier he demanded, and got, solid observation towers for his men, with internal armour plate to protect them. They were laughed at by the superior public school boys, and called 'MacIntosh's mushrooms' but none of his men were ever killed in them from enemy gunfire. The policemen who were later killed in a flimsy police post on the frontier, built after Duncan's time, might have lived had there been a little bit of armour inside the bricks! Years after he retired many Chinese people said he was a rough man to cross but a good practical policeman. . . but only the Chinese said it!

In July 1954 an unarmed, civilian, passenger aircraft, a C-54 Skymaster, was shot down into the sea without warning by three Communist Chinese Air Force fighter planes causing the deaths of ten of the people on board, including the Scottish Flight Engineer G W Cattanach. The aircraft was fifty miles off the coast of China, thirty-eight miles outside China's territorial waters when the attack occurred. No explanation for this grotesque murder of innocent people, flying in international air space. was ever given, although later, the Chinese government did pay out nearly six million Hong Kong dollars in compensation.

In April 1955 an Air India Lockheed Constellation, carrying among its passengers eight Communist Chinese delegates to the Afro-Asian conference in Bandung, suffered an air explosion as a bomb went off in the baggage compartment, as they approached Sarawak. The Indian pilot, Captain Jatar, landed the plane in the sea by superb skill and airmanship. Sixteen people including the brave Captain, and all the Communist delegates, died. The bomb had been placed on board by a Nationalist agent who had obtained a job with the aircraft cleaning and maintenance company in Kai Tak airport. The Hong Kong Police offered HK $100 000 reward for his capture but he had already escaped to Taiwan in another aircraft.

Hong Kong had, however, undergone a beneficial change in the period following the communist victory in China. The Korean War had begun in 1950 and China allied itself with the aggressor North Korea. As a result a UN embargo was imposed on China in May 1950. It was a disaster for Hong Kong, as a port dealing almost exclusively in goods going to and from its giant neighbour, but it was a blessing, by forcing Hong Kong to become an industrial producer. From such unlikely beginnings, Hong Kong, rapidly, became one of the world's most energetic and successful producer-countries and a place of, dizzying, financial wizardry, soon to be handed over to, politically backward, China.

Two

FIRST IMPRESSIONS

On first arriving in Hong Kong I knew as much about it, or as little, as any other Scotsman of my generation. Having served my King and, later, my Queen in much of Britain's dwindling Empire, I had learned that you could not judge any man by the colour of his skin or by what he said, only by his actions and the way he, consistently, conducted his life. My friendship and respect were reserved for people who ranged in colour from the almost blue-black of Sam in the West Indies, who taught me how to survive in the jungle, to the almost albino blond Pieter from Cape Province in South Africa, who taught me that former enemies could be good and honourable friends. But I knew nothing more about Hong Kong, and the Hong Kong Chinese people, than could be learned from reference books and a brief chat with a man at the Crown Agents in London.

My fellow passenger in the next seat on the BOAC Stratocruiser, to Hong Kong, was an Englishman, John Guy, ex-Royal Air Force, also on his way to join the Hong Kong Police and I was relieved to discover that his knowledge of the Colony and its people was as limited as mine. All, we thought, we knew was a garbled mixture of reference books heavily overlaid, with almost subliminal, memories of movies starring Charlie Chan, Sydney Greenstreet or Peter Lorre!

Our first, terrifying, oriental experience was, actually, landing on the old Kai Tak airport. The magnificent Kai Tak airport of today, with its nearly one-and-a-half mile long runway extending into Kowloon Bay, did not then exist. From the air, all that passengers could see in the approach run was a couple of tiny landing strips looking like match sticks lying in the bottom of a soup bowl, made of rock. The airport was hedged, around two thirds of its perimeter, by an arc of mountain peaks, the other third being the waters of Kowloon Bay. One strip extended into a main road, full of traffic, and the other, seemingly, into cliffs or the Bay! The, incredibly, skilled pilots would always try to land on their first approach as it was rumoured that many passengers would take just one look at where they were supposed to be landing, and either have heart attacks or, if Americans, demand to be taken back to Manila!

On our approach, it was apparent that the July winds were fickle and it took two tries to get the plane down. It was, finally, accomplished by the pilot skimming a mountain peak then, seemingly, stopping all four engines and letting the huge plane drop like a stone, until he was satisfied with his height. We were convinced we would just make a gigantic crater in the concrete, but the engines buzzed merrily again, and we touched down safely, several times, before staying down. The aircraft rumbled along the runway and I noticed John's jaw muscles tighten as he looked out of the window. Glancing out we could see that we seemed to be crossing a major road swarming with coolies carrying huge loads of vegetables in baskets hanging from bamboo poles. There were red and white striped barriers lowered across the road to control traffic, but the coolies just ducked under them, then under the aircraft's wings, and carried on happily down the road in both directions.

We turned round and trundled back, eventually, coming to a stop with the engines turned off. It was pleasing to note that everybody, including my new ex-RAF friend, looked as pale green as I felt. There was a hushed silence in the passenger compartment until the intercom clicked and the Captain told us we had arrived in Hong Kong, he hoped we had enjoyed the flight, and he wished all the Americans on board a 'Happy 4 July, we hope you have a nice Independence Day'! There was a wild burst of half-hysterical laughter from everybody, including the Americans who had probably forgotten what day it was during the landing.

On disembarking from the plane, we were taken to some run down utility buildings and huts, where we were met by an incredibly fit looking Welshman, Inspector Taff Lloyd, the PT Instructor from the Police Training School. He saw us through Immigration and Customs, then took us out to a car for the trip to Hong Kong Island.

It was a trip of dazzling and exotic contrasts. Kowloon's teeming streets, especially the main thoroughfare, Nathan Road, looking like a would-be Manhattan, caught up in the bamboo scaffolding web of an oriental time warp! As far as the eye could see, were Chinese traditional tenement buildings three, or more, storeys high, built of brick, stucco and wood. Their verandahs, some with awnings made of rain proofed oiled rice-paper, were crowded with boxes, unidentifiable goods, and people. Almost all of them held a variety of cages, some containing singing birds, others a small battery of hens, incongruous, in such an intensely urban setting. Now and then, the odd cockerel would let out a loud crow as if calling on its tightly packed owners to compare their own existence with the battery hens, who at least had some room to move. Each row of old houses looked like ancient teeth being extracted at random by cosmic dentists. There were buildings in the course of being demolished, by swarms of coolies, some empty gaps waiting to be filled, some with the roots of new construction visible, and others with the towering, alien, skyscrapers that now symbolise Hong Kong for foreigners.

The streets were densely packed with seemingly suicidal people doing body swerves, that would have done credit to the best of Spanish matadors, right under the vehicles' radiators. It was not suicide they were seeking, it was safety, as any ill-intentioned Dragons following behind them would be deflected from them and follow the car.

To reach the car ferry terminal we turned off the main road and plunged into Shanghai Street. Nathan Road had seemed busy, this was a chaos that had a strange discipline to it. More than anything, it resembled the bloodstream of a living creature as seen under a microscope. Clots of people and vehicles swirled and swerved, and avoided each other, whilst still flowing along an invisible base course to somewhere. Individuals, like independent protective micro-organisms, zig-zagged through mainstream flows, and disappeared to their target destinations. Rickshaws bearing humans and loads of goods, pulled by thin, sweating, rickshaw coolies with huge leg muscles, wearing sweat cloths, like identifying fraternity scarves, swerved and weaved their way, at a run, through almost stationary vehicles, signalling their presence, or displeasure, in verbal klaxon blasts of ripe Chiu Chow invective from the puller. The 400 and more goldsmiths shops lining the street, each with its own shotgun armed, turbanned, Sikh guard, gave a glittering medieval market flavour, to the journey, reinforced by the hundreds of bamboo poles filled with drying laundry protruding from overhead verandahs like the multi-coloured banners of ancient chivalry.

Colour and noise in stunning, dazzling, mind-altering, profusion. A parade of proof, in three miles of slow progress, that the arrogant statement 'All Chinese look alike,' is not just a lie, it is a stupid lie. China's wonderful mixture of races and racial groups was evident wherever the eye fleetingly rested. Tiny, full grown, men from south China, weighing no more than 110 pounds or so, jostled on the pavement with towering, broad-shouldered men from the north, six feet and more in height. The colour of skin, that, impenetrable 0.1 millimetre barrier, between races, ranged from dark walnut brown to a beautiful translucent white. Glimpses of eyes varying in shape from the heavy epicanthic folded slit of the northern deserts to the exotic almond shape of Soochow and the wide Slavic slant of eastern Europe. The only stereotypical sight was, almost universally, black hair, and that would only be commented on by pale, fair, people from northern latitudes.

Colour abounded, from the exuberant dazzle of 'lucky' red and gold, through the brilliantly aesthetic decoration of figure hugging Cheongsam silk, the black and white of amahs' uniforms, to the jet black of the common Chinese 'pongee' top and trousers.

Every group of shops had its unique identifying smell, leather, spices, Chinese wine, smoked and barbecued meats, candles, charcoal, fish, kerosene for cooking stoves, strong Chinese tobacco, silk carpets, a profusion of various perfumed teas, all blended together with the smell of people and an overloaded sewage system.

And the background, like a modern symphony of discordant yet organised noise under the baton of a titanic conductor, noise of traffic, noise of people, noise of construction sites, and the noise of movement everywhere, ceaseless movement.

In the car-ferry to Hong Kong Island we stood on deck, smoking, and looking about us, even Taff LLoyd, who had seen it a hundred times. From the harbour the sheer unlikeliness of the development of Hong Kong, from pirates' haunt to one of the world's greatest entrepôts, was starkly evident. Out of the Colony's 398.25 square miles barely one eighth, fifty square miles, could be used for agriculture in acid, unfertile soil, only 12 square miles was available for house construction, and the remainder was mountainous, rocky scrub land. The 3.75 square miles of Kowloon, through which we had just driven, was the largest area of flat land in the colony. The 29 square miles of Hong Kong Island ahead of us reflected in miniature the physical nature of the whole Colony. The capital, Victoria, situated at the foot of the 1800 feet high Victoria Peak, with a narrow strip of residential and business development spreading away to east and west on the harbour boundary. The whole of Wanchai built on reclaimed land. Houses creeping up the mountain sides, in search of living space, clinging to the easily friable soil with deep foundations. The tall towers of the Hong Kong and Shanghai Banking Corporation and the Bank of China in Central District, barely a hundred yards from the harbour side, the source of their great wealth, visible evidence of the uneasy marriage of convenience between socialist East and capitalist West brought about by simple economics.

The scene in the harbour itself was a maritime rerun of Shanghai Street. Fleets of sailing junks, most of them with sails seemingly made of holes loosely joined by strips of patched and tattered canvas, wallowing by, through flotillas of small power boats darting to and fro like pond skaters on a village pond. Merchant ships of the world, from small Pacific Island traders in need of paint to the glittering liners of Peninsular and Oriental (P&O) with their cargoes of wealth, some lying secured to buoys and surrounded by cargo junks being loaded and unloaded by strings of sure-footed coolies, others lying in privilege alongside piers with famous company names Alfred Holt, Blue Funnel, Ben Line, Jardine Matheson. Hong Kong Harbour was, and is, the most fascinating and colourful harbour on this planet.

We disembarked into Connaught Road in Victoria and headed into the Western District at a snail's pace in heavy traffic. Different from, yet similar to, Shanghai Street, in the overriding limitations to haste imposed by the press of people. The traffic speed was dictated by hundreds of sweating coolies loading and unloading cargo from junks. We looked with unbelieving eyes as a full-sized, Steinway, grand piano moved briskly down the pavement in a vertical position, seemingly self-propelled. Closer inspection revealed two pairs of feet, belonging to the carrying coolies, underneath. We entered an area of heart-stopping stench, strong enough to make the eyes water and the stomach heave. In response to our agonised request to tell us what the hell the stink was, Taff replied casually that we were in the street of dried fish merchants, and pointed out the dozens of shops displaying what looked like ovals of drying cardboard, Chinese dried fish. We were glad to get clear of the town and into Pokfulam Road leading from Hong Kong University to Aberdeen and the Training School. The contrast between the town areas and the countryside so close nearby was startling and memorable.

Obviously expensive single houses and three-floor high blocks of six luxurious flats could only be glimpsed, in passing, through gaps in their plant and shrub screens. Contented looking Friesian dairy cattle in the fields of the Dairy Farm Company, stood chewing cud and watching working water buffaloes below with the seeming casual superiority of the pampered over the worker.

Aberdeen was approached with a swoop down a hill, passing the dock built by early Scottish entrepreneurs, who found its native name of Heung Kong Tsai too difficult and named it after the Scottish Granite City. No greater contrast could exist than that between the cool northern discipline of busy Aberdeen in Scotland and the hot, steamy, bustle of Aberdeen in Hong Kong. The Far Eastern town was fish and fishing in all its guises, from catching it to cooking it, even exporting it to America. The harbour, sheltered from typhoons by Ap Lei Chau Island, served the needs of the colony's more than 8000 fishing vessels ranging from tiny one man prawning boats to huge ocean going fishing vessels. Everything that could be trapped, netted, or caught by long line, would end up on the auction blocks of the non-profit making Government Fish Marketing Organisation. Except for the big, sad-looking, sea turtles, which were sold to the Buddhists, who, after painting prayers on their shells, released them back into the sea. The crowded harbour had permanently anchored floating restaurants of various sizes, some like small junks, catering for a handful of customers to the huge two storey Tai Pak decorated in exuberant Chinese style even to the big, curling, dragon excluders on her roof points, able to furnish banquets for hundreds. All selling every variety of fish dishes known to mankind.

We could see that the harbour was so full of junks that they formed a pontoon causeway almost to Ap Lei Chau as we drove on to Wong Chuk Hang. We turned off the main road and dived down a side track well populated with pigs, chickens, and bare-bummed Chinese children. John and I looked thoughtfully at each other, it certainly did not look like the approach to any Training establishment we knew, neither HMS Ganges, nor RAF Cranwell, but it was a good introduction to one of the basic Chinese facts of life in Hong Kong, in life as in good cooking, sweet and sour always go together. We approached a gate where an immaculate sentry nearly blinded us with the reflection of the sun from his brilliantly polished boots as he leaped to attention and saluted. We had arrived.

Three

EARLY DAYS . . .
AND FIRST LUMPS!

In the 1950s the Hong Kong Police Training School did not look quite as grand as its name suggests. Before the Second World War it had been a collection of godowns (warehouses) used for the storage of rice. During the war it had gained an infamous and much feared name as a place of detention and torture by the Japanese secret police, the Kempetai. The godowns were also used as places of detention for many thousands of Chinese who were reputedly murdered by the Japanese by being loaded into old junks and secured down below with sealed hatches. The junks were then towed out to sea and sunk, drowning their hapless passengers. Few ever managed to escape from the sinking ships but those who did make it to the surface were used as targets by Japanese military personnel and shot dead. It is hardly surprising that the School was reputed to be heavily haunted by the spirits of these victims of Japanese genocide.

The Training School which was commanded by a Scotsman, Superintendent Bill Todd, was situated at Wong Chuk Hang on the outskirts of Hong Kong's major fishing port of Aberdeen and separated from the town by an odoriferous sea inlet named Staunton Creek which was full of Chinese refugee squatters in sampans, small junks, and numerous strange wooden structures which seemed to float. Wong Chuk Hang village a few hundred yards down the road, had a population of sturdy, pro-Communist, pig farmers who probably bred more pigs per square foot than any other pig breeders anywhere in the world. The pigs were traditional Chinese black pigs, perpetually escorted by squadrons of buzzing flies as they majestically trundled their pot bellies along the ground peering short-sightedly from under their huge floppy ears as they searched for tit-bits, happiest when rooting with their retroussé snouts for secret delicacies in any available filth, and always stinking to high heaven. To sit in a lecture room or stand on the parade ground in the hot season, could have qualified in America, or any other civilised country, as cruel and unusual punishment. The hot, heavy, steamily humid, summer air always carried a powerful blend of pigs and fish and, if the tide

27

was out, a horrific overlay of stinking creek mud mixed with the domestic sewage of the squatters strong enough to stun a polecat. Surprisingly, it only took a day or so to become so accustomed to the smell that it passed unnoticed, although an American friend reckoned that even the skunks from his home State would have declared the Police Training School a no-go area in summer!

The accommodation provided for the trainees was built in accordance with the basic British philosophy that it would be morally corrupting, bad for discipline, inducive of hedonism, a waste of public money, and possibly cause the collapse of the remainder of the Empire, to give recruits anything but the most Spartan of shelters in which to survive their months of training. After all, they might quit, or die, half way through. Besides, many of the senior British officials in Hong Kong had spent their early childhood and adolescence in the tender care of the British Public School system, an experience that had provided them with the survival characteristics of Hottentots and Eskimos, the digestive systems of ostriches, the cunning of horse dealers, the money sense of Mafia loan sharks, and, reputedly, peculiar ideas about sex. What had been bad enough for them was good enough for recruit police officers.

The police constables were housed in dormitories, while the officers, probationary sub-inspectors, shared dormitory type rooms. The general construction of the accommodation was to an old, much cherished, Imperial recipe that guaranteed maximum noise, dust, heat in summer and cold in winter, plus free access for meals to every blood-sucking biting insect in China. Presumably in the interests of building character and self-control the bathrooms were designed to provide cold water in winter and tepid water in high summer. Fortunately for all there was a superb beach at Deep Water Bay within easy walking distance of the Training School and, in summer, it was well patronised by many of the recruits. The water was clean, and the beach looked as beaches always do in Tourist brochures but rarely in reality, it also had what seemed to be a resident population of stunningly attractive Chinese girls in modern swimming costumes. Parked unobtrusively on the beach perimeter was a Chinese entrepreneur with an ice cream tricycle from which he innocently sold a wide selection of excellent ice creams to the public in general and, illicitly, ice cold beer, mainly to the Police recruits! It was rumoured that this had nothing to do with corruption but that he had helped to save a policeman's life some time in the past, a rare event in the Colony, and that this was his unofficial reward.

Most of the British and Commonwealth officer candidates had served in the armed forces before going to Hong Kong, some as regulars and some as national service men doing their compulsory service time with the colours. To all who had survived the rigours of service training in Britain the training regime in Hong Kong was reminiscent of roast beef and Yorkshire pudding done in a sweet and sour sauce, very British with an oriental flavour! The British and Chinese instructor officers were astonishing in the fact that they resembled every hard bitten recruit instructor ever seen in any recruit training centre anywhere in the world. Incredibly smart uniforms with razor sharp creases, standard military haircuts only a millimetre from baldness, boots polished to a glittering glory unattainable for recruits. They carried themselves with the straight backed ease of guardsmen and as they marched across the parade ground, or even to the toilet, with their swagger sticks tucked under their left arms, it was easy to imagine hearing in the air the faint sound of the military bands celebrating the Relief of Mafeking. Until better known, all of them had official issue, anonymous, emotionless, instructors' faces, only displaying a hard determination to survive the horrors of months of training brainless, uncoordinated, stumbling, fumbling, uniformed idiots to an acceptable British standard. Each of them, without exception, had the eyes and world weary demeanour of a Jesuit priest who has served too long as father confessor in a sailors' church!

If it is accepted that the basic reason for training men to march in step, and manoeuvre as a disciplined formation, is to teach them to work together in an organised manner as a cohesive group engaged in a common endeavour, then our first day was a total disaster. A number of factors combined to defeat the best efforts of the British and Hong Kong Chinese Drill Instructors. The greatest of these was the fact that it is necessary to get all the members of a drill squad to march at the same speed and cadence, advance, retire, turn, and halt, together, all in response to commands given by the Drill Master. The British ex-servicemen were accustomed to the fast pace and cadence of British military drill, carrying out manoeuvres swiftly and snappily in response to sharply uttered commands, at least all those who had served in the Army and Air Force, not so the solitary former sailor from the Royal Navy more accustomed to different naval drills designed to be carried out in restricted confines aboard ship. All of the Hong Kong Chinese officer recruits were fluent in the English language but had never done drill in their lives, nor had they ever

29

needed to respond immediately to commands uttered sharply, and forcefully, in the English language, but they were keen.

The constables, on the other hand, were mainly Cantonese speakers although they came from a wide selection of China's wonderful variety of peoples, Cantonese, Shantung, Fukienese, Hakka, Chiu Chow, Hokklo, Tanka, and others, all of whom speak vastly different dialects. The scale of the problem of communication may be judged by the fact that, although the population of Kwangdung (Canton) Province is barely 6 per cent of the total population of China, there are some ninety-six different dialects in spoken Cantonese alone and the constables were drilled from their first day with English words of command accompanied by explanations in the Cantonese dialect. Adding to the obvious potential for disaster, in this linguistic Tower of Babel, was the design of the parade ground. In area and shape it was a standard parade ground such as can be found anywhere in the world. Where it differed from most was that it had been built by filling in a steep slope at the foot of Brick Hill, with the result that two sides of the parade were level with the main camp, while on the other two sides, the land sloped sharply down from the edge, to sports fields and weapon training ranges, respectively; the ranges being separated from the rest by a deep gully in which ran a small stream. Need it be said that the stage was set for disaster?

The Chief Drill and Musketry Instructor of the Hong Kong Police Force was Chief Inspector Les Guyatt, a former Sergeant-Major in the British Army and an outstanding example of the best of that much maligned, but truly irreplaceable component of British military excellence. Mr Guyatt was known to most Chinese, police and civilian, by his, honourable, Chinese nickname, 'General Ninety Thousand Dragons', principally because his body was completely covered from neck to toes in the most beautifully artistic, brightly coloured, tattoos drawn during long service in India. Also because he resembled the Chinese War God 'Kwan Ti' in the ferocity of his features adorned with a spiky military moustache, his rotund but immensely strong physique, and in his honest, frank, and forthright dealings with men of all ranks, races, and creeds. Les was a formidable figure in every respect but his innate kindness and immense knowledge of all things police and military was shared freely and warmly with anyone who asked for his assistance, whether to pass a promotion examination or just out of interest. He was also much admired for his off-duty ability to consume vast quantities of 'Black Label' Scotch whisky without displaying any signs of intoxication, smoking his cigarettes in Indian fashion, and taking huge sniffs of lethally strong 'Top Mill' snuff with no evidences of distress or discomfort! As a young soldier, in India, he had taken part in the Waziristan campaign against the Ipi of Wa, and was the only person any of us had met with the Waziristan campaign ribbon. We were very impressed.

The Commandant's office was situated higher on the slopes of Brick Hill about one hundred feet above, and overlooking, the parade ground. On the same level were the instructor-officers' common room and the officers' lecture rooms. It was almost a tradition that the Commandant and all available instructors would gather in front of the offices for the first parade drills of the new recruit intakes. It was also customary for the Chief Drill and Musketry Instructor to stand on the roadway some fifteen feet above the parade ground to observe and estimate the degree of incapability of co-ordinated movement displayed by the suffering recruits below. Cooks, room boys, gardeners, and loafers of all descriptions would also congregate out of the Commandant's sight in every available lurking place to enjoy the fun. Our recruit group gave them a memorable day.

It was a typically humid, stuffy, July morning, following two days of heavy monsoon rains. The rain had stopped the previous night in time for the early sun to create a morning mist that turned air to the consistency of clear steam. The recruits, officers and constables alike, shambled on to the parade ground in what was supposed to be platoon formation looking for the marks painted on the concrete on which to take up their formations facing towards Victoria Peak with their backs to Brick Hill and the assembled camp staff. All looked smart enough with peaked caps, starched khaki shirts and shorts, and boots and gaiters burnished to a high shine by our room boys. There were three platoons, one of officers, and two of constables, numbering in all approximately one hundred men. Our platoon had an Irish drill instructor formerly of the Irish Guards. The constables' platoons each had two very experienced Hong Kong Chinese drill instructors, one giving the drill orders in English, and the other assisting with the explanatory Cantonese. We began quite well. While standing still, known as 'at the halt', we managed to come to attention and stand at ease with remarkable facility in response to the commands shouted at us in a clear Irish accent. The trouble began when we were required to turn left and then right, still at the halt. British Army drill demands a peculiar, almost masochistic, habit of raising the moving leg to an astonishing height, until the thigh is parallel to the ground, then smashing it down with spine jarring force

31

so that the sole of the boot makes a very loud noise when coming in contact with the ground. Both the force of the impact and the loud noise of gravel being crushed seem essential to the good health and mental well-being of Army-type people. Lack of these effects induces reddening of the face, screaming fits and hoarsening of the voice in all drill instructors, regardless of nationality or race.

The Royal Navy has not only, traditionally, been far more aesthetically minded than the brutal and licentious soldiery, Admirals have always had to bear in mind the fact that even steel decks can suffer damage if thundered upon by hundreds of feet crashing down in unison. Even worse, light bulbs have been known to eject themselves spontaneously from deck-head (ceiling) light fittings to smash expensively on 'tween decks when subjected to the percussion effects of unnecessarily enthusiastic foot drill from above. Naval drill has, therefore, always been a matter of smart but limited physical movement, the soles of the shoes, not boots, never rising more than one inch from the deck in the course of drill movements. Even the Royal Marines, those splendid military hybrids of lethal amphibian tendencies, always had to curb their enthusiasm and develop schizophrenic drill movements, moving gently and in a civilised manner on board ship and only reverting to their crashing, earth shaking, nature on shore in special reservations provided for them in places such as Deal, in Kent.

Most of my life had been spent in the Royal Navy, much of it in submarines where there is really very little room for drill even if anyone was dotty enough to want it, so my drill movements were at variance with those of the military types. So it transpired that while every member of the squad, including the enthusiastic Chinese officers, was happily pointing knees skyward, thighs parallel to the ground, and loudly pounding the concrete into dust in approved military manner, I was the only person moving with the discreet and delicate movements demanded in a ship.

The drill instructor spoke to me about this at some length. His voice ranged interestingly from a quiet scream to a bellow, and he accompanied his tirade with appropriate drill movements, demonstrating the actions and movements he required with great physical vigour. He looked rather odd under the hot morning sun, sweating copiously, shouting loudly at himself and smashing his feet up and down in response, all on his own. It was mentioned to me later that these demonstrative spasms of enraged concrete crushing by drill instructors were always most frequent in the early weeks of training. It was fascinating to note that the instructor's face had quickly assumed the purple colour of an enraged baboon's bum, and remained so for some considerable time. Naturally, in the interests of good order and discipline, keeping my new job, and the instructor's blood pressure at a less perilous level, I agreed to perform military drill and did so from that day. It was unfortunate that this episode had been witnessed by the eagle eyed Mr Guyatt as he personally gave me some extra drill instruction, in my off duty time 'in order to assist me in speedily adapting from swaying decks at sea to stable parade grounds on land' as he delicately phrased it!

By the time the demonstration had ended, and the drill instructor had us marching about on the parade ground, the other recruit squads were also on the move. All went quite well considering the fact that we were recruits, and after thirty minutes or so we were dismissed for a tea break with instructions to reassemble on the parade ground afterwards. When we returned to the parade we noticed that a platoon of fully trained recruits had already fallen in on one side of the drill square, well away from where we were due to carry on drilling. They were there as a drill squad for the benefit of a number of officers who were taking their drill examinations as part of their promotion routine. We began drilling as far away as possible from the examination squad. It was unfortunate that one of the officers being examined had a good powerful voice but was not so good at remembering which orders should be given for appropriate manoeuvres. He became so confused over which command to give in order to move the platoon where he wanted them that, inevitably, his platoon strayed in among ours. Shouted orders seemed to be coming from all directions at once and we obeyed those we could decipher. This resulted in a brief scrum in the far corner of the parade ground as four platoons came together, followed immediately by the individual squads pouring off down the steep slopes like a migration of clockwork lemmings, heading in the general direction of the sports fields, the ranges, Staunton Creek, and distant Aberdeen. The drill instructors rapidly had us back under control. The officer under examination, who was a CID man, was not so fortunate. The most fiendish aspect of the much dreaded drill examination was that the drill squads were specifically instructed beforehand to obey to the letter every order given to them by the candidates, no matter how bizarre the result, unless to do so would endanger life. After months of rigorous training, and strict discipline, the recruits were only too delighted to obey, and looked forward to the examinations as to a light-hearted frolic. In this instance we all watched with fascination as the drill squad marched steadily and with almost theatrical inevitability in the direction of the ranges and the boundary stream, while the demoralised CID officer tried to get his act together. By the time he screamed a despairing 'Halt' he was too late, the whole squad, grinning from ear to ear, had gone over the edge of the gully and splashed happily into the cooling waters of the boundary stream.

Life became a round of hard study, hard drill, and hard play. Our Commandant set a high standard in everything and displayed very Scottish characteristics in his attitude to learning. Not everyone was a natural student, and few of the Europeans could match the incredibly high marks obtained in examinations by the Chinese officers, but all Mr Todd demanded was that everyone tried their best. He gave decent encouragement to the less gifted and he gave hell to any loafers! He also, in marked contrast to some other senior officers, seemed to acknowledge the fact that major characteristics looked for by the recruiting officers, when they interviewed would-be recruits, was youthful initiative, enterprise, spirit, and leadership potential, and he took this into account when, occasionally, we got up to some of our sillier pranks.

The weekend was always a dangerous time for corporate recruit idiocy, especially so if someone's birthday happened to fall on a Friday or Saturday! Some long-awaited redecoration and modernisation had been done in one of the old classrooms adjoining the Commandant's office, with the work being finally completed late on a Friday afternoon and everything closed up ready for the official reopening on the following Monday.

By chance one of the chaps had his birthday on the Saturday following, and celebrations started quite temperately after lunch. By the evening the party spirit was rather more overt, including a splendid dinner in a floating restaurant in Aberdeen harbour, with party streamers, bangers, and other aids to enjoyment, including a moderate amount of alcoholic liquors. Everybody was roused out of bed at an indecently early hour on the following Sunday morning by a very irate Duty Staff Officer with the information that we were all required to be up outside the Commandant's office in full uniform within seconds, or dire consequences would result. Considering the hung-over condition of most of the officers it was miraculous how quickly we were all assembled as ordered. We could see before our startled gaze the formerly pick and span, newly decorated, class room, now a disaster scene of the utmost desolation, covered in what appeared to be mountains of goat manure, with desks and chairs scattered about all over the place and the blackboard hanging by one corner.

The Duty Officer told us of the unexpected arrival of a Very Senior Person (VSP) early that morning. It appeared that the VSP was on his way to play golf at the Deep Water Bay Golf Club and had decided to pop into the Training School to have a brief look at the newly refurbished classroom before the reopening next day. The Duty Officer had been up and about and was only too pleased at this break in the usually uneventful Sunday routine. They had gone up to the classroom and he had opened the door only to be knocked off his feet by an outpouring of bad tempered goats unaccustomed to spending a night locked up in close quarters! It was quite apparent also that they were not house-trained. The VSP was a very decent man who had undoubtedly been young once, as he merely commented to the, by now, distraught Duty Officer that he hoped all would be ready for the opening the following morning and left to keep his golf appointment.

Hazy memories were beginning to percolate the guilty minds of the assembled suspects, memories of a jolly and rather 'liquid' return to the school in the early hours of the morning. Sergeant Major Chan Chor-choi, the senior Sergeant-Major at PTS, usually kept a herd of goats high on the slopes of Brick Hill and in the early hours of the morning the goats had been, unusually, in the grounds of the school. It had been quite a chilly night and it seemed only humanitarian, to some well-watered idiot, to shelter them under cover until the morning, hence their presence in the class room. No one admitted culpability but it was immediately agreed that we would clean things up and restore the room to a condition suitable for the next day's ceremony. No one could have believed that only twenty to thirty medium-sized goats could have produced so much manure and other unspecified mess in what could only have been five or six hours of captivity! It took us until late afternoon before we felt able to invite the Duty Officer to inspect the results. He did so with grim faced efficiency and then declared himself satisfied.

We began to relax a bit and started collecting up the buckets, scrubbers, cloths, and other cleaning gear we had borrowed from the coolies whose usual task it was to keep the school clean. As we came out on to the lawn in front of the classroom to be dismissed by the Duty Officer, there was a loud bang from one of a pair of old cannons flanking the saluting dais on the parade ground and from its muzzle poured forth a huge quantity of party streamers and other bits of coloured paper normally seen only on festive occasions. We all glared at one of our number who had been involved with bang-making in the British Army, and had been expounding at well-oiled length on the subject of delayed charges at the party the night before, the obvious culprit! Without a word being said the beaming cleaning coolies produced brooms, brushes, and dust pans, and handed them to us. We eventually finished our second clean up job as the sun was going down, and retired from the parade ground, weary but satisfied, to our quarters.

The following day the reopening ceremony passed off without a hitch but we were told that the participants had commented on a smell of goats that seemed to be lingering in the air! It says much for the character, decency, and understanding of young men, of Commandant Bill Todd, and the Very Senior Person, that we never heard a word from them about the goats or the gun. In any case, by the following Wednesday the Police Force had far more to worry about, the Double Tenth Riots!

Wednesdays were always good days at PTS as the afternoons were usually devoted to sport, swimming, sometimes visits to Police Stations. Wednesday, 10 October 1956, started off no different from any other but by nightfall Kowloon was in flames, and many of us were fighting for our lives in ferocious hand to hand struggles in the dark of alleyways and seething resettlement estates. By about three o'clock in the morning, I was in the 33rd British Military Hospital in Kowloon, blinded and suffering various other injuries after a vicious and extended action in the Tai Han Tung resettlement estate.

The first day of October is celebrated by Communists as the anniversary of the formation of the Communist People's Republic of China. The tenth day of October, usually referred to as the Double Tenth, the tenth day of the tenth month, is usually celebrated by non-communist Chinese to mark the anniversary of the creation of the first Chinese Republic in 1911. Both days were commonly treated with caution by the Hong Kong authorities as they were regarded as patriotic holidays by Communist and Nationalist sympathizers. Tension always arose as a result of large organised rallies, speeches, strings of 'lucky' firecrackers being exploded in celebration, and provocative displays of the opposing national flags, the Communists', a red flag bearing one large and four small yellow stars in its top left corner, and the Nationalists', a red flag with a blue square containing a white sun with twelve rays in its top left hand corner.

On this particular Double Tenth all police leave was cancelled as usual and both Regular and Auxiliary policemen were held in reserve on 'stand by'. No one was aware that the Hong Kong government was about to face its greatest challenge since the defeat of the Japanese and all because a junior official in a Resettlement Estate allegedly tore down a few Nationalist paper flags pasted on a wall. The flimsy paper flags cost, at most, five pence but the civil disturbances resulting from their removal cost approximately £3.25 million in damage and lost trade, plus a high price in human life and injury before peace was restored.

That day – 10 October 1956 – was just seven years after the 1949 victory of Mao Tse-tung's Communist People's Liberation Army in China over the Nationalist Army led by Chiang Kai-shek, and the majority of the population of Hong Kong, at least a million of them, were refugees from Communism. Many had arrived in Hong Kong with no possessions other than the clothes they stood up in, and had endured seven long years of grinding poverty, hard work, and unending effort, just to keep themselves and their families alive. They hated Communism and Communists with the hatred known only to those who have suffered bitter exile from their homeland. Many had further cause for hate in the executions, and deaths in prison and labour camps, of relatives and friends accused of being pro-Nationalist, anti-Communist or just an 'exploiter' of the people. It is against that tragic background that the events of the Double Tenth Riots must be judged.

The first that the recruits in PTS knew of what was happening in Kowloon was when all outings were cancelled and we were told that there was serious trouble in Kowloon. Police patrols had been out in strength throughout the colony but trouble that had started at the Li Cheng Uk Resettlement Estate over the paper flag incident had grown and was in danger of getting out of hand, as Triad gangs had become involved.

The Hong Kong Triads claim to be descended from the ancient Chinese secret societies, devoted to the freedom of China from foreign rule, but they are just gangs of criminals who use a bastardised form of the old rituals. They have none of the old Triads' honour of professed purpose, they are just thugs involved in murder, drugs, prostitution, protection rackets, and any other profitable illicit activity. They even stoop to squeezing protection money out of the street hawkers who are among the poorest of Hong Kong's poor. Failure to pay up on demand is punished with the utmost brutality and, in contrast even to the Mafia, Triad members take a positive delight in murdering, raping and mutilating the wives and children of their victims. These were the people who leaped at the chance to stir up trouble on 10 October 1956.

In PTS all of us who had completed the basic riot drills were formed up with full riot equipment and moved over to the Kowloon Police Headquarters as evening fell. We were ferried over the harbour in marine police launches and driven up Nathan road in police trucks driven by civilian drivers. The air stank of tear gas and the smoke of fires. There were large numbers of heavily armed, weary looking, policemen at all the major road junctions. Weapons could be heard being fired from time to time.

At the Kowloon Police Headquarters we were placed on immediate stand-by, as all of the Kowloon reserves were already fully committed so great, widespread and organised was the disorder. The Head-quarters complex was like a disturbed wasps nest, with people hurrying to and fro with set faces, and vehicles coming and going all the time, loaded with armed policemen. Chief Inspector Guyatt was talking to me when a senior officer came up to him and ordered him to take me and two of the Police Training School sections he indicated, two NCOs and fourteen PCs, to the Tai Hang Tung Resettlement Estate where it had been reported that a small group were threatening the Police Post in which there were three police officers. Mr Guyatt said something to him, I believe it was to the effect that the two sections were only equipped with riot truncheons and shields – no firearms, and he was sharply told to get on with it as we were going to deal with a handful of louts not a riot!

We embussed in transport and were driven to Tai Hang Tung Resettlement Estate where we debussed on to the estate approach road in standard riot formation, or what would have been standard formation at that time if the other forty-eight NCOs and PCs armed with gas grenades, gas guns, shotguns, and rifles, the standard riot platoon at that time, had been with us!

The estate looked like Dante's Inferno with smoke writhing in the flickering flames of many fires. Figures could be seen darting about, and numerous groups of people coalescing breaking up and reforming quickly, like a film being speeded up through a projector. The civilian drivers took one look at the scene, turned the transport round, and, despite being told to stay, drove off never to be seen again. They did not even take the trouble to inform headquarters that instead of facing a small group we were facing a full scale riot. The NCOs and

PCs were magnificent, they stood ready, facing the front watching the mob from which occasional individuals ran forward towards us from time to time. Mr Guyatt and I discussed the situation and decided that we were honour bound to check the fate of the men in the Police Post, and in any case we might be able to use the post's communications to call for reinforcements. Our men showed great courage and discipline and marched confidently forward towards the mob between us and the post when ordered to do so. We charged and charged again at the mob as we were attacked with every missile and weapon they could lay their hands on. We had to keep to the centre of the road as furniture, refrigerators, and the odd petrol bomb rained down from every balcony above us in the unending blocks of flats. We finally broke through to the Police Post only to find it empty, ransacked, and burning. We found out later that the Post NCO and his men had, with commendable common sense, estimated their chances of holding the post against a mob of approximately 3000 demented rioters as being something less than zero. They had changed from their uniforms into black Chinese clothing, concealed their pistols in their pockets with their fingers on the triggers, tucked the important official records into the tops of their trousers, and strolled off into the mob, eventually reaching safety. Unfortunately, when their report of the events and extreme violence in Tai Han Tung reached Kowloon Headquarters no one connected it with us, in fact nobody seemed to know we were there!

We caught our breath in the uncertain shelter of the post, and carried out what little first aid we could on each other, as we planned our next moves. We had to make our way back through the mob to the approach road, then go up the approach road to the main Tai Hang Tung Road. That was the only way out for us as any other route just took us further away from any possible escape or reinforcement. Mr Guyatt and I decided that, at a point near the Tai Hang Tung Road junction, where the road narrowed so that the mob would be forced to attack us on a narrow front, we would take a stand with our, and the NCOs, pistols, and delay the mob for as long as possible to let the NCOs, who were both married, and the young PCs make their getaway. We checked our available weapons and ammunition. We each had a three foot long riot truncheon and rattan riot shield. Mr Guyatt, the NCOs and I had Colt .38 revolvers and some spare ammunition. We also had four C-tear gas grenades. Not a lot for dealing with a howling mob in excess, it was estimated, of 3000 people but enough for a disciplined group of men to have a go at it! We tidied ourselves up, had a drink of water, and set to. We burst out of the area of the Post in a series of sudden furious charges catching the mob off balance, and gaining precious yards in the direction of the approach road. A hail of bottles, some containing acid, some petrol, stones, and other missiles constantly poured at us from the mob, some of whom we could see were armed with Chinese fighting irons, and spears. There were occasional explosions but we could not be certain if they were from big Chinese fireworks, bombs, or weapons.

Time seemed to go into slow motion and the world narrowed down to the people immediately in front of us, faces distorted with hate to the extent that they did not look human. The air had a stink of smoke from scores of fires, tear gas, hate, fear, and human sweat. The night was darker in a strange way than any night I had ever seen before. Faces rose and fell in front of us lit by uncertain light, seeming at times to explode into blood, bone and teeth as the truncheons hammered down, to a chorus of screams of rage and pain from them and us. They tore at us with clubs, knives, metal bars, spikes, and bamboo spears, we responded with truncheons, the rough edges of our riot shields, kicking and heeling with our boots, butting with our riot helmets, and meanwhile big stones launched at us by two man catapults, rained down. They were trying to kill us, but we were determined to stay alive. We charged as sections, either Les Guyatt or me leading one NCO and seven PCs at a time into the attack, then fighting our way back to the slim shelter of the other waiting section, standing alert, on guard and catching its breath. Each time we charged, we gained ten or twenty yards in our long advance to the road junction.

A sudden increase in the volume of missiles raining down on us from above, and the sides, signalled the fact that we had fought our way to the corner where we would turn towards the approach road and our route out of the main estate. The mob organisers, Triad members wearing identifying arm bands and head bands, could be seen redoubling their efforts in the crowd, whipping them up and encouraging them to attack us. If the Triads could have killed us all on the first day of the riots it would have been a great victory for them and could have had a major effect on both Police and public morale in this first major direct confrontation between the authority of the Hong Kong government and the covert power of the Triad societies.

Before we had been attacking and advancing, now our tactics had changed. We were attacking and, each time we withdrew, retiring round in to the approach road a few yards at a time. The mob's fury seemed to be growing. Each charge was replied to with a more furious response as they charged us in turn. The battle changed tempo as we finally stood facing the crowd ready for our fighting retreat down the approach road. The Triads in the mob knew that if we could make it they had lost the game, so they redoubled their efforts and formed up a large group at the front of the mob with the obvious intention of swamping us. We had to hit them hard and quickly before they could settle down as an organised group. We charged into them full tilt with no warning catching them by surprise and drove right into their middle. We used our truncheons, the edges of our rattan shields, our boots, and our bodies. They lost their cohesion, but we, through training and discipline, kept ours and that was our salvation. The rioters immediately in front of us began to break and try to back away from us, the mob behind them were still pushing forward and preventing them from escaping, so those at the front began fighting with those behind them to get clear of us. We knew that this was a crucial moment for us to impose our moral superiority over the mob and we redoubled our efforts.

As we did so, there was a loud banging noise, and I became blind. I automatically put up my hand to wipe my face and eyes and found that my face felt like minced meat. I managed to see a little from my left eye but nothing from the right and every few seconds the left eye filled with blood rendering me completely blind. The section had started to retire when the PCs realised that I was still in the middle of the crowd being battered from all sides and defending myself vigorously if inaccurately. They immediately charged back in to my rescue and saw at once that I had been badly hurt. They knew that I could not see properly as I had nearly brained them at first. Two PCs formed up on either side of me and guided me back up the road where we did some quick first aid. We could not let the mob see that one of the two officers was out of action, as it might have encouraged them, so I carried on with charges, closely accompanied by the PCs who had rescued me from the middle of the crowd. When I could see hazily from my left eye all was fine, when it filled with blood or just blinked out, the PCs would grab my belt and we would retire in good order with them steering me by the belt.

To my amazement, during a brief breather in the midst of this bloody shambles, I heard the PCs having a bit of a giggle and one of them told me it was because they felt a bit like jockeys at the Hong Kong Jockey Club steering a bad-tempered horse each time they guided me by my belt into and out of the mob. This was overheard by the other men, and they also had a laugh, to the amazement, I was told later, of those of the mob within earshot.

We carried on until Les Guyatt told me we were at the narrow bit of the road where we had agreed to take our stand to cover the escape of our men, and this was the only time on that terrible night that we had any doubts about them obeying orders, as they made it abundantly clear they were not going to abandon us to the mob. It all became a matter of hypothetical interest as there was a sudden burst of gunfire from gas guns on the main road and salvos of gas shells flew over our heads into the crowd. Chief Inspector Jack Hayward had by chance been passing with a riot column and had seen the trouble we were in. He deployed his men and soon had the mob driven back into the estate. His first-aiders patched us up then he had to be off to a reported emergency elsewhere. His radio report about us to headquarters caused some consternation as they apparently did not know that we had been sent out over two hours before!

We marched wearily back to the HQ compound where we were received with some astonishment at our appearance. We were covered in blood from head to foot, faces black with dirt and smoke, uniforms torn and disarrayed from hand to hand fighting, and everyone had cuts, wounds, bruises and scratches. We went to get a cup of tea and I suddenly found myself sitting on the steps of the hut from which tea was being served. A senior officer who was passing by, Mr Dawson, took a look at me and ordered me to be taken to hospital. Every civilian hospital in Kowloon was under attack from mobs and being defended by police so, to my great good fortune, I was taken by armoured car to the 33rd British Military Hospital.

Army medical people have traditionally been portrayed in Britain as being specialists only at dishing out laxatives, telling patients to say 'ninety-nine' and 'cough.' That was not my experience. The casualty reception area was full of people, but as I walked in, a strict looking lady in a Queen Alexandra's Royal Army Nursing Corps uniform took one look at me, and instructed orderlies to attend to me at once. In no time at all I was lying on an examination couch with two military doctors bending over and examining me, paying special attention to my eyes and face. Somebody stuck a hypodermic needle into me as I was asking about going back on duty, and I woke up much later in a bed, feeling clean, in a lot of pain, and bandaged up like an Egyptian mummy. There were bandages covering my eyes and I could not tell if it was night or day, but as soon as I moved a man's quiet confident voice told me where I was, that I had been involved in riots, that I had been severely injured, that I had received initial treatment, that my superficial wounds and injuries had been dealt with, and that one of the Army's top eye specialists would examine me in eight hours' time. I was given a drink of water and as I finished it another damned hypodermic needle was stuck into me and I went to sleep again. That orderly could have made a fortune as a slick crimp in a Barbary Coast brothel giving sailors Mickey Finns before Shanghaiing them!

The next time I woke up it was to be examined by a Colonel Grant, a fellow Scot from Rumbling Bridge in Perth only fifty miles or so from Aberfeldy, reputedly my, unknown, natural mother's home town. It was rumoured that the Colonel, who was an outstanding eye specialist, was in Hong Kong simply by chance as he was on his way to Japan to attend to an important patient there who suffered from an unusual eye condition – according to the orderlies' gossip – the Emperor. The Colonel performed numerous operations on my eyes, and other Army specialists attended to my rather battered face and the other bits of me that had been mistreated by the rioters. No one knew for certain exactly what had caused the injuries to my face and eyes, it might have been stones launched at great velocity by some sort of machine or two-man catapult, or it might have been some kind of explosive device, containing stones and other material as shrapnel. Whatever it was it was effective as, twenty years later in Edinburgh, Scottish eye specialists took tiny fragments of metal out of my eye with a new magnetic device.

During the course of the operations on my eyes in Kowloon I woke up once with someone sitting on my hospital bed, it was the Colonel. He told me it was two o'clock in the morning and he had visited me as he had a decision to make that was very important to me but that it was a decision only he could make. In reply to my question, asking him what was wrong, he told me that he was certain that he could save the sight in my left eye but my right eye was in such a bad state and so heavily infected that he had to consider removing it in case it made the left eye blind. He was concerned that removal of the eye could mean loss of my job as a policeman with all the uncertainty for my future that could mean but that failure to do so might result in my being totally blind. I trusted the Colonel although I had never seen him and I was willing to go along with whatever he thought best, and I told him so. I also said that as long as I had one eye I could always go back to sea, if necessary as a pirate! That made him laugh. Contented, and full of pain killing drugs, I went back to sleep. He didn't, but neither did he remove the eye.

One day the bandage on my left eye was taken off. I could see and the first person I saw was the gorgeous Sister Coral Peake-Cottam, unfortunately she was engaged to be married to some fellow to the anguish and despair of most of the males in the 33rd. The right eye was too badly damaged but, where a lesser man might have followed standard practice and removed it, as it was horribly ripped and infected, the Colonel performed numerous painstaking operations and patiently put the fragments of the eye back together, so it was still my own eye in the socket. Even if it does wander off in different directions from its partner from time to time, to the consternation of onlookers, it is my own and not a bit of glass, and I am very fond of it!

While I was loafing in hospital my colleagues in the police force, backed up by the Army, were battling against enormous odds to get the Colony back under control. The riots were mainly confined to Kowloon and parts of the New Territories and involved nearly sixty major actions, and uncounted minor clashes, between the Police and rioters by the time order was restored.

The main trouble began in the Li Cheng Uk Resettlement Estate in the northern part of Kowloon. As was so often the case in Hong Kong, the whole thing started over a piece of bureaucratic nonsense, dreamed up in an office and slavishly applied by junior officials. The Hong Kong government never wanted to become a landlord, and was only forced into building Resettlement Estates by events beyond its control. When the first starkly utilitarian blocks were built, the bureaucrats of the Resettlement and Housing Departments created a paternalistic bye-law or nit-picking rule for every shovel of cement used, or so it seemed. This meant that the junior bureaucrats in charge of the day to day running of estates containing as many as 36 000 tenants could make absolute pests of themselves to the residents at any time, and could always find a valid justification for it in the voluminous Book of Rules. The Chinese are a remarkably patient people but petty dictatorship over a period of years can build up a remarkable charge of latent hostility in any society. One of the bye-laws had sensibly been designed to prevent the unlawful posting of advertisements in public places and was basically similar to the 'Stick no bills' laws in Britain. In Hong Kong there is great competition between illicit bill-stickers who can cover an entire district with advertising bills secured to walls, doors, and any other flat surface, with a glue that is almost impossible to remove save at great expense. It was a bye-law designed for these nuisances that was the justification for the ill-considered action of the officials in Li Cheng Uk.

As usual on 10 October every year, China National Day, some of the pro-Nationalist residents in Shek Kip Mei Estate, about quarter of a mile from Li Cheng Uk, had pasted paper flags on the walls of the residential blocks but took them down when asked to do so, in reasonable manner, by officials. After all, they were still able to fly flags from their windows, verandahs, washing poles, and ropes slung between the blocks. In Li Cheng Uk other housing officials removed the pasted-on Nationalist flags and other political symbols themselves. That was enough to start the trouble. A crowd of approximately 500 people quickly gathered demanding that the officials replace the flags. Frightened officials called for police assistance and a patrol was sent to the scene. By the time they arrived the crowd had swollen to over 2000 and two of the officials had been seriously assaulted and were badly beaten up. Police reinforcements were sent and were greeted with barrages of stones, bottles, and anything else that could be thrown. With the assistance of further reinforcements and the use of tear gas, the mob was dispersed, but only for a time.

Later, in the early evening, a bigger and uglier mob began attacking the police in a more organised manner than before. Nationalist flags were used to direct rioters, as banners were used to direct soldiers in popular Chinese historical movies,and rioters repeatedly charged the police formations using any weapons to hand. Four full riot platoons totalling, at that time, 240 men, were sent to the scene and the whole area was cordoned off. Sporadic outbreaks of disorder began to be reported outside Li Cheng Uk and it was soon known that Triad members were busily engaged in stirring up trouble throughout Kowloon not just in the Resettlement Estates.

By eleven o'clock that night police were being attacked over a wide area by small groups of men who would hit and run. Any advantage gained by setting up police road-blocks on the main roads, was rapidly nullified by the sudden appearance of these hit and run gangs, who moved about via back streets and alleyways. By the late evening it was obvious that rioting had spread well beyond the bounds of Li Cheng Uk, and was widespread throughout the whole of Kowloon. The mobs did not just attack police, they quickly widened their targets to include the Fire Service, Ambulances, and any other official vehicle. One fire engine driver was knocked out by a missile, and his machine skidded into the crowd, killing three people and injuring five. Many fires were started deliberately, to draw fire engines to a scene where they were immediately attacked, this then brought the police who were attacked in turn. Casualties among police, fire, and ambulance service personnel began rising rapidly.

Looting soon emerged as the primary purpose of the Triads in particular and the rioters in general. Mobs began attacking business premises in northern Kowloon looting and burning shops by the score. No sooner was this brought under control by strong police action than it broke out again in Mongkok. Massed gangs, mainly Triads, made their way down Nathan Road from Sham Shui Po and Mongkok towards the popular tourist and shopping area of Tsim Sha Tsui, looting and burning as they went. Police were waiting for them in strength at Austin Road, the northern boundary of the tourist area, and they hammered the mobs with everything they had, gas, riot guns, truncheons, and rifle fire. The mobs were dispersed and many were arrested.

A few had infiltrated one part of the area and had set fire to a taxi in which the Swiss Vice-Consul Fritz Ernst and his wife were about to drive off. Mrs Ernst died of burns and Fritz was burned severely about the face, arms, and chest. Fritz was a fellow patient with me in the 33rd Hospital later. One of the gang who set fire to the taxi died from burns he received as he ignited the petrol tank which exploded spewing burning petrol all over him. His four accomplices were eventually hanged in Stanley Prison for Mrs Ernst's murder.

Communist schools were looted and set on fire. People were bullied into buying Nationalist flags at ridiculous prices for fear of being beaten up or killed. Looting and extortion became the obvious motivation for the continuing violence, and the Triads were the obvious organisers. Sham Shui Po police station underwent a sustained attack from a huge mob. The policemen beat them off with gunfire again, and again. They were finally dispersed by a police armoured car. Police in Hong Kong do not usually shoot to kill but during the Double Tenth riots they were forced to do so to prevent murderous mobs killing at will. The night of 10 and 11 October 1956 was a night of unmitigated savagery deliberately created by the Triads.

By lunch-time on 11 October the police were exhausted, had suffered many casualties, and were out of reserves. They did not even have any

A typical stilt hut in a typhoon shelter.

Smoking opium in a divan.

further reserves of trained recruits as they had already been committed to the battle. The Army was asked to assist the Civil Power and they did so, enthusiastically. The Army provided three battalions who were immediately deployed and added new strength to the forces of law and order. Curfew was imposed, ferry services stopped, and the curfew was rigidly enforced. With army assistance sweeps were carried out and hundreds of rioters were arrested. Force was met with force as in one incident in Kowloon where three rioters were shot dead and 400 more were arrested after a fierce police action.

By the third day of the riots, 12 October, the human wave tactics of rioting masses of people directed by Triad men had given way to vicious street warfare between groups of Triad gangsters and the police. In this type of action the gangsters could not use their previous cynical tactic of putting little children at the front of the mob to force the police to fire high, and they began to pay the price for their evil actions. In one fracas in Mongkok three of them were shot dead leading an attack on a food store where the proprietor had bravely stood his ground against them in defence of his family. In one series of sweeps through bars, brothels, gambling schools, and known hideouts on 12 October, police and army rounded up over 3000 Triads and rioters for detention and processing. General curfew was lifted on 14 October but night curfew was enforced in Shum Shui Po, Shek Kip Mei, Li Cheng Uk and north western Kowloon until 17 October.

The rioting had not just been confined to Kowloon. Serious rioting of a different sort had erupted in the factory town of Tsuen Wan in the New Territories on 11 October but these were more overtly political even though Triads were involved. Most of the workers in the factories lived in dormitories owned by the companies they worked for but they were divided by their membership of mutually hostile pro-Communist and anti-Communist trades unions. Violence was mainly directed against the pro-Communist union members at least five of whom were killed. Looting, extortion and arson were rife. At one Nationalist rally sixty unfortunate members of a left-wing union were savagely beaten, kicked and punched into unconsciousness for the entertainment of the mob. Police foiled an attempt by a gang to set fire to a dormitory of 300 left-wing girl workers, where the gang had blocked all the exits from the building. Tsuen Wan Police station was attacked but the attacks were repulsed. The army used military vehicles to crash through barricades and a strict curfew was clamped on the town. Before order was restored at least eight people had been killed, over 100 seriously injured, some 700 arrested.

No one will ever know for certain how many people were killed and injured during the 1956 riots. The Chinese people have learned from their history never to get involved with officialdom, as to do so eventually turns out to be against your family's best interests. As a consequence of this, if members of the family get shot or injured during a riot or civil disturbance it is plain common sense to have them medically treated, or buried, privately! As a matter of interest, about a week after the riots ended a dead Chinese man who had obviously been involved in the riots was found under a hedge. He had been wounded and had treated his wounds with red 'lucky' paper. It wasn't so lucky, he had died of gangrene!

It may be helpful to bear in mind, that the usual rule of thumb employed by cynics in the Far East is, always divide official figures projected in positive reports by ten, but multiply official figures given in negative reports by ten! The final report on the riots gave the following figures: fifty-nine people killed, 500 injured, financial cost approximately £3.25 million (HK$50 million) in damage and lost trade, 6000 people arrested, over 1200 sentenced to prison, 4 hanged for the murder of Mrs Ernst. In all the sweeps and operations carried out, approximately 15 000 people were detained. Bureaucrats should be taught to think twice before creating and enforcing piddling bye-laws!

I spent a few weeks in the Army Hospital and became friends with two of my fellow patients, Fritz Ernst the Swiss Vice-Consul, who bravely endured immense pain from his burns, and Brigadier Bill Barlow, then Commander British Forces Korea, who was in hospital with a leg injury. Bill Barlow was in a wheelchair. Fritz Ernst had his arms fixed out horizontally from his shoulders and could wear no clothing on his chest. I had my eyes, part of my face, hands and arms done up like the invisible man. When we were together, usually plotting how to foil the prohibition on alcohol in the hospital, we jointly added up to just about one functional human being! The QARANC chief nurse, Major Holton a New Zealander, should have been employed by Elliot Ness in Chicago as she could detect a sealed bottle of Glenlivet or Remy Martin at 200 paces! But she was a superb nurse and we presented her with a silver tray on her retirement. Part of the hospital wall was covered by a climbing plant with pretty flowers and one day when one of my visitors had secretly delivered me a bottle of Glenmorangie Malt whisky, I had the brilliant idea of hanging it out of the window on a piece of stout string where it was well hidden from the Major's eagle eye by the thick foliage. Bill and Fritz were quite impressed by my cunning and we all repaired to my room for a wee dram. We had barely entered the room when the Major marched in, bade us all good afternoon, marched over to the window produced a pair of scissors and cut the string to the precious bottle. As we heard the faint sound of shattering glass from far below us she gave a quick glance at our horrified expressions, bade us a smiling farewell, and marched triumphantly out. The damn woman had alcohol ESP! This just spurred us on and increased our thirst. Through one of my visitors, a constable whose family lived in the area, we discovered an oasis, a superb little coffee house one street away from the hospital. The hospital staff were soon much impressed by our sudden desire for fresh air and exercise. So keen were we to exercise muscles grown soft in our invalidity that medical people of all grades became accustomed to the sight of our weirdly assorted trio going out for our constitutional, one in a wheelchair being pushed erratically by one with bandages over his eyes who was being directed loudly, in a thick German accent, by one with his arms in the air like a flightless bird. It was too good to last. We met the Major on the return from one of our health-seeking excursions and one sniff of our breath meant the end of our walks!

It is difficult to calculate just how much one owes to medical people, but I know that I owe every interesting day for the last thirty-three years to the Colonel, doctors, nurses, orderlies, and the other staff serving in the 33rd Military Hospital Kowloon in October and November 1956. On my return to the Police Training School, some three weeks after leaving for Kowloon, I had to work hard to catch up on missing studies as my future career hung in the balance due to the nature of my injuries. I had to prove I was fit to continue as a policeman. A major problem was the fact that all Hong Kong Police Officers have to be well trained in the use of firearms and well skilled in their use. Hong Kong is so crowded with people that a poor marksman let loose in their midst would be a disaster. I was quite a good shot but I was right-handed and my right eye had always been my dominant eye for shooting. Now I had to learn to shoot left-handed using my left eye. Failure to pass all the requirements of the School examinations, including the use of firearms, could mean being dismissed from the Force. There was also the matter of getting accustomed to doing ordinary

49

things, normally taken for granted, without the benefit of bifocal sight. Even now, at dinner parties and other social functions, it is my custom to move my wine and water glass into my field of view as soon as I sit down. It is no pun to say that it puts a damper on civilised social intercourse if the first thing one does is knock glasses of wine and water into one's neighbour's lap because they were standing in the blind spot on the table!

It was fortunate for me that the School Sergeant Major was Mr Chan Chor-choi who, with immense patience and skill, helped me to adapt quickly. He even taught me how to aim and fire a Bren gun using my left eye, a skill any former soldier will confirm is very difficult as the rear sight is offset to the left and because the ammunition magazine is set on top of the gun! Mr Chan showed equal patience helping me to learn to judge distances and angles in my car, how to eat with chopsticks in public places without arousing hilarity; generally how to adjust.

On one occasion, battered and bruised and feeling stupid from misjudging distances on the assault course, tired and depressed after a truly stressful day, I just felt like packing it all in. Mr Chan sensed my depression and, good practical psychologist that he was, said that 'they' would be delighted if I quit or failed the course, 'they' being nameless senior people in headquarters who didn't quite know what to do with me. That was enough for me as I have always detested universally nameless 'theys' who push people around, I caught my wind and cracked on with my work. As a result of all the help I received from Sergeant-Major Chan, combined with the firm insistence of Commandant Bill Todd that I pass all the examinations on my own merits, I was able to qualify as a Probationary Sub-Inspector on the same basis as my classmates and started my career differing from my colleagues only by the fact that I was the only one wearing a black patch.

A year or so later when I passed my Hong Kong, China Coast Ship master's Certification examinations, I telephoned Mr Chan to thank him for all his help and encouragement. He was a good man, and I remember him with gratitude although he is no longer with us. He was my first truly personal contact with the Chinese people, and the greatest lesson I learned from him was, the enormous fund of friendship and good will they are willing to share with any reasonable person.

As a postscript to the events at Tai Hang Tung, while in hospital,

I had written a report about the events in Tai Hang Tung and sent it off to my superior officers. In the report I had said truthfully that in my opinion, and based on my previous experience in the armed forces, it was solely due to Mr Guyatt's coolness, skill, and leadership qualities that our two sections had fought their way out of Tai Hang Tung without suffering serious casualties or death. As is the tradition in the British armed forces I intimated that some recognition should be made of Mr Guyatt's exploit; in other words, a medal. I spoke about this to the NCOs and PCS, when they visited me in hospital, they agreed wholeheartedly with me as they knew what we owed to Les. After some days I received a visit from a senior officer who suggested that I change the content of my report and tone down my praise for Mr Guyatt. In reply to my questioning him why I should, he told me that it was not my place to write such a report, and in any case the matter was under investigation, as my continued service as a policeman would be, considering the fact that I had only one eye. He was told bluntly, in naval language, that I would not change one word, and he left in a huff.

Les called on me later and suggested that I agree to change the report. He was grateful for what I had done but he was worried that it might have some effect on my own future. Stubbornness is a Scottish characteristic and it has been suggested that I have my share and more. I never did change the report. Les Guyatt did not get the medal he should have been awarded, he was praised faintly with a 'Governor's Commendation'. Special Branch men used to get Governor's Commendations for putting in reports with correct spelling, especially when they contained difficult words like accommodation! This was my first experience of the strange internal politics of the Hong Kong Police Force.

As was invariably the case, some time later at his retirement party, while well lubricated with Scotland's major export, a senior person-in-the-know told me that my report had started a real 'flap' in the higher echelons of the Police Force. If Mr Guyatt had been recommended for a medal all the facts would have to be revealedd and embarrassing questions may have been asked. Questions such as: Who sent two sections of recruits armed only with truncheons into Tai Han Tung Resettlement Estate when a full scale riot was going on? Once they had been sent why was Kowloon Control not informed? How was it that the senior officer who sent us there did not connect the evacuation of the Police Post in the

51

face of a huge mob and our presence there? And many others in similar vein.

Les's 'Governor's Commendation' could be arranged quietly in Hong Kong without embarrassing questions. A medal would have involved London! What a rotten way to treat a brave and deserving man, just to cover up for some careless senior officer!

Four

FROM ASS TO ARSON

The first policemen in Hong Kong were Marine Police, created, shortly after the cession of Hong Kong to the British Crown, to control crime in Hong Kong harbour. The problems they faced then were similar to those still existing today; piracy, thefts from ships, warehouses and docks, smuggling in general, including illicit drugs and gold, illegal immigrants, and a whole range of other criminal activities.

My first operational posting was to the Marine Police Division of the New Territories and Marine Police Command. Where, as I discovered, I was regarded with considerable suspicion because I had served in the Royal Navy and had only one eye. At that time just one other marine policeman had served in the Royal Navy, a burly Englishman nicknamed 'Great Water Buffalo', who was a first class seaman and a good and decent man if a trifle short-tempered. The remainder of the officers had no previous sea going experience except for one who had reputedly been a Third Mate in the days before Radar, and another who, I was told, was at one time an apprentice.

My first meeting with the Chief Inspector, Marine Police was not a happy one and established a pattern for all future meetings. It resulted in a heated argument about my fitness to command police vessels with only one eye. My mention of Horatio Nelson, and a number of other one-eyed persons of repute, were less than enthusiastically received but eventually I was accepted as a marine policeman under sufferance. It was pointed out to me in a mock humorous manner that meeting an armed vessel with a Commander who was wearing a black eye-patch could frighten the hell out of the Captains of any innocent merchant vessels approaching the coast and might give rise to emergency calls about pirates. My politely expressed doubts that merchant ship Captains would have been so deeply impressed by Captain Hook from Peter Pan that they would scream for protection as soon as a sea-going black patch was sighted, were furiously ignored. As the patch was worn mainly for cosmetic reasons, because my dead eye bothered some people, it was taken off there and then and never put back on again during my service in Hong Kong, even though those who wanted it removed in the first place suggested that it should be replaced after they had viewed the result!

My first duty in Marine was as Officer in Command, Marine Police Drug Squad. This was a fascinating job and it gave me my first personal experience of the impressive standard of loyalty, dedication, toughness, efficiency, and decency of the Chinese police officers I would work with for the next eighteen years. It also demonstrated the appalling level of man-management and training in the Force at that time. Like most new officers I had no previous experience of commanding drug raids, and it might be thought that some introductory training should have been routine but that was not so. I was very lucky in having Sergeant 'Tommy' Ying as my second-in-command and I learned more from him in a week about the practical side of the work, than could be gleaned from months of studying the Police General Orders Manual containing some 6000 miscellaneous orders, quirkily indexed when indexed at all.

The Drug Squad had a wider field of responsibility than its title indicated. The legal authority of all officers of the rank of Probationary Sub-Inspector and above was vested in a General Warrant, and statutory powers, that covered drugs, firearms, gold, white slaves, illegal immigrants, and so on, just about anything illicit. We even had powers under the Cruelty to Animals Laws to deal with persons in possession of fighting crickets!

Armed with these immense legal powers and a few days study of drug intelligence reports, files, and information lists I prepared to set out on my first drug raid leading my squad to raid premises allegedly being used as an opium divan. The address was of a modern building within the Marine Police area of authority but it was unusual in the fact that due to the speed of reclamation and development, the area was also policed by a land division. My sergeant had suspicions about the raid as the information had apparently come from a source involved in an internal wrangle going on privately between senior officers within the force. Sergeant Tommy took a risk with me as a 'new boy' and unknown quantity and told me of his fears that I might have been 'set up' simply to do someone else's dirty work. In reply to my questioning he gave me my first unofficial briefing on how some corrupt practices were being conducted within the police force and gave me fair warning that junior officers were frequently caught between competing factions of more senior officers, like peasants trapped between competing barons. In this instance what was happening was that land reclamation areas were being rapidly built upon as a result of new developments in construction techniques unique to Hong Kong. As a consequence some corruptly lucrative areas containing drug divans, gambling and prostitution, were being transferred from the Marine Police division to various land divisions, to the financial loss, it was alleged, of some corrupt officers in the New Territories Headquarters and in the Marine Police Division. In most instances agreement had been reached that the 'pay offs' would be split for a time but in this case no agreement had been reached. I took this information into account as, even in the training school, I had heard rumours that this kind of thing was going on.

Well after dark one evening I hired a 'Walla Walla', a water taxi, and headed off into the harbour with my squad. We wandered about in a purposeful manner for twenty minutes or so until I was sure we were not being followed then headed to make a landing near the target building. As we made a cautious approach to the building on foot it was obvious that some activity was going on, with people, all men, coming and going. The building was three floors high and the suspected opium divan was on the second floor. We had made a provisional plan of attack based on the original information supplied but it was quite clear that modifications would have to be made. A complete reconnaissance of the building proved that the main entrance was the only way we could get in. All the windows on the ground floor were protected with steel bars and there was no rear entrance of any kind. My main objective was to seize the opium pipes, opium, cash, documents and receipts, and arrest the man who was running the den. Any other arrests or seizures would be icing on the cake. Some squad members were posted to secure the opium pipes and any other evidence that might be thrown out of the windows on our entry. The remainder of the men accompanied me and we entered the building silently and unseen.

On the second floor, the air was heavy with the sickly sweet, treacle-like, smell of opium smoke and we could hear a low murmur of voices from behind the divan door. The door looked like any modern standard door but I was aware that divan keepers traditionally secured them with many locks, bolts, and bars, however this door looked as though a solid charge at it could split the wood enough to force a quick entry. In a moment of temporary mental aberration I decided to break down the door myself as the tiled hallway was very narrow and two men would only obstruct each other to no useful effect. The sergeant and the rest of the men were set to follow up any advantage gained.

THE ONE-EYED DRAGON

I went back as far as I could and charged full tilt at the door like a kamikaze pilot, hitting it square on with a satisfying crash and taking it off its hinges. My satisfaction was short lived though, as the cunning owner of the divan had fitted a strong horizontally pivoting bar across the middle of the door and this held long enough for the bottom of the door to fly forward, the top to fly back, and the whole door to fall on top of me with some force knocking me to the ground.

For a moment I lay flat on my back under the door with the breath knocked out of me and was then held down by the weight of what felt like a herd of buffaloes, the opium smokers, stampeding over the door seeking escape. I felt like Charlie Brown in the 'Peanuts' cartoons as I lay there struggling to get up, felled in my brief moment of glory on my first raid. My discomfiture was compounded by being able to see sideways and noting that my loyal men were busy trying to make arrests, and gain entry, while disabled with laughter, tears of mirth running down their faces. What was worse was the fact that even the drug addicts were being hampered in their escape by giggling hysterically, and I was the cause. The rush eventually subsided and I was assisted to my feet by the sergeant who desperately tried to keep a straight face as he checked that I had suffered no injury, other than bruising from head to foot plus badly dented pride. It was noticeable that the remainder of the men did their best to keep their backs to me but the suspicious heaving of their shoulders indicated either mirth or St Vitus Dance, and I knew they were all fit.

At least fifteen smokers had managed to escape but we had arrested the divan keeper and half a dozen smokers, seized four opium pipes, a large amount of prepared opium, several hundred dollars in cash and some documents which later proved of interest to our CID. In the final analysis my first raid had proved a qualified success and I had been given the first of many lessons in how not to charge like a bull at a gate! I invited the squad to join me for a drink to celebrate my first operational duty in the Hong Kong Police, and they all accepted. They took me to a small Chinese floating restaurant where we celebrated in style with good food and drink for a ridiculously low price.

I learned much that, farcical, night. Not just about charging doors but about the Hong Kong Chinese people, particularly those serving in the police force. Like most Europeans I had accepted the stereotype of the 'inscrutable Chinese' and I discovered that they were extremely 'scrutable' when their boisterous sense of humour was engaged. They told me over the meal that they had only recently seen the Marx Brothers movie where about sixty people had been crammed into one small cabin aboard a ship until eventually the door had opened and they fell out. The scene at the opium divan, especially the expression on my face, had irresistibly reminded of this and they had started laughing. Just talking about it set them off again and we ended up roaring with laughter, attracting some attention from the other diners. Our next raid was not as amusing.

There are two major typhoon shelters for junks and small craft in Hong Kong Harbour, one at Causeway Bay in Hong Kong Island, the other at Yaumati in Kowloon. In the Kowloon typhoon shelter, over a period of many years, wooden huts were built on stilts stretching out into the shelter from the sea wall and foreshore, mainly in the Mongkok area. They eventually formed a maze of structures linked precariously by a spider's web of springy wooden catwalks which could be laid in place or removed in seconds. The huts were ideal as drug divans as access could be gained by customers from the land via the catwalks which would be raised and lowered as required, or from the waters of the typhoon shelter by sampan. They were almost impossible to raid as every access point was guarded by lookouts equipped with an electric bell push with which they signalled warnings to the opium divans. Even the sampan girls were paid for giving an arranged visual alarm if they were suspicious that their passengers might be policemen. Even if a drug squad managed to sneak in part of the way, one shout was enough to empty every divan leaving the police with only the most comatose of the addicts as prisoners and only scraps of opium as their prize.

A problem with raids in the Mongkok typhoon shelter was that responsibility for the huts was shared by Marine Police and the Mongkok, Land Police sub-division, part of the Yaumati Police Division. If the Marine drug squad scored a success in the divans the Land sub-divisional inspector was criticised by his superiors and if the Land drug squad scored a success the Marine sub-divisional inspector was criticised by his. This pattern of unfair criticism ran right through the Hong Kong police as senior commanders tried to protect their own records at the expense of their juniors. In such a no-win situation it can hardly be surprising that, over the years throughout the Police Force, a succession of sub-divisional inspectors and other junior commanders, came to arrangements that guaranteed none would be subject to unfair criticism as a result of any action by the other! If some corrupt policemen took advantage of these arrangements to make money, the responsibility lay with the system under which the police force was run, rather than the hapless SDIs. This put quite a burden on drug squad commanders who were, invariably, quite junior officers who quickly learned never to fully trust anyone, including senior officers, with full details of any raid being planned.

One day we were given a series of addresses of properties in the stilt-hut community in the typhoon shelter and told to carry out drug raids on them. A reconnaissance of the area over a night or two from the roof of a high building near the foreshore proved that the 'addresses' were quite useless as there was no rational lay out to the unnumbered and unmarked huts or the routes in to them. Through binoculars it could be seen that the wooden planks of the catwalks were raised, lowered, and moved from place to place, in no discernible pattern, and that access seemed to be provided only to those people who were recognised by the look-outs or were introduced to them by acquaintances. It was also obvious that the sampan women were doing a good trade ferrying passengers into the drug dens. Some successful drug raids had been done in the huts in the past but for the life of me I could not see how. The only possible way to make a truly surprise raid on the drug divans seemed to be to go in late at night over the mud flats and filth under the stilt-huts. The raid would have to be carried out on a night when the tide was very low and there was enough wind and, hopefully, rain to keep the look-outs and sampan girls under cover.

Shortly afterwards, on a night when conditions proved perfect for our enterprise, we discovered why no one had ever been stupid enough to go in by the low route so far as we could discover. The huts had stood high on their big bamboo stilts over the waters of the typhoon shelter for many years. Strongly constructed of sound timber, and well sheltered, they were able to survive the passage of typhoon after typhoon but they had no modern plumbing nor did their inhabitants have any rubbish collection service. They did, however, seem to have an insatiable appetite for shellfish with large, sharp, shells. We gained access to the foreshore some two hundred yards from the nearest of the huts and under cover of lashing rain driven by a strong wind we made our way under the huts without being seen. Our target was the largest of the huts, built as strongly as a fortress and set smack in the middle of the maze. As we made our way towards the target it quickly became patently obvious why no one had ever been stupid enough to use that method of entry before. It was a nightmare journey that seemed never ending. Beneath us was a foetid, squelching, horrible mud, that stank, and felt, like a ghoulish amoeboid thing, sucking at our limbs.

On top of the mud, in layers, was the accumulated evidence of years of 'hole in the floor' toilets, 'over the side' rubbish disposal, and small mountains of fish shells all with sharp, cutting, edges. On all sides squeaks and rustling rushes betrayed the presence of rats disturbed by our progress. At one stage someone went to the toilet as an unfortunate constable was just passing beneath and his furious disgust was sympathetically felt by all. We progressed slowly in the pitch dark, with only occasional flashes of a small pen torch to keep us in contact and on course. In the brief light of one flash we saw the body of a man with his face set in a death grin and with rats feeding on him. From his appearance it could be seen that he had been a drug addict in an advanced stage of emaciation so he had almost certainly died of malnutrition as a result of having to spend all his money on drugs and not food. He had probably died in one of the divans while smoking opium and then been thrown into the water by the divan owner, like just another piece of rubbish. We mentally marked the spot to collect him afterwards but the corpse was washed away later by the rising tide never to be seen again. Our nightmarish journey took over an hour, and we traversed an almost unbelievable trail of foulness rarely seen by modern man. Arrival under the target came almost as an anti-climax. Overcoming the stink in which we lay was the hot, sweet, treacle toffee smell of opium smoke. We could hear the shuffle of feet on the floor above our heads accompanied by the characteristic droning murmur of the voices of the smokers as they drew the dream smoke into their lungs.

The tide had turned and the strong wind was beginning to drive the rising sea in under us as we began our climb up the stilts to the boardwalk surrounding the hut. Two of the constables were very fast and a short fierce scuffle took place overhead followed by a splash as the burly divan look-out fell into the water. Noise from nearby huts and the sound of the wind prevented the people inside the hut from hearing what was going on. We took up prearranged positions and prepared to force entry. Some reminiscent grins were directed my way as, like some sort of door-flagellating masochist, I prepared to force the door open, determined not to end up underneath it imitating a constabulary beetle on its back!

We moved simultaneously and crashed into the divan through the windows and door as a synchronised group to the absolute horror and amazement of the divan keeper, his strong arm man, and the smokers as they lay in a stupor on wooden slat platforms with opium pipes in their hands sharing opium lamps. There was a brief but furious resistance from a few of the livelier smokers but our entry had been so sudden and unexpected they were totally unprepared, and all were shortly handcuffed together sitting quietly, and resentfully, on the floor.

Only then did the squad members get a chance to look at each other. We looked awful. We stank to high heaven. We were covered in filth from head to toe. We were also covered with blood from dozens of cuts and scratches sustained from the thrice dammed shells under the huts.

The squad had seized eight opium pipes, nearly a pound of pre-pared opium, HK$2000 in cash, numerous receipts and papers, plus seven opium lamps, and fourteen prisoners. It was necessary to send for reinforcements to help us take our haul to the land police station so one constable was sent off to find a telephone and call for assistance. It was necessary for him to walk all the way to the police station as everyone he approached took one look at him and slammed the door in his face thinking him one of the numerous filthy madmen, mainly tertiary syphilitics kicked out of China by the Communists, who haunted the streets of Hong Kong with torn clothes and matted hair, at that time. Even at the police station the unfortunate constable Chan had to produce his official warrant card before he could convince the station guard and the Duty Officer that he really was a policeman.

Our departure from the stilt-huts was watched with interest by the assembled residents, braving the wind and rain to watch our progress across the swaying catwalks to the waiting police van. It was one time when even the sorriest looking drug addict looked much better than the arresting police officers. Even at the police station, men of all ranks gathered to look at us with sheer disbelief.

My satisfaction at a very successful raid conducted under difficult circumstances dimmed swiftly as I saw my men under bright electric lights. All of us then went to the Queen Mary Government Hospital in the early hours of the morning and were treated by a scandalised Chinese Doctor who injected us with anti-tetanus serum followed up by a mixed bag of antibiotics. At breakfast, before going off duty, my appetite was small as I looked at my colleagues sitting round the table chattering animatedly about the raid, looking like a team of cartoon mice who had just done three unsuccessful rounds with a mob of heavyweight alley cats, festooned in sticking plaster, bandages, and iodine stains.

My feelings were of guilt at exploiting their loyalty and exposing them to the possibility of a whole variety of awful diseases in order to pull off a successful raid in a difficult place. Had I done it that way, I wondered, from devotion to duty or vanity? This guilt feeling was reinforced when the case came to Court. Each prisoner was fined an average of HK$15 except the divan keeper who had to pay HK$150 a total of HK$350, the equivalent at that time of the cost of a meal for two in a good restaurant! The case before mine was a bar owner who was charged with breaching his licence for selling two bottles of beer twenty minutes after the legal closing time. He was fined HK$700! It was a neatly appropriate demonstration of the Hong Kong Judiciary's scale of priorities at that time.

Some time later, in stark contrast to the purgatory under the huts, we were standing in bright sunshine on the deck of an immaculately smart Marine Police patrol launch heading west out of the harbour in the direction of Tsuen Wan, a New Territories industrial town approximately five and a half miles from north Kowloon. The launch commander was a Eurasian friend of mine and I had thumbed a lift from him. It seemed that the whole world and its dog knew that we were heading for the New Territories but we did not mind. Many people in the police force had been taking too great an interest in our movements since the raid in the typhoon shelter at Mongkok, as our methods of operation apparently did not conform to previous standard procedures, although they did comply with the laws of Hong Kong. It may have been purely coincidental but from the time this interest in us became apparent our drug seizure success rate began to decline!

In Tsuen Wan we boarded an illegal taxi-bus and proceeded east across north Kowloon to an excellent beach in the Port Shelter area where we rendezvoused with some girls we knew, and spent most of the day swimming and enjoying ourselves. Our newest squad member, Constable Ma-yee, was a keen young chap substituting for a man who had been injured on a raid, and he was obviously puzzled by our activities as they did not fit in with the reputation we had gained for being a hard working, if non-conformist, group who had recently had a run of bad luck and poor results. He displayed his intelligence by asking no questions and keeping his mouth shut.

As evening fell we left the beach and walked to the village of Hang Hau where we had a meal and picked up my car which had been driven there and hidden the previous night. We then drove towards town until we turned on to dirt roads leading to within two miles of Lei U Mun. We parked and started walking. The whole day had been set up to deceive watchers and give us a chance to raid an opium divan near Lei U Mun village.

The divan was located in quite a large traditional Chinese style wooden house set on stone foundations, and had reputedly been owned by a well known local family for many years but this could not be proved. What was undeniable was the fact that it had been an immensely profitable opium divan for at least twelve years and most of the drug raids it had experienced had results of the two opium pipes and two prisoners variety.

In the area there were a number of deep holes some reportedly leading to caves, and excavations, and these had traditionally been used as bolt holes and escape routes even before and during the Japanese occupation of the Colony. Our information was that the valuable opium pipes and cash were slung into one or another of these holes when an alarm was given, sometimes hanging down into the dark on thin steel wires, sometimes lowered swiftly to collaborators waiting below to spirit them away.

We took our raid equipment bags containing jemmies, bolt-cutters, and other tools, out of the car boot and made our way to the divan. It was a dark night and we managed to get into position without being heard before bursting in on the surprised opium-smokers. Quick as we were some of the pipes were thrown out through a secret panel in the wall and disappeared into the night closely pursued by our energetic young constable. We had managed to seize six very old pipes, worth a lot of money to the divan owner, HK$1600 in cash, five ounces of prepared opium, and ten prisoners.

However, there were at least eight opium lamps on the wooden slat divans, so it seemed that we had lost about ten pipes through the secret panel. We began our usual procedures and finally had the prisoners and the exhibits, except for the oil lamps, ready to go down to the village pier to await the arrival of a police launch to convey us all to the harbour police station.

Suddenly the whole building shook and swayed from side to side as though hit by an earthquake. We immediately rushed the panicky prisoners, and the exhibits out into the open air from where we could see that the building was swaying to and fro in a remarkable way for such a substantial structure. We could see from their lights that houses in the village nearby looked perfectly normal, just standing there without movement as buildings are supposed to do, so it meant that we were experiencing either a remarkably localised earth tremor, or the building had somehow parted company with its foundations!

As we watched, the whole divan crashed down into a huge heap of tumbled wood wreathed in dust. Sergeant Ying was just saying something about the lighted opium lamps, left behind when we fled the building, when the first flicker of flame appeared. The wood was very old and dry and within minutes was roaring like a furnace. It was fortunate that there were no structures close enough to catch fire as it took nearly thirty minutes for fire-fighters to struggle to the scene, only to find that there was no water supply within half a mile. It did not matter really as all that was left of the building was a large mound of red hot cinders piled on top of the stone foundations some of which had cracked in the intense heat.

There was nothing more to be done at the scene, so I went to collect my car, accompanied, at the sergeant's insistence, by Constable Ma-yee. He looked rather harassed and uncomfortable, and in reply to me asking if he felt OK, he told me what had happened to him from the time I saw him piling out through the secret panel after the opium pipes. He had followed a running man who appeared to be carrying a bag, presumably with the pipes in it. The fellow stopped briefly only a few yards from the divan then continued running. Ma could see that he had stopped by one of the holes leading to the caves so he checked to see if there were any wires or ropes hanging down and found a wire cable which he tugged at but it was immovable. Ma then went back to the divan, took a bolt cutter out of one of the raid bags, returned to the hole in the ground and cut the cable.

It was not until the free end of the cable whipped violently past him that he realised it was secured to the ridge pole on the roof and before his horrified gaze the whole building began swaying to and fro. He saw us piling out in a rush, and the house collapsing and realised that he was still holding the bolt-cutters with which the deed had apparently been done. Purely by reflex, he dropped the cutters and, as it was obviously not his day, they hit the edge of the hole and dropped down into the darkness, apparently, into the middle of the earth, as he could hear them hitting the sides of the hole for a long time. It was only when he saw the first flames appearing from the remains of the divan that he forgot about the loss of the expensive bolt-cutters and just stood, transfixed, looking from the burning building to the hole in the ground and back again to the burning building. He was simultaneously trying to calculate how long it would take him to pay for the building by instalments of HK$25 out of his pay of HK$175 per month, if he was sued for compensation by the owner, and had arrived at the answer of 833 years!

THE ONE-EYED DRAGON

My sense of humour is weird and has got me into a lot of trouble in my time, and as Ma was talking the black humour of the events he was describing took charge of me, I started laughing and couldn't stop. Ma was quite a serious young man and the more I laughed the more solemnly puzzled he looked, and that made me laugh even more. We reached the car and set off on the long drive to the car ferry in Kowloon to return to harbour police station in Hong Kong island. On the way I explained to him that he had nothing to worry about as I was the officer in command of the squad and if anyone was held responsible for the destruction of the building it would be me not him as he was acting under my orders. Instead of looking happier Ma looked even gloomier at this and pointed out to me that such a defence had availed nothing for the people who were put on trial for war crimes after the Second World War this set me off laughing again.

It was customary to inform one of the senior officers in Marine Police headquarters on the conclusion of any unusually successful raid, or one where anything unusual had occurred. This raid qualified on both counts so I telephoned my immediate boss on arrival at Harbour station and reported to him in 'good news, bad news' style – the good news being the successful raid, and the bad news the fact that the building had fallen down and burned to a cinder. I anticipated all sorts of problems, demands for explanations in writing, disciplinary proceedings, an official enquiry at the least but all I got was a remarkably satisfied grunt of approval and the comment that the place had been rotten with termites for years, that it was just a question of time until it fell down, that it was a notorious opium divan and the fire had undoubtedly started as a result of illicit opium lamps.

That was an end to it as far as officialdom was concerned but rumour spread among the divan owners that I was a dangerous man to tangle with, and hinted of arsonous tendencies! It did not matter as Lei U Mun was my last raid as officer commanding Marine Police drug squad. It seemed almost theatrically appropriate that my spell on Marine drug squad had started with the farce of the door falling on me and had ended with a dramatic blaze. A week later I was in Marine Police Launch No.1 under the command of the redoubtable 'Great Water Buffalo' and busily learning that Marine Police work differed quite considerably from the Royal Navy.

Five

'DOWN TO THE SEA . . .'

Marine Police Launch No.1 was a Second World War utility tug, transformed into a Marine Police Gunboat. She was one of the Admiralty-type tugs hastily designed and built at the height of the U-boat campaign against British merchant shipping. These steam-powered tugs were used to tow in any torpedoed ship that had not sunk, simply in order to obtain any of the cargo that was salvageable. It was said that they were so cheaply built they only had to rescue one merchant ship to pay for themselves!

When I first saw Launch No.1 she was at her buoy in Yaumati Typhoon Shelter, squat, powerful, smartly painted, and clean, she was no beauty, but she was purposeful. Later, in a typhoon, she proved to be a superb sea boat, in the very capable hands of her Commanding Officer, Inspector Jim Cunningham, an ex-Royal Navy man, known to the Chinese by his nickname the 'Great Water Buffalo', and to Europeans as 'Bull Moose' or 'Moose'. Jim was a big man who always reminded me of King Henry VIII, and the bluff blunt sailors of the Elizabethan era, although he was reputedly of Scottish descent. He was also one the finest seamen I ever met in eleven years at sea, and many Chinese people, fishermen and refugees, owed their lives to his personal and moral courage and outstanding ship handling ability. Within thirty minutes of going aboard Launch 1, it was obvious that Jim knew his stuff. We slipped away from the buoy and threaded our way through the busily teeming waters of the harbour without fuss, or hesitation, like an eel through reeds.

We headed East through Lei U Mun Pass into our main patrol area in Mirs Bay from where, on 27 April 1898, after being ordered out of Hong Kong by the Governor, the American Navy launched its victori-ous assault against the Philippines during the Spanish-American war.

In contrast to my deployment in the drug squad, Jim gave me a very full briefing on all the duties we would be performing and went over the charts with me pointing out pitfalls and telling me in detail all about the sea and land patrols we would be doing. He also mentioned the unofficial tradition that all officers slept with their pistol to hand in their bunk. Some years before, following the Communist victory in China, two members of the crew aboard one of the large patrol launches decided to hijack the launch and take it to the Chinese mainland. It seems that they had visions of being greeted like heroes and rewarded with good positions in the Communist hierarchy. It may also have been that, as frequently happened, rumours had been circulating in the Colony that Mao Tse-tung was contemplating the occupation of Hong Kong. Whatever the reason the two traitors planned their treachery well. Late one night when the launch was at anchor in the Mirs Bay area the conspirators were the Duty Watch charged with keeping guard and look-out for four hours during the night. In the engine room there was only a drowsy engineer on watch. The two men gained access to the ship's armoury and obtained automatic weapons. They locked the other sleeping crewmen down below in their quarters then went to the cabins of the Commanding Officer and his second-in-command and shot them both dead in their bunks. Under the threat of being killed by the two mutineers, who had nothing to lose, having killed their officers, some of the remaining crew men, were forced to get the launch under way, and it was steamed across to the coast of Kwangdung Province where they handed it over to surprised Communist officials. Instead of being given a hero's welcome they were immediately placed in detention; while the minor officials of the local Party bureaucracy quickly passed this international hot potato up through the chain of command to Peking. The loyal crew men were kept on board with their dead officers and the launch was later sent back to Hong Kong. What happened to the two murderers was not known, for certain, but it is generally believed that they did not receive any reward of any kind for their actions, on the contrary, they were last reported as being seen working hard in the fields as part of a labour battalion. To the best of my knowledge, this is the only case of its kind where Hong Kong policemen have turned against their officers. They have been, consistently, outstanding in their loyalty to the British Crown, and their officers.

It seems to be my fate always to drop a clanger at the beginning of any new job, and Police Launch No.1 was no exception. The day after we started our patrol we headed for the northern end of Mirs Bay to Laichee Wo, an isolated rural community near the Starling Inlet, connected to the modern world only by a motorised junk used to carry their goods to market.Information had been received that trouble was brewing.

As the name indicates Laichee Wo is one of the best areas in the whole of China for growing a particularly popular variety of the valuable lychee fruit. Valuable, because it can earn more money per tree, on each thirty feet of land used, than almost any other legitimate crop. The delicious, translucently white, one inch long fruit in its brittle skin, has been the favourite fruit of the Cantonese people from ancient times.

However, at this time, weather conditions in southern China had not been good in the main lychee growing areas, and there was a reported shortage of fruit. Prices were at an all-time high and competition to buy was fierce. As sometimes happens, the bad weather had freakishly missed Hong Kong, so any fruit growing in the Colony commanded a premium price. There had been friction in Laichee Wo, sometimes leading to bloodshed, for many years, allegedly over a long past, oriental, Romeo and Juliet incident, but the main source of disputes was quarrels over which laichee trees belonged to which family. About fifty varieties of lychees exist of which the 'No Mai' and 'Haak Ip', described to me by one villager as 'delicious Rolls Royces', are considered the best, and these were the type mainly growing in Laichee Wo.

Jim Cunningham anchored well off shore before briefing me carefully and sending me off in the dory to find out what was going on. The last thing the authorities wanted so soon after the Double Tenth riots, was a 'lychee war' – who would believe it anyway?

We secured the dory at the village pier and I set off to see the village elders, together with another police officer, Lee, who knew the local people quite well. Before going off, I told the men in the dory to circulate around in the village and see what useful gossip they could pick up. It was unfortunate that, I did not specify who was to circulate and who was to stay with the dory.

As with so many calls upon village dignitaries in Hong Kong, etiquette took up much of our time. European brevity is not regarded as efficiency, just bad manners and poor upbringing. By the time we had finished drinking our numerous cups of delicious China tea, exchanging felicitations, inquiring politely about the state of crops, water supplies, the price of fuel for their generators and junk, heard of new births of boy-children, and a great deal more, much time had passed. We eventually angled the conversation round to recent events, and gradually approached the subject of potential trouble in the community. As briefed by the knowledgeable Jim Cunningham who, in my opinion, knew the people of his area better than anyone else, we were not so crass as to put the question bluntly or even gently – in fact we did not put it at all. It was mentioned to the elders that the police had heard rumours that certain persons from across Mirs Bay, the Communists, had been making surreptitious visits to the more isolated islands and communities on our side, to the extreme consternation and dismay of our hard-working and law-abiding farmers and fishermen. For this reason, they were told, Mr Cunningham had decided that the area should receive his undivided protection, night and day, for the foreseeable future, that he would be putting out well armed land and dory patrols, at all hours, thus ensuring that no one disturbed the Queen's Peace to which they were all entitled! This seemed to me to be well received by the elders, who expressed their gratitude to the Queen and Jim Cunningham at great and flowery length and then saw us ceremoniously off.

We had been with them for well over an hour and, as we walked back to the pier, I asked my Chinese colleague what, exactly, we had accomplished? Mr Lee grinned at me and told me that we had delivered 'Moose' Cunningham's message which was, in essence, 'Right you bastards, I know you are set for another 'lychee war' and I won't have it. I am going to cover this area with policemen, like manure over a paddy field, and at one, just one, hint of aggravation from your would-be warriors, we'll kick the living shit out of you!' What then, I asked, was their rather long reply? Lee's grin was even wider as he told me their answer which was, in brief, 'OK, don't worry, we'll keep everything under control, and your ears really are as big as a bloody water buffalo's if you heard about this so fast!' My sense of satisfaction at this was short-lived. When we arrived at the pier I could see the dory high and dry on the mud surrounded by the crew who were radiating extreme consternation. The tide had gone out and no one had remained with the dory to ease off the securing line so that the boat stayed afloat for our return. The fault was entirely mine, as I was senior officer present, and my failure, as a former seaman, to remember the ebb tide was especially galling to me. To compound my disgrace, I was the one who had instructed the men to circulate, as spies, on the gossip circuit. I had been so busy, being James Bond, I'd forgotten Horatio Hornblower! Even from the pier Moose Cunningham could be seen on the bridge of the Launch, radiating fury, his face bright red with anger. It took us nearly half an hour to get the boat into the water, and on the way back to the launch I felt like a right, royal, eighteen carat, twit. We had provided the local water people with a yarn to keep them amused for months, probably still, and all my fault.

The author with Staff Sgt. Chan Chor-Choi after the 1956 riots.

The Hongkong Standard

Bird's eye view of Cheung Chau.

In private, Moose gave me the finest dressing down I have ever received in my life, good enough for the *Guinness Book of Records*. His face was red but his voice was quiet, though impassioned. He never repeated himself, every word he said was true, and I still remember it. When he had finished I apologised, without excuses, for my negligence. He accepted my apology and the matter was never referred to again. He was a good commanding officer.

Perhaps on the same principle as used in bygone times, to ensure that children remembered boundary markers by beating them heartily by the boundary stones, to make 'beating the bounds' an unforgettable occasion, Moose sent me off with a search squad to search a huge, Kwandung-type, distant water, fishing junk, over ninety feet long and carrying a family crew of at least eighty men women and children, we never were quite sure of the total number as the children never remained still for long enough to be counted.

They stopped dead in the water when we signalled them to halt, possibly encouraged in this unusual promptness for Cantonese, by the sight of the gun-crew standing casually by the uncovered for'rd Browning which they had been cleaning. We scrambled aboard her and checked her ship's papers watched by grinning adults and wide-eyed children obviously unaccustomed to the sight of a white 'foreign ghost'. Just smiling, in a friendly way, at one tiny child brought such a howl of terror from him that his big sister snatched him up, with a scowl at me, and Moose looked over to see what was going on as the crew of the junk roared with laughter.

The junk was beautifully built for long fishing voyages, and was equipped with a marine-diesel engine in addition to a full set of sails. Her crew lived in quite comfortable quarters, in the after part of the junk, with single men accommodated forward in the bow. When fishing was in progress the children were kept clear of operations, for the rest of the time they, with the exception of the very tiny toddlers, swarmed everywhere. These were prevented from falling over the side by being put in a small creche, or popped into small wooden barrels, on the after end of the junk, secured by cord tethers, and under the strict supervision of 'older' girls, usually about eight or nine years old!

My straight-faced corporal invited me to lead the search below, and we lowered ourselves into the dark 'tween decks. The combined smells of fish and bilges were strong enough to stun a cart-horse! There were six good-sized holds, full of fish, and two containing the fishing nets. We conducted a fairly short, but efficient search, as it was obvious from the genuinely amused attitude of the crew, plus the fact that all of the families were aboard, there was little likelihood of any illicit cargo being found. In any case, they were genuinely delighted, when we told them that their catch would fetch a good price ashore, as there was a temporary shortage of fish in the markets, at that time. We returned to No.1 and they were cast off to resume their voyage into harbour. As they pulled away a huge Ray nearly knocked me out, thrown over as a gift from the smiling junk skipper, and as they sped off, we could still hear the howls of the little boy, making his dislike of foreigners known to the world!

Soon after this, when a typhoon hit the Colony, Moose showed what a magnificent seaman he was. After Laichi Wo we continued with normal patrols, stopping and searching junks, visiting isolated fishing and farming communities, sharing tea and gossip with the inhabitants and thereby picking up snippets of useful information for our intelligence reports. We made arrangements for medical teams to visit isolated communities, and occasionally evacuated sick people to clinics or, if seriously ill, to hospital. At times we steamed down the eastern side of Mirs Bay parallel to the coast China, occasionally seeing miserable gangs of prisoners in patched blue clothes being marched along to the site of forced labour. Ping Chau Island was the farthest east of the British islands in Mirs Bay separated by barely a mile of sea from the nearest commune. We called there at regular intervals as it was known that Communist militiamen, in the guise of fishermen, occasionally landed there, with weapons, to terrorise in hopes of corruptly obtaining food, clothes, and other things, difficult to obtain in the People's Republic. There was always the possibility, too, of finding illegal immigrants, but this did not happen very often, as the local communes were liable to be penalised by the District Commissar, if anyone made an escape from their area. The Launch's funnel had a few patched up bullet holes in it, resulting, I was told, from Moose going to the rescue of refugees in the sea.

One night Moose had taken No.1 on a patrol over to Ping Chau. As they rounded the island, from the north, they heard gunfire, then a number of people, forty or more, were seen swimming in the water, together with debris from a sunken boat. There were three or four commune junks around them and the crew of No.1 thought they were rescuing the survivors until they saw, to their horror, that militiamen in the junks were smashing the swimmers' heads, in with boat hooks and metal bars, as they desperately tried to save themselves. What added to the horror of the scene, if that was possible, was that many of the terrified people were children who were being dealt with as ruthlessly and cruelly as the adults. The water was red with blood and floating bodies, and the commune junks were being deliberately manoeuvred to chop people with their propellers and smash them with their hulls. Some of the Cantonese policemen were enraged, as they saw one militiamen using a fish gaff, a barbed fishing spear, plunging it into the body of a young woman, with a baby on her back, treading water with hands stretched up pleading for rescue!

Launch Commanders had been given confidential instructions, devised by bloodless bureaucrats and politicians, 'to avoid unnecessary and politically embarrassing contacts with the Communists' but, thank God, Moose was too fine a man, and too good a seaman, to allow that to stop him from doing his moral, and seamanlike duty. According to the admiring NCO, who told me the story, he sounded gun action stations and steamed towards the scene of slaughter. The militiamen could be seen yelling at the junk masters to go back to shore as No.1 bore down on them, and they smashed into each other in their panic as they turned to run for it. Moose ignored them and eased his way in among the terrified swimmers, his crewmen lowered the boarding ladder, rope ladders, and ropes. Men dived into the water and brought weak swimmers to the side where they were pulled to safety. The ship's dory had been quickly lowered and her two man crew busied themselves gathering people up, bringing them to the ship, and going off again on their mission of mercy. The militiamen fired at the ship from a safe position near the beach, where they felt secure, as it was common knowledge that no Police vessel would deliberately open fire from a position where their fire might land on the sovereign territory of China. The sea gods had the last laugh as two of the militia junks sank as a result of colliding during their panicky retreat. All of the living who could be found were picked up and cared for on board. Corpses were still floating in the sea already being attacked by what was thought to be sharks and barracudas, no one was certain in the darkening night. In any case, No.1 had to head for Hong Kong to get the many shocked and injured refugees to medical help.

The story they told the crew men was one that was common at that time, as it is today with refugees from Vietnam. Some ninety people had been aboard the illegal immigrant's junk trying to flee China for Hong Kong. The local militia leader had been paid a bribe to ignore them but had double-crossed them instead. He took the money, then led the attack on them shortly after they had set sail. A commune junk had deliberately rammed and sunk their boat, then the militiamen on board had fired at them with Kalashnikov rifles as they floundered in the water, competing with each other for the number shot in the head. They had started to smash at them in the sea just before No.1 came on the scene. What shocked some of the survivors was the fact that the militiamen were laughing and obviously enjoying themselves as they killed the poor people in the sea, boasting that they had done this to many traitors in the past. Thirty-four survivors made it in to Hong Kong out of the ninety or so who had embarked in the escape junk!

My informant told me that they had heard that Moose had been reprimanded verbally for risking an incident but that he had replied that he would prefer a disciplinary tribunal to a bad conscience. Whether true or not, it fitted his character as I knew him. It certainly did not change his humanitarian attitude, and anyone he saw in peril in the sea at any time, and regardless of bureaucracy, he went to rescue. Horatio Nelson would have been proud of him!

We received weather information one day that a typhoon had brewed up off the Philippines and was heading our way. These were the days before transistor radios, so we had many duties to carry out as soon as possible. We warned isolated villages, and tiny inter-village ferry junks, by displaying typhoon signals to warn fishermen to take shelter, herding stubborn, or stupid, small boats into safety and, generally charging about like a purposeful, but overactive, sea-going collie dog. We had our own main typhoon station at No.1's buoy in the typhoon shelter at Yaumati. If caught out for any reason our next best place was at anchor in the four mile square Plover Cove, now a huge reservoir, one hour's steaming time down the length of the Tolo Channel.

For people who find it difficult to understand the sheer power and full effect of a typhoon, compared with a full gale, the reservoir builders calculated that it would take at least four years for Plover Cove to fill up with fresh water on completion of the dam, one year for each square mile of area, it was actually full and running over after just one tremendous typhoon!

Wind and seas were increasing rapidly, as we set off on the way to our typhoon buoy when we sighted a large sea-going fishing junk lying upside down in the water with the family crew hanging on to her. We went to take them aboard but were told that there were still people alive trapped in the hull. We could not dive into the junk to rescue them as the seas were roughening so Moose decided to tow her into sheltered waters which we did. Within an hour the junk had been beached safely not far from Plover Cove, actually on a small secluded beach at the foot of the District Commissioner's garden much to the displeasure of his wife.

We were, prudently, preparing to anchor in the Cove when we received a radio message reporting a large junk with many people on board in trouble well down the coast near High Island. Moose set off, immediately, and we steamed as fast as we could to the reported distress scene. The typhoon was beginning to blow with growing force as we steamed down the coast, so strongly that we began taking a tremendous battering from seas hitting us broad on the beam. Moose had to alter course and take us in an extended dogleg miles out into the Bay, first taking the sea at an angle on the port bow, then after he had made a superbly judged turn on a huge wave, on the port quarter as we steamed back toward the land. We were being pounded by the waves as we arrived at High Island and found that the report had obviously been a hoax. Later it was confirmed to be. The drug and illegal immigrant smugglers would make false reports quite frequently in bad weather, in the hopes of having a police vessel sunk or damaged, as any patrol area with reduced police coverage gave them a better chance of getting their illicit cargoes through. Marine Police were well aware of this but it was still a matter of duty, and pride, to go and see, regardless of the danger, and sometimes the reports were true.

The weather had become so bad we could make it to neither Plover Cove nor the typhoon shelter; even to go back out into Mirs Bay would have been suicidal. Although we were near the entrance to the Port Shelter area, we could see that the freakish prevailing winds were sending huge seas running down through the shelter to break in foaming surf on the arms of land protecting Hebe Haven at the end. Moose calculated that the typhoon would veer off into the eastern part of Kwangdung province and took us in behind Basalt Island where we dropped anchor. The second anchor was prepared to be dropped, instantly, if the first was lost, and an anchor party stood by. It was a brave decision arrived at through sound sea instinct, good seamanship, and confidence in his own knowledge of the vagaries of Hong Kong's typhoons. If he was wrong, we would probably, all be dead by morning ! We spent a whole evening and one of the longest nights of all our lives, behind that island. If hell was water instead of fire it would have been little exaggeration to describe it as a hellish night! We kept full steam up, and the chief engineer and his crew stood by the engine controls to respond instantly to any orders, on the telegraph, from the bridge. Moose had me leave the bridge from time to time to check on any damage, and to visit the engineers in order to keep them in touch with what was going on up top. Going down the engine room ladder was quite an experience. The heat and strong smell of hot oil was overpowering, the movement of the ship was magnified, and the bangs and rattles that went unnoticed on deck became booms and clangs down below, as though a gang of seagoing scrap merchants were tearing No.1 to pieces. None of this seemed to bother the chief and his oily crew, who always seemed quite unconcerned by what was happening outside their real world of gleaming brass and gauges, and perpetually engaged in some arcane activity that involved much hammering and squirting of oil, at things, from cans with long spouts, like humming birds' bills. The same calmness was displayed by crew members, off watch, in their mess. Some were sleeping, some playing cards, some quietly reading, to the background noise of the Hong Kong radio station broadcasting pop music and up-to-the-minute news reports of immense damage being wreaked everywhere by the typhoon. Their calm attitude had nothing to do with inscrutability or fatalistic oriental acceptance of their fate, everyone simply trusted Moose!

Many times that night, we had to steam ahead just to stay in position, at anchor. The strong winds battered the upper works of the launch, carrying away the radio antennae damaging the enclosed bridge, and much else beside; loosening the funnel which swayed within its wire stays until the bo'sun and his team secured it, after a struggle. At one stage things were so bad everyone was ordered to wear life jackets, and the engine-room was reduced to a skeleton staff including the chief engineer, but the danger soon passed.

By dawn, it was obvious that Moose's calculation of the progress of the typhoon was correct, as it moved gradually into China. By early morning we were under way, still in heavy seas, heading into harbour for repairs and also to let headquarters know we were still afloat. As we sailed through the harbour we received some friendly and admiring waves from merchantmen, as a respectful, and well-deserved salute, to Jim Cunningham's seamanship.

On our next patrol, we spent a pleasantly warm afternoon in the Port Shelter area, near Shelter Island, tidying up the ship and swimming. These occasional 'make and mend' afternoons were the nearest thing to time-off in ships, usually arranged after everyone had been working hard for an extended period, and taken in a place where the crew could relax. The site of this one had been arranged as a result of a chat with the bo'sun, and through him the rest of the crew, and it had arisen from my last run ashore.

In the course of having a drink in the Marine Police Officers' bar, a passing comment of mine expressing my admiration for Jim Cunningham's seamanship had revealed an unexpected, and quite startling, well of spiteful dislike against Moose, among some of the senior Marine men, surprising in the fact, that most of them were very friendly to him when he was there. My views of his ability were treated with scorn and a great performance was made of a story alleging that he had smashed the propeller of No.1 when he hit a well-charted rock, and then compounded his offence by claiming that the rock he hit was not the one on the chart. Repairs, they said, had necessitated a spell in dry dock, and considerable expense, before No.1 could resume patrol. They sounded off like a sanctimonious bunch of beer-filled sea-lawyers, until I got bored with them, and offered one particular big mouth a knuckle sandwich, before vacating the bar at the request of the senior man present!

Together with the crew we decided to clear Moose's name. Our dory was pressed into use as a swimming boat and some of us, including the bo'sun who had been on the bridge at the time of the incident, went off in it. The bo'sun dropped a small anchor at the spot, and I dived to the bottom with snorkel, face mask, and flippers. Apart from having worked under water in the Royal Navy, I enjoyed underwater swimming, so this was a pleasant way to look for the truth. Within half an hour, we had found the blade from the propeller, lying on the bottom, near a rock on which deep marks clearly showed where the propeller had struck and been broken off . . . it was not the rock shown on the navigation chart, which was about two cables, 400 yards, distant. We tied a marker buoy to the battered rock and returned to No.1, where the propeller blade was presented to the 'Skipper'. He was not the type of man given to great displays of emotion, but he could grin well. On my next run ashore the bar went quiet and chilly when I asked if they sold 'sour-grape' wine, so it seemed only diplomatic to beat a quiet retreat!

That was my last trip with Jim Cunningham, as I was given my own Command, Launch No.27, based in Cheung Chau island on the western side of the Colony. We were never particular friends, we were too different in character and in our interests, but my respect for him then, as a good seaman and a good commander, is unchanged to this day. There can be few men who have saved as many lives in their time, as the 'Moose'. He taught me a great deal, both directly, and indirectly by observing the way he did his work.

My service under his command proved unexpectedly to my benefit in Edinburgh nearly twenty years later. From No.1 Moose used to send me in charge of regular patrols in isolated communities to make sure that the people were not being intimidated or 'squeezed' by Communist militiamen making clandestine bullying visits from across the bay in China, and also to see if there were any illegal immigrants present. These checks used to mean that villagers and genuine visiting fishermen and their children had to be identified to us when necessary. All Hong Kong citizens, sensibly, had identity cards which they carried at all times, but occasionally someone would forget and leave their card in their junk or at home, and would then be detained by us until identified and vouched for, by some known and respected local. As a result of this, all children were given the day off school when we visited their community. Tap Mun village, in Grass Island, at the entrance to Tolo Channel, used to receive frequent and irregular visits from us, as Tap Mun people had a regular, ferry-junk service to Tai Po Gau on the mainland of the New Territories. Tai Po Gau was also a stop on the Kowloon Canton Railway from which illegal immigrants could catch the train straight into town. The checks were always done in a friendly way and the villagers were nice people who accepted that we were just doing our duty. They were also grateful for the fact that our visits reduced their chances of being exploited by the militiamen.

One day, in Edinburgh, I went with my favourite cousin, and her husband, for a meal in the Silver Bowl Chinese restaurant in Comiston Road. We were enjoying superb Chinese dishes when we became aware that there was much surreptitious talk going on, behind the beaded curtain that separated the kitchens from the dining room, and that we seemed to be the subject under discussion. Eventually, the curtains parted and a young man came to our table and said, rather than asked, 'You are the one-eyed Dragon aren't you?' I replied that had indeed been one of my nicknames in Hong Kong. He called his wife and the others and they came to the table and began talking to me. They were from Tap Mun and had been children at school during our searches. Even all these years later, and thousands of miles from their island home, they still recalled their unexpected holidays from school with glee. We were kept supplied with a constant stream of glasses of Remy Martin Cognac, 'on the house', while they chatted with us, and they did not want me to pay for the meal when eventually we left. It was a tremendous pleasure for me, after all the years that had passed, to realise how much our visits to Tap Mun had been appreciated, at least, by the schoolchildren!

Six

FIRST COMMAND

While serving under the Command of Jim Cunningham, in Launch No.1, I had studied for my China Coast Master's Navigation Certificate examination and my Radar Navigator's Certificate. Both were set by the Hong Kong Marine Department to the highest British standards. Before being allowed to begin the courses, I was sent off, like everyone else, for an eyesight check. Theirs, generally, took about twenty minutes, mine took over an hour, but I passed it, to everyone's surprise. I bore no resentment for this, as being put in command of ships with twelve and more men on board, it was only right that my medical and academic fitness for the job should be established beyond any reasonable doubt. Following my discharge from the Army hospital in 1956, my medical treatment had been entirely the responsibility of Dr Dansey-Browning, a Hong Kong Government eye surgeon, and he had done well by me, well enough for acceptance by the Marine Department, as fit to command a police vessel, in the most crowded waters in the world. Horatio Nelson and Blackbeard jokes were, naturally, part of the cross that had to be borne, in order to gain the cherished 'ticket to command'. So I tholed my nautical assizes, with scowls at my fellow students' pathetic attempts at humour; and, weakly, ingratiating smiles, at those of the instructors! Yuck! Friends helped me to celebrate my acquisition of the certificates, perhaps not wisely, but well, as this represented a victory for me as the only one-eyed person, at that time, to have been awarded his Master's ticket in Hong Kong! My posting to command Police Launch No.27 came through, it was based in Cheung Chau Island, the most westerly base in the Colony covering the Ferry routes to Macao.

Out of the Marine Police fleet of some twenty or more craft, at the time, the seventy foot, Thornycroft-designed, patrol launches were the most popular with young commanders. They were good, manoeuvrable ships, able to get in and out of restricted places, and easy to take alongside the many differently built craft that had to be boarded and searched. They were strongly constructed of strong timber with bullet-proofed wheelhouses, equipped with radio and radar, with a galley, a crew's mess, and a private cabin for the commander. Their twin-diesel engines were powerful, but delivered only eleven knots, except in extreme emergencies, when engineering legerdemain could produce an extra knot or two. Their main armament was an American, belt-fed, 50-calibre Browning, heavy machine gun, firing a one and a half ounce bullet that could penetrate light armour, and could chop a sturdy pirate junk into matchwood. A Bren gun and a variety of light arms made up the weapons complement.

Barring breakdowns, or refits, there were normally three or four launches at sea, at any given time, night and day, patrolling the Colony's 400 miles of coastline, and 730 square miles of territorial waters. All the sea lanes around Hong Kong are perpetually busy, but those on the western side are the busiest. Launch 27's patrol area covered the whole of the western side of the Colony, and most of the islands. Some days, when patrolling our boundary, visually and on radar, we plotted over sixty vessels, in forty miles of sea space between Hong Kong and Macao! However, most of the big merchant ships used the eastern approaches, with the exception of tankers, and the ships with dangerous cargoes, who generally, went to their special anchorages from the west via Lamma Channel. Almost all of the smaller craft preferred the western approaches avoiding the big ships.

On arrival in Cheung Chau I met my colleague and co-commander, Mike, and settled into the police bungalow we shared. The following day I accompanied him for part of his patrol to get the feel of No.27 and to observe how she handled. She was a beauty, with no built-in vices. Her berth was a reserved space on the Government pier in the harbour.

Like everywhere else in the Colony, the harbour was always crowded and busy, perhaps more so than some, as Cheung Chau was the nearest port to the western fishing areas and did a thriving business with fishing boats whose crews did not want to spend the extra time and fuel needed for running the two to three hour journey to Aberdeen. It was also very handy for the fishing junks from Chinese communes, whose catches were grabbed by the commissars as soon as they arrived back, who wanted to sell some of their fish for cash to buy small western luxuries, or even just imported Chinese foodstuffs unobtainable at home.

Every week end and public holiday, Cheung Chau was inundated by visitors arriving by ferry from Hong Kong and Kowloon to eat seafood and buy dried fish. The island had rows of stalls covered with dried fish of all kinds and it was said that, in bad weather, if you could not see the harbour all you had to do was sniff, and navigate in on your nose!

The crew treated my first day in command quite formally, after all, they did not know me, but I discovered later that the bo'sun had followed, a well-established routine, and had partaken of dim-sum dumplings, and tea, with the bo'sun of Launch No.1 and Sergeant Tommy Ying from the drug squad, during which, purely by chance conversation, my nature, character, and general background were discussed!

The moment of truth was taking the ship away from the pier, out of the harbour, and into the open sea, without any disasters. Getting away from the pier went like a dream, the engine-room responded immediately to every telegraph order, and we slipped away as smoothly as an Admiral's barge. We had successfully threaded our way through a water-borne maze of junks, sampans, and barges without hitting anything and were approaching the harbour limits when a heart-stopping outburst of fierce Chinese invective came from the stern. I looked back and could see my corporal and a senior constable leaning over the safety rails whacking at the ears of a number of grinning and giggling youngsters standing up in the bows of their little sampans, who were hitching a ride by holding on to our fender, as children used to do on their bicycles, hanging on to the backs of carts or lorries, when I was a boy in Scotland. There was a tensing of the atmosphere in the wheelhouse as the bo'sun and other crewmen waited to see my reaction, and as I laughed at my Scottish memories they all relaxed and grinned. The sampan kids let go and stood waving to us, as we headed out and started my first patrol in command. It was a nice send off and, although I lectured them many times later, on the dangers of playing about near our propellers, they paid no more attention to me than we did in Edinburgh, to horror stories about the dreadful fate of naughty children who were crushed under lorry wheels when catching a tow up Robertson Avenue!

Within the first hour at sea we stopped and searched a very fast, small, junk heading towards Cheung Chau from Silvermine Bay in Lantau Island. It turned out to be the unofficial ferry run by the villagers of Mui Wo village, virtually all of whom were members of one extended family, the Yuens, whose patriarchal head lived in miniature castle. Mr Yuen proved to be very well known, indeed famous, throughout the islands, and I was gradually given, unverifiable, details of his past history during the course of my time in No.27. The family had been in Silvermine Bay for as long as anyone could remember, before the British came according to some, and had been fishermen and farmers, struggling for decades to make a living from the sea and poor soil, much like the old crofters of Scotland. Everyone lived in extreme poverty, barely at subsistence level, a situation that could have been rectified to a considerable extent by a few bags of lime, potash, and superphosphates, but those were not available.

It was alleged that he had been a successful pirate between the wars, but no evidence was ever given, other than a reported comment of his that he would never, by any such activity, embarrass or 'cause loss of face' for his 'elder brother', King George VI for whom he had a great respect and admiration. What was provable fact, was the anti-Japanese activity which Mr Yuen and all the Mui Wo people were involved in during the Japanese occupation of Hong Kong. In 1940, before Japan was at war with Britain, numerous junks were equipped with engines to enable them to run the Japanese blockade of the China coast with much-needed supplies for the Chinese Army. The Japanese treated anyone employed in this patriotic, and profitable, trade with extreme cruelty, and death, if captured. It says much for the skill of the water-people that few were caught, although, many died when their junks were fired upon by Japanese forces. During the later period of the war the reverse was the case, the Japanese lost some ninety-nine per cent of their merchant fleet to Allied submarines and aircraft, and were compelled by necessity to rely on motorised junks to maintain their communications. The water-people used this to their own advantage. The operators of the cargo lighters in the harbour detested the Japanese but played along with them, seeming to co-operate in exchange for privileges. In fact, they stole food and medicines from the cargoes, they were carrying, and hid them in specially prepared false-bottomed boats for later distribution to their compatriots ashore.

The Mui Wo people, under Mr Yuen, made daring deliveries of food to some British prisoners-of-war existing under atrocious conditions in Japanese hands. Junks from Mui Wo slid into bays near Stanley POW camp and passed over food, and medicines, at great danger to themselves. They kept in touch with the clandestine British Army Aid Group in China and carried out sabotage attacks, such as the one on the main Kowloon Canton Railway bridge over Waterloo Road in Kowloon.

When the war was over many old scores were paid off. Many back alleys, and typhoon drains, contained the shredded remains of Chinese people who had betrayed their compatriots to the Japanese. It may have been rough justice, but for the tens of thousands, who had been murdered by the Japanese, there had been no justice. As it was explained to me, in most cases, they were identifiable by the fact that they were well-clothed and well-fed, even when disguised in tattered clothing, their sleek physical appearance caused them to stand out, like beacons, amongst the starving remnants of the Hong Kong Chinese people.

It was said, that many Japanese collaborators in Hong Kong sought to escape post war retribution by fleeing the Colony, in junks, for destinations in China where they stood a better chance of escaping justice by disappearing into the chaos of a huge population. Passage money was paid, in gold, to junk masters skilled in avoiding patrols and penetrating sea blockades. According to one old inhabitant of Mui Wo, all of them, that he knew of, had been delivered to Chinese soil all right, that part of it, that made up the beds of West Lamma Channel and the Pearl River Estuary. He chuckled as he said that there was a glut of shark's fin soup, as the sharks were so fat, from 'collaborator stew', they were unable to swim!

Mr Yuen's remarks about King George had been made, it was said, when he had refused the offer of an award in recognition of his efforts on behalf of the British. His reference to the King as his 'elder brother' did not mean that he was claiming a family relationship, everyone knew that it was the natural Chinese use of familial terms when showing great respect, demonstrating, publicly, that his duty to the King was as a duty to an elder brother. Chinese people could identify with that more easily than with abstract and impersonal concepts such as applied to constitutional monarchs.

An invitation was given to me to visit Tai Yu, 'Great Fish' Yuen, in his castle at Silvermine Bay and I accepted. Chinese people rarely invite strangers into their homes so this was a great honour for me and gave me much 'face', not only in the local community but among the fishermen and water people generally. The house was, truly, like a small Chinese castle as seen in old paintings. Solidly built, with great gates and doors of solid timber bound, and reinforced, by wide bands of iron. The roof parapets were crenellated, and there were windows narrow enough to be loopholes for firing weapons at enemies. The approach to the front door was made over a bridge that spanned a small moat, generally, referred to as the duck pond, as it did, always, have flotillas of ducks swimming up and down, bickering in duck language, or duck-stepping about the muddy margins looking important, and occasionally fluttering out of reach of bad-tempered guard dogs.

It was a fascinating occasion, meeting this man who figured so largely in every one's conversation. He was tiny and looked quite frail, but he radiated energy, determination, and what used to be called 'power of command' in the armed services. Over time I met his whole family and they were wonderful, down to earth, people. His eldest son was a strong powerful, happy-go-lucky, man. His eldest daughter had a brilliant business brain and would have made a great diplomat. She had been behind my invitation, not because she had any personal interest in me, but because she had heard through the 'Bamboo Telegraph', the ever-efficient gossip channel, about my eye, and the operations I had been given to save my sight. Her father had cataracts developing, one had already made him blind in one eye, and she knew, without him complaining, how much he was missing his full and active life. She eventually mentioned to me that he was visibly growing older as his blindness progressed. Over a number of visits I spoke to him about Dr Dansey-Browning, how much I trusted him, how much he had helped me, and how cataract surgery could restore sight, given appropriate conditions. The upshot was, that he made his first visit to Kowloon, in twenty years, and after an interval, had the cataract operation performed by Dr Dansy-Browning. It was a complete success and Mr Yuen's eyesight was restored, so was his very busy life as head of his clan, chief village elder, and leading figure in Silvermine Bay. I was delighted to have been able to help by introducing him to the doctor, and was honoured to be adopted secretly into the clan. From then on I was his 'nephew' and he was 'Uncle Yuen'. My Commissioner would have been horrified if he'd known.

One of the islands in my area was the 'Leper' island. We received orders to go there one day as, according to somebody's information, there was 'heroin dealing going on'. Orders are orders, as someone once said at the Nuremburg Trials, so I went. My crew were not too happy about it as they, sensibly, had man's universal fear of leprosy but the chosen squad went ashore with me when we arrived at the pier. We met the staff and the lepers. The information had obviously been false. We saw nothing but amazingly dedicated people giving their lives, and doing their damnedest, to help the most cruelly afflicted people I had ever seen. We all managed, I hope, to keep our feelings hidden as we met some of the more extremely affected people, suffering from awful deformations, but we were all shaken by what we saw. It was interesting to note that the medical centre had its own well-stocked pharmacy including opium-derived pain killers. There was no market for anyone dealing in heroin here. In any case, where would these poor people get the money to pay for drugs? We turned what was supposed to be a raid into a, for them rare, social visit, and left. My bo'sun, I discovered later, made it his business to find out where this information had come from and established that it had originated from an officer who had been involved in my little discussion about seamanship some time before, in the Marine Police Officers bar. It had been a malicious parting gift to me, as he went off on nine months' leave. By the time he returned I had transferred to Land Police but I heard that fitting retribution did overtake him in due course. Marine Police crews do not like being messed about over other people's disagreements.

Every day food poured into Hong Kong from Kwangdung Province in China, without it the Colony would have gone on short rations, and without the Colony as a cash market, China's foreign exchange reserves, at the time nearly sixty per cent earned through Hong Kong, would have dropped dramatically. They would also have gone on short rations through their inability to pay in US dollars for essential grain from abroad. Much of the Colony's food, especially perishables, came by rail from Canton via the Kowloon Canton Railway, but by far the greatest amount came from Canton down the Pearl River Estuary in long strings of cargo barges, some of them six, eight or ten pairs long, towed by steam-tugs. These tows had regularly to be stopped and searched. Everyone accepted that, but the place this was done was crucially important. Tows are difficult things to handle at the best of times. Even in canals, rivers, and sheltered waters, it requires the highest standards of seamanship to get them under way, steaming quietly in a straight line, and stopping slowly under control. Any sudden or jerky moves and the whole string of barges would immediately go in all directions, like a string of 200 ton beads being played with by a giant kitten. It could not only take hours to straighten out, but also could cause death and serious injury from snapping towing cables and hawsers whipping viciously about the decks where the crew would be trying to bring things under control. Voyaging down a busy estuary in all kinds of weather, then turning in open sea to enter Hong Kong waters, took outstanding seamanship, and the crews had it! We had a high respect for their abilities, and no desire to make their job any more difficult than need be, nor to delay food from getting into port in time for the daily markets.

My first search was carried out off the coast, near Castle Peak Bay, on their route in from Chinese waters, in a position that gave them nearly ten miles of open sea to stop in, and gave us nearly sixteen square miles of clear water in which to conduct our search. The target was a string of eight barges being towed by a very old, but smart, steam tug that had left Canton City more than a day before. We flew flag 'K', the signal to stop, from the yardarm so that the tug skipper could see it in plenty of time to do a controlled slow down and stop.

As they lay stopped in the water we went alongside and I jumped aboard with the search team. I was completely taken by surprise by the fact that the captain of the tug was a girl, dressed in the dowdy Mao uniform of the time, but undoubtedly a girl and a very attractive one at that. My unthinking male chauvinism took a further dent when I found that all of the crew were girls, in fact all of the crews of all of the tows to Hong Kong . . . were girls. There was nothing particularly significant in this politically, it was just that they were all excellent seamen – seawomen – sea persons, and happened to be the best qualified people for the job! The female engineer did not betray the ancient international order of seagoing engine wallopers; she came up on deck from the engine room wiping her hands on an oily rag, and with grease on her face, the proper identifying signal for engineers, as originated by the world's first real marine engineer aboard the *Charlotte Dundas* in Scotland in 1802.

As soon as we had secured alongside, the tug's equivalent of a political commissar had, with a stern face and properly upraised right fist, given us a brief official harangue from Mr Mao, on the ultimate victory of communism and the total defeat of western-Imperialist-capitalism, then, duty done, she grinned and asked if we'd all care for a cup of tea. The engineer had been told by one of the search party that I was a Scot and I was promptly taken down into the spotlessly clean engine-room, full of brightly clean brass work and smiling female stokers, to be shown the engine and boilers made in Glasgow in Scotland before the First World War. They built them to last in those days! She told me that the tug had originally been used in the Yangtse River and Shanghai and, though very old, the engine worked 'like a good sewing machine'. She invited me to tell this to the workers in Glasgow. It must be admitted that I would prefer to deal with an everyday riot of a few thousand whirling dervishes brandishing curved swords rather than tap on the shoulder of a

Glasgow boilermaker, and tell that I had a message for him, from a female, Chinese, ship's engineer, who thought that her engines ran as smoothly as a 'good Singer sewing machine'!

We met and searched them frequently and got to know the crew quite well. I was always fascinated by the fact that at least two of the huge barges were floating fish tanks, filled with fresh water and shoals of fat freshwater carp for the restaurants of Hong Kong. They appreciated that we were doing our duty and that we did our work as quickly as possible, consistent with our remit to ensure that no prohibited goods, or illegal immigrants, came into the Colony concealed in their cargoes.

One clear calm day we stopped them off the Brothers Islands and began our usual search. The crew list was handed to me as part of the routine, although it never changed. On this particular day I ordered that the engineer be called on deck as there was an error in the list that had to be investigated. This caused great consternation and the engineer came on deck, as usual wiping her hands on an oily rag and with grease on her face. Surrounded by her chattering and worried crew mates I pointed out to her that she was described in the list as being twenty-four years of age, and that was not true. She immediately protested that she was until I pointed out that it was her birthday and she was twenty-five years old that day. They all laughed and I explained that one of my men had the same birthday, and had noticed the coincidence during a previous search. One of my men, the one with the same birthday, then presented her with a small 'Max Factor' make-up kit we had all contributed to buy, and offered it to her 'for use as a cosmetic rather than engine grease'. She was quite flustered and was reluctant to accept it until the political commissar gave her an elbow in the ribs and said the Chinese equivalent of 'take it you daft besom while you have the chance'. We cast off to resume patrol with the girls waving and applauding, and as we moved away from the side of the tug we were bombarded with fat carp, as a thank-you for a bit of fun.

These hard-working women, and their sisters in Hong Kong, women farmers, women construction workers, women road-menders, women painters, sampan women, women handling harbour cargo junks, women in all trades, made me look at some of my own unthinking, and insulting, presumptions about the idea of describing some professions and jobs as 'men's work' and other things as 'women's work'. It seemed to me then, as now, that it is a stupid system that bars nearly half of the population, in a world short of greatly needed skills, from work they are perfectly able to do as well as any man, simply because they are not men!

It was not long after this that my good eye began giving me trouble as a result of much exposure to the effects of sea-blink, the reflection of bright sunlight from the sea, combined with the strain of night patrols. My transfer to land duties came through and off I went.

Seven

'ALL GOD'S MEN . . .'

The Christian Church in all its versions has been active in Hong Kong since its beginnings as a Colony. Missionaries of all denominations have contributed in varying degrees to the general well being of all its people, some showing more Christian common sense and understanding, than others. The American Maryknoll Fathers, the Poor Clares and the Caritas charity have been especially active, so too have the much loved Salvation Army. Many religious people fled from China to Hong Kong in the 1950s after the Chinese Government's announcement of its official policy of state atheism. Despite a declaration of tolerance for all religions, many missionaries were detained and expelled. Devout Chinese believers were harassed and often accused of the serious charge anti-Chinese activities, a charge bearing a possible death penalty. Malicious informers could have their enemies arrested and sent to horrific prisons and labour camps, to die, on accusations of being Christians. Many Christians had to flee from China, and many of the most wanted would never have made it without the aid and assistance of the 'Chinese Pimpernel' who, like Baroness Orczy's fictitious *Scarlet Pimpernel* of the French Revolution, was sought here, there, and everywhere, by the Communist Secret Police, Commissars, and Militia . . . but they never caught him. The 'Chinese Pimpernel' was a small but well built Chinese man, quiet, gentle, devout, a man of great 'presence'. His name was Lee, Dom Paulinus Lee, and he was the head of a Chinese group of the silent Order of Trappist monks who built a monastery in Lantau Island.

Lantau Island is the biggest, some sixty-five square miles, and westernmost island in Hong Kong. It is hilly and rocky with the second highest mountain, Lantau Peak (3061 feet), in the Colony but it is thinly populated because the land is poor and it was difficult to get to the urban areas of Kowloon and Hong Kong Island.

The Trappists had been forced to make a daring and dangerous escape from Communist China. Because of their intense devotion to their Catholic faith and their vow of silence, which they never broke even under torture, they were especially hated by the Communists, though much respected by the simple peasants to whom they always displayed Christian charity. When they arrived in Hong Kong after their hazardous journey from the mainland, they created the Tai Pak monastery and dairy farm on an isolated, scrub covered, hillside on the north western slopes of Lantau Island near Tai Pak Bay, and the tiny fishing hamlet of Cheung Sha Lan. The monks built a steep track down to the sea below the monastery but it was no easy place to land even in good weather. They received some assistance from well-wishers in America, mainly in the shape of superb American dairy cattle, but their outstanding achievements were wrestled from the unfertile land by the sweat of their brows and sheer hard physical labour. Where there had been scrub and thorn they created lush pasture. Where there had been rocks and bare earth they created gardens with fruit and vegetables. They laboured hard in truly biblical fashion and they made a mountainside flourish. After their faith their most prized possession was a magnificent, pedigree bull, a gift from friends in the United States. The monks had come mainly from agricultural backgrounds and they had started their dairy herd to supply much-needed milk to the burgeoning population of the Colony. Before their arrival there had been only one supplier, the HK Dairy Farm Company, and their output of milk could just about fulfil the demand from wealthy Europeans and Chinese. The milk was so expensive it was generally sold in bottles containing about one third of a pint for a price that could buy you two pints of Chinese beer! Poor Chinese, especially nursing mothers who were suckling babies, but were running dry due to bad living conditions, could not hope to afford cow's milk as a substitute. The monks' aim was to furnish a source of cheaper milk, and they did.

Marine Police Launch No. 27 was the most westerly based police vessel in Hong Kong, based in Cheung Chau Island about an hour's steaming from the monastery through a tricky stretch of water full of rocks, shoals, and mini-islands. Her command was shared evenly, in alternate periods, between myself and Inspector Mike Newton. We also shared a bungalow in the grounds of Cheung Chau police station.

Early one evening the launch was alongside Cheung Chau pier when a message, that one of the monks had been seriously injured and urgently needed to be evacuated to hospital, was relayed to the police station from Peng Chau, an island about one mile to the east of the monastery. The weather was not particularly good as a typhoon was brewing up, but I decided to go as quickly as possible to see

89

what could be done. A considerable worry was that the little beach below the monastery was difficult to approach and my seventy foot launch would have to anchor well out, while I went ashore in our tiny motorised dory. Mike, who was amazingly fluent in many Chinese dialects, offered to come along to assist, and I accepted gratefully. My engineer managed to get more speed out of our diesels than they had developed on her acceptance trials – it is strange but true, marine engineers can always get more out of engines when they feel it is necessary – and we hurtled on in the dark, threading through the rocks and shoals to Tai Pak at a greater pace than I usually proceeded in daytime.

When we arrived off the monastery's shingle beach, we could see that the wind-blown seas were breaking on it heavily. They had sensibly lighted a fire as a beacon for us, and there was a half moon of monks holding lanterns standing round the perimeter of the small bay, to give us guidance so that we could approach the shore as close as we dared. We still had to anchor a quarter of a mile off shore but it vitally reduced the distance we had to travel in the dory through very rough seas. My fully qualified sergeant-bo'sun was left in command of the launch as we set off in the dory to pick up the injured man.

Rain was pouring down and there was a stiff wind as we approached the heavy breakers. We could not risk them straight away as our little boat was equipped with a fairly low powered engine, so we drew off and considered how to make it ashore. There was a lifebelt and a coil of rope in the boat so we secured the rope to the lifebelt and made another approach to the breakers. Mike stood up making a stupendous throw that nearly took us overboard, while I held on to his waist, but it carried the lifebelt near to the beach where monks caught it and waited for our next move. We waited a moment for a suitable wave then the mechanic revved up the engine and, with monks hauling heartily on the rope, we charged through the breakers arriving at the beach with a thump. The monks pulled the dory clear of the breaking waves under my direction, taking her up the beach and placing her facing the sea ready for our departure.

As a Scot, raised as a Protestant, I did not know much about Trappists other than the fact that they were a silent Order, however, I need not have worried, the Founders of the Order had made provision for emergencies. One of the senior brothers had been given a special dispensation to speak to us and he greeted us warmly when we landed.

As we climbed up the dark steep track to the monastery it struck me very forcefully what a medieval scene we presented. A black, windy, night, rain pelting down, a long double line of robed and hooded men, with two strangers in their midst, walking in procession up a rough path, illuminated palely by the flickering light of candle lanterns held by monks. At the monastery door we were met by Dom Paulinus Lee himself who expressed his gratitude at our arrival. We were taken to see the injured monk who was being attended by the infirmary brother. It was obvious that the patient was very seriously injured and in extreme pain, yet he smiled and acknowledged our arrival with a nod of his head.

We were quickly given a brief report of the events leading to the accident. The injured man was the cattle man and his principal task was to look after the prize bull, with whom he had always had a special affinity, having been his keeper since his arrival in Hong Kong. Earlier in the day there had been some heifers in the yard too young to be served by the bull. Somehow the bull had escaped from his stall and was in the process of trying to mount one of the immature heifers when the brother had tried to intervene. The bull had not gored him but had squashed the monk against a concrete post with his head, crushing his rib cage and causing severe internal injuries.

It was quite obvious that we had no time to waste, we had to get him to hospital as quickly as possible. I was deeply worried as I knew that he would suffer greatly from the movement of my ship and the vibration of her diesel engines but there was nothing else to be done. I had taken our canvas emergency stretcher ashore with me but it was unsuitable for a man with crushed ribs and severe breathing difficulties, However, the monks made a hurdle stretcher with raised sides in a matter of minutes and we carried him out to a tractor and conveyed him as gently as possible to the beach.

The wind had picked up while we were ashore and, looking at the waves breaking on the shingle, I was concerned about getting the dory off the beach with the injured man, Dom Paulinus, the infirmary brother and the mechanic, not counting Mike and myself. I reckoned that, with the help of the monks, we could launch the dory and her passengers into the water straight from the beach, as life-savers do in Australia and Hawaii, and, provided the mechanic could get the engine started quickly, the overloaded boat could get out to the launch with Mike and I swimming in the sea, hanging on to the grab lines round her sides. I anticipated quite a struggle

91

fraught with possibilities of disaster but I had not calculated on the immense strength of the hard-working monks, nor their devotion to their injured brother. The plan was quickly explained to everyone and, to my astonishment, accepted without comment. Even the mechanic swore that the engine would start, and that, in my experience, was a very rare guarantee from any seafaring person involved with engines! The stretcher was laid fore and aft in the boat, held and supported by the passengers who had climbed in and sat in the bottom, the mechanic was poised with his hand on the engine starting handle, ready to swing her, hopefully, into life. Mike and I prepared to help to lift the dory but were gently dissuaded by the monks who indicated to us to hold on to the grab ropes. They bent down and raised the boat to shoulder height with one smooth movement and walked steadily with her into the sea until the water was above shoulder height. As they released her the engine burst into life and the triumphant mechanic steered us out in the direction of our launch. As we headed out into the dark I took a brief look back and in the tractor's headlights I could just see one of the monks making a sign of benediction in our direction as others waved farewell.

The bo'sun had been watching the shore closely, worried at the way the weather was developing and the sea building up. As soon as he saw us going down to the beach he began preparing to get under way and hauled up the anchor. As we approached the launch he manoeuvred her superbly and made a perfect lee for us to come alongside. From the water I could see that the side of the launch was manned by every man aboard, including the cook and as we touched her side, the stretcher, Dom Paulinus, and the other brother were plucked on board, with Mike and I following.

We immediately set course for Cheung Chau and the nearest doctor, heaving the dory and the mechanic aboard as we went. The stretcher with its uncomplaining occupant was laid in the shelter of the wheelhouse with him propped on his right side. If he lay back or to the left, his lungs filled up with blood and he could not breathe. We made record time to Cheung Chau and the Doctor was waiting for us at the pier as arranged by radio. He examined the patient and told me that he had to be taken immediately into Queen Mary Hospital in Hong Kong Island as that was the only place capable of dealing with such severe injuries. He left his colleague in charge in Cheung Chau and came with us to do all that he could for the patient on the way in. We radioed ahead and asked for an ambulance to be waiting at one of the piers in Western District usually used by cargo vessels for unloading their goods. Arrangements were also made for a Harbour Police Launch to make sure that the pier was unobstructed.

During, the hour and more, that it took us to get to Western, the whole of my crew, at one time and another, visited the injured monk who was lying on his side in my wheelhouse, slowly drowning in his own blood, showing their concern, sympathy, and support for him in a most remarkable way. I worried that this might overstrain him but both the doctor and Dom Paulinus told me that it was doing no harm. Dom Paulinus came to me as we, at last, approached the pier and told me that his brother wished to see me, so I went and kneeled down by his side. He could not have spoken if he had wished to, I could hear the blood in his lungs bubbling as he breathed laboriously, but he raised his hand, gently drew a cross on my forehead with his finger and smiled at me. As I prepared to take the launch alongside the pier where the ambulance was waiting there were tears trickling down my face and I didn't give a damn. Every man in my launch had been touched deeply by the quiet dignity, uncomplaining fortitude and serene faith of this humble, rough-handed, simple, monk. He died quietly in the company of his two brothers one and a half hours later, despite the best efforts of one of the finest hospitals in the world and, contrary to police regulations, we flew our ensign at half-mast in his memory.

This was not our last contact with the Trappists. Not long after, various bureaucratic requirements having been satisfied, the Tai Pak monastery was licensed to have its own burial ground. The dead brother who had so affected us all was to be the first person interred in its soil, close to his home, his brothers, and his beloved cattle. Mike and I were invited to attend his funeral ceremony. This is, apparently, rarely done and we both accepted.

On the day of the ceremony Mike was unable to go so I went on my own. Again a typhoon was threatening and no boat could safely approach the beach so I went over the ship's side beyond the breakers and swam ashore, being plucked out of the sea like a small child by welcoming monks. They dried me with rough towels and gave me soft, warm robes to wear and stimulating cordials, and I was then taken to the chapel. They knew that I was a Scottish Presbyterian but they gave me the privilege, as a welcome stranger not of their faith, of sharing their grief for their dead brother and their joy at his transition. I respect the privacy of the Trappist monks of Lantau. My memories of the ceremony will always remain; I was deeply moved. The man I have always remembered as the "cattle" monk was huge,

93

over six feet tall, a strong, simple, gentle, northern Chinese, brave in his belief, whose memory, now, so many years later, can bring the warmth of unaccustomed tears to my eyes. This is, in its way, a eulogy to a dead monk. If remembrance is a blessing, then he is blessed.

The New Territories Command of the Hong Kong Police has always been unique, bearing as part of its ordinary constabulary duties, in its more than 200 square mile rural district, the responsibility for controlling an international frontier, the twenty-two mile long Sino-British Frontier between Hong Kong and China. Although members of the Hong Kong Police, the policemen who serve in the New Territories have traditionally been a bit different from their colleagues in the urban areas, perhaps more individualistic as is only to be expected of men who work in isolated areas and have to be capable of dealing with any situation on their own initiative. It is interesting to note that most of the expatriate people who prefer to work in the New Territories are individualists, men of strong character who do their jobs with dedication but are dismissive of pomp or posturing. The only occasions on which I served in there were once as a Traffic Branch officer, once during a particularly heavy flood of refugees over the Border, and twice in Riot Companies.

Like everyone else in the police force, I had heard of the 'Flying Priest', not a daredevil in a biplane doing stunts but an Italian priest with a Lambretta scooter that could, if you believed the reports, go faster than any racing car. Father Polletti was much loved by the Hakka farmers of the New Territories who always smiled if you mentioned him; smiles of warmth and affection. He was fluent in several Chinese dialects but his English was of the type usually only heard coming from comic Italian-American characters in 1930s movies. His parish was up close to the frontier and his sphere of interest and concern was wide. He was devoted to his work and to people, regardless of their religion or lack of it.

Stories about him abounded. One officer told of me a night when, as frequently happened at the time, the whole of the frontier was in a state of uproar with guns being fired and flares soaring into the air on both sides. He and his patrol were exchanging fire with their opponents when he heard the sound of a motorbike engine popping rapidly towards them, it was Father Polletti riding flat out, beard, hair and cassock blowing in the wind of his passage, to attend to one of his parishioners. As the Lambretta approached the scene of the firing they heard him yelling in English 'No shoota da guns pleez

Man of God passing!' and he disappeared into the dark at high speed laughing like a drain. The police also started laughing and, shortly after, the firing died down and peace returned to the border. Some of the men claimed that the frontier guards on the other side were also laughing!

During a particularly bad typhoon that devastated a large area of the New Territories, flooding much of the Yuen Long district, my Riot Company was deployed to assist in the urgent task of rescuing some 3000 villagers from a low-lying flooded area, before a high tide swept in and drowned them all. It was good and satisfying work, better by far than shooting at people, but it was exhausting and dangerous. Most of the roads in the Territories are raised on banking well above the level of the surrounding paddy fields, keeping them above the general water level.

We were up on the banking, catching our breath, and drinking tea, before returning to the flood waters, when we saw a cloud of spray coming towards us at tremendous speed, occasionally being blown from side to side by gusts of strong wind, but always returning to a straight line course in our direction. It finally arrived with a tremendous skid, a Lambretta scooter, and out of the spray we saw the beaming face of the good Father, hair and beard plastered down with rain and cassock absolutely sopping. He had a leather case hanging on a strap from around his neck which, I was told, contained his 'Tools of trade for peoples', apparently wafers, holy water, and other things for his priestly duties. It was also commonly rumoured that he had as many pockets in his cassock as the 'Temple of Ten Thousand Buddhas' had statues, many of them allegedly containing what he called 'restorative cordials', known to the laity as alcoholic drinks, as well as a seemingly limitless supply of sweets for the village children.

This, of course, was not believed by outsiders, but, when he spotted that one of my men was bleeding from a deep scratch, and immediately whipped a wound dressing out of some inner pocket to bandage the wound, our belief was confirmed. He wished us farewell and started up his scooter but before moving off he took a small bottle out of his cassock and handed it to me saying 'Some a firsta aid for you'. It was Hennessy brandy and the equivalent of a good-sized double! Grinning, widely he revved up and shot off in his own personal cloud of rain. We could hear faintly floating back in the Lambretta Doppler effect his parting words 'God'sa blessinks on your good a work chaps!' and we all laughed. The brandy was shared round, a sip each, and we tackled our 'gooda work', refreshed in body and spirit. We were also pleased that we now had our own story to add to the myth that the good priest had the only cassock bar in the world! His work in the area was much appreciated by all, even by Traffic Policemen who never gave him a ticket!

As ships steam into the Lei U Mun Pass to enter Hong Kong harbour they pass, on their right hand side, a six mile long sea inlet known as Junk Bay. Some two-thirds of the way up the western side of Junk Bay was a squalid, dirty, disease-ridden place, a refugee area called Rennie's Mill Camp, the last retreat of a defeated army, their wives and children, some 8000 of them in all, filled with despair, sick, beaten, angry, people abandoned by their former leaders and regarded with justifiable suspicion by the authorities and Hong Kong public alike.

These men were the remnants of Chiang Kai-shek's Nationalist Army. Completely routed by the Communist army and militia in 1949, and in many instances deserted by corrupt officers who fled to Taiwan, they were fortunate to be close enough to Hong Kong to seek refuge over the border, most of them still carrying their weapons and ammunition. The roads and tracks through Kwangdung Province leading to the Sino-British Frontier were strewn with dead, dying, and badly wounded men. Marine policemen on patrol off the Chinese coast could see Nationalist soldiers, in scenes reminiscent of Dunkirk in the Second World War, on beaches and in bays trying to bribe boat people into ferrying them across to the sanctuary of British territory. Many, without money for bribes, tried to swim across, at places like Starling Inlet and Deep Bay, but few made it. There were corpses of drowned men in the sea for weeks. Many did manage to cross over, in still-disciplined and organised groups, sometimes led by good officers or senior NCOs. Many of these buried their arms and ammunition, well greased and protected, in old oil drums at secret places, to be recovered and used for their 'return to the motherland'. They never could return but the weapons became a major threat to the people in Hong Kong when they were later used in crime.

These were the men grudgingly allowed to establish their miserable encampment on the site of, a Scotsman's long past enterprise, Rennie's Mill. Like most defeated armies, they ran up their Nationalist flags and lived on memories of past victories, mainly imaginary, and vain hopes of a victorious return home. The reality of their existence was badly treated wounds festering many of them into chronic ill health or their graves. Tuberculosis was endemic. Typhus, typhoid, gastro-enteritis, malnutrition, and despair took a steady toll. Suicides were frequent as the reality of the completeness of the Communists's victory in China overwhelmed them, and as they were forced to accept the fact that Chiang Kai-shek's corrupt government in Taiwan had no intention of sending for them, or even helping them. They knew that they would never return and the knowledge gnawed away their will to live. Drug addiction became widespread, mainly among the men, in an attempted escape from reality, but it only added to the misery.

The camp was isolated and ignored. Without a proper water supply or decent sanitation, water-borne diseases flourished. There was no electricity supply, so candles and paraffin lamps provided ample sources for many fires that destroyed their miserable shacks. Rats swarmed about even in daylight spreading yet more disease. There were no roads just rocky tracks through the steep hills and a junk ferry for the long and expensive trip through Lei U Mun Pass to Hong Kong Island and Kowloon.

Into this medieval scene of squalid filth, disease, and despair came Annie Margaret Skau, an Oslo-born Norwegian, a missionary nurse of the Mission Covenant Church of Norway. A strong, tall, happily good natured, dedicated Christian woman, who had suffered detention, persecution, and maltreatment in mainland China, a refugee herself from the Chinese Communists she was uniquely qualified to understand, and help, the people of Rennie's Mill.

Sister Skau had been active from the late 1930s, in an agricultural region in Shensi in north-eastern China, the only western-trained medical worker in an area of some two million people. She was never betrayed to the Japanese invaders of China nor was she ever denounced to the Communists despite the offer of rewards. They threw her in prison anyway and only released her when she was near death from her ill-treatment.

When she arrived in Rennie's Mill she had been convalescing in Norway for nearly a year and a half. With another nurse, who had created a small clinic in a hut measuring barely eight feet by ten, they began treating some 600 and more patients a day. Their patient numbers rose and rose as people gave up hope, and tuberculosis spread like wildfire in a community with no money, no food, and appalling housing in wood and cardboard shacks. They were barely holding their own in the hut clinic and it was obvious they needed better accommodation if they were to make headway against the endemic ill health of the refugees.

Annie found a site for a chapel and a rest home and sanatorium but had no money to build; every penny went on patients and medicines. As a result of publicity in the United States about her work at Rennie's Mill funds began to come in as Americans displayed their usual generosity, and a rest home was built, just bare walls and a roof at first, but the foundation of the justly famous Haven of Hope Sanatorium and nurses' training school, with over 200 beds, and a rehabilitation centre for forty patients.

Rennie's Mill Camp was gradually transformed, with water and electricity supply, proper sanitation, modern buildings replacing wooden huts, new schools established by Catholic and Protestant missions, buses running to Kowloon on regular services on new roads. Nationalist flags may still be flown but the children of Rennie's Mill are Hong Kong Chinese!

Sister Skau and I only met once, although I had heard much about her. My drug squad had raided a heroin distributors in a wooden shack. We had arrested four men, obviously heroin addicts themselves, sitting round a rough wooden table in a squalid hut, packaging heroin in retail size paper packets. One had been the former Nationalist Governor of a Province in China, another had been his aide, the third had been a Colonel in the Nationalist Army, and the last had been a Captain in the Chinese Navy, who had trained for a time, before the Second World War, at the Royal Naval College, Dartmouth, in England! We were taking our prisoners down to a waiting police launch when we met this immensely tall, about, six feet six inches, European woman with a kind but careworn, face, Sister Skau. She looked at our prisoners, whom she recognised, shook her head, and said, softly, 'What a waste!' She could have been pronouncing Hong Kong's epitaph for 1997!

At one time during my career, a senior officer with a sense of humour posted me to a duty known colloquially as Officer-in-Charge, Bars and Brothels, Wanchai. The work was interesting but hell on one's social life, as duties always began when everybody else was quitting for the day to go and enjoy theirs.

Through this job I came into contact with one of the most interesting and hard-working men I have ever met, a Maryknoll priest whom I shall call Father Sam. Sam had been a missionary priest in China and had suffered much for his beliefs when the Communists took over. There were stories that, in addition to the standard physical abuse and maltreatment handed out by the Communists to Christ-believers, Sam had spent much of his time in detention, locked up in solitary confinement in a dark, ill-ventilated cell in an attempt to break him down. He did not break down because he had two secret weapons, his faith and, what is possibly Scotland's second most famous invention, golf! Sam is a mad keen golfer and he plays the game well.

According to whoever is telling the story, Sam would spend part of his time attending to his daily devotions and observing the appropriate special and holy days, in addition, aided by an excellent memory, he worked his way through the books of the Bible. For relaxation he would play, in his imagination, increasingly interesting games of golf with various people, starting with well-known golfing personalities of the time, then moving on to other sportsmen such as, baseball player Babe Ruth, boxer Joe Louis, and others, then politicians, historical figures, and so on. It is alleged that he even played his way through all the Saints in the list but was, fortunately, booted out of China before becoming too ambitious!

After recovering his health, Sam began working in the Maryknoll mission in Hong Kong. One of the most brilliant innovations in Hong Kong owed much to the clerics. A major factor in the expense of standard school education was the prohibitively high cost of scarce building land, the expense of construction on it, and the need for high fees to recover the cost. Some of the Maryknoll men including, it is said, Sam, reputedly looked up for inspiration and saw empty rooftops. With some help from American sources, some favours from old friends, and some discreet arm-twisting, the colony suddenly sprouted rooftop schools, and play areas. To give some idea of the hunger for education, some schools worked a two shift system, some even a staggered three, so students were categorised as 'A' shift, 'B' shift, or 'C' shift!

Soon after becoming OC Bars and Brothels, during a call at the American Shore Patrol Office, I was introduced to Sam who, in addition to all his other numerous tasks, was the Catholic Chaplain to the American Fleet when ships were in the harbour. He also acted as a Welfare Officer for any US military personnel. We became good friends. He was, and still is, an incredibly sane and fair-minded man in an increasingly dotty world. He was very concerned about drug addiction in Hong Kong, and the rapid rise in drug use in the USA and the in Western countries generally. We shared common ground in believing that, unless the drug traffic was nipped in the bud quickly, before it could develop further, then drug abuse would become a global problem . . . as it is today.

We met often, sometimes in connection with official business, sometimes with other clerics for a meal and good conversation. On occasion, I would just drop into the Shore Patrol office for a mug of good American coffee and a chat. Official business, I discovered, is frequently better done, and more quickly, completed over a mug of coffee, than through bureaucracy. This proved so when there was a possibility that all US Navy ships would stop coming to Hong Kong for rest and recreation. At the time this could have been a financial disaster for the Colony as American servicemen were spending up to US$2 million a day ashore, a significant part of the Colony's foreign earnings. What had happened was that two sailors had gone back to their aircraft carrier after a run ashore. They were later found dead in their bunks and it was suspected that they had been the victims of a Communist poisoning plot. Father Sam told me of this shortly after the event, and just as official discussions had begun between the US and Colony authorities. We got cracking in Wanchai with other officers from the Division. From a bar girl, the police got the information that the sailors concerned had bought heroin through an intermediary, one of the casual workers in the bar, and had gone off with it to their ship. The man who bought the heroin was quickly brought in and, admitted getting the heroin for the sailors. two bags of 99 per cent pure Thai heroin. It was the purity that solved the mystery. It was established that the men had been using heroin in the USA and the Philippines, where the average purity had been 7.5 per cent, or less. They had injected themselves with a dose nearly ten times stronger than they were used to and had, in effect, taken a massive overdose. The information was relayed to the Admiral immediately through the Maryknoll coffee cup route, and was confirmed through regular channels a day later. Post-mortem examination confirmed the cause of death as drug overdose.

Sam had always wanted to go on an opium raid, not in the spirit of a police 'groupie', but because he had so often dealt with the tragic outcome of opium addiction and its effects on family life, but had never actually seen the inside of a divan.

Later I was appointed as OC Hong Kong Island drug squad, and I was given the opportunity of taking Sam along on an opium raid on an alleged opium divan in an almost impregnable situation in among huts and pig sties in Telegraph Bay on the western side of the Island. The little collection of sturdy huts that housed the Bay community was tucked in below sandstone cliffs several hundred feet high, with only one small steep track leading down to it, easily watched by a look-out and impossible to approach without being seen. Attempts had been made to raid the place from the sea but they had been unsuccessful as whenever a strange boat was seen approaching the beach the alarm was sounded. We had studied the area discreetly and noticed a large pipe that went down from the top of the cliff to just behind one of the huts and we thought that, given the right conditions, a dark rainy night for example, we could possibly slide down the 200 foot pipe and catch them by surprise. As the information about the divan had come through official channels we kept our plans secret.

On the evening of the 27 December conditions were perfect, it was a pitch dark night with thick clouds and unusually heavy rain, and we decided to go for a raid as two of my men had spied out the area from the cliff tops and seen a lot of unusual activity going on in the Bay below. Sam had been briefed by me and was ready, dressed in dark clothes and wearing gym shoes. We drove to the area and hid our cars then approached the cliffs on foot. The weather became worse by the minute and the rain teemed down. We arrived at the top of the pipe and I decided to go down first with Sam following behind me. The trip down the pipe was hair-raising. It had looked difficult but possible in daylight but it was horrendous and nearly impossible in the wet dark night. What was not observable from the heights of the cliffs, was the fact that the angle of the pipe steepened drastically about three-quarters of the way down, and this, combined with the slipperiness of the wet pipe was our, literal, downfall. We had been inching our way down the pipe flat on our stomachs, arms around it, and gripping it tightly between our thighs, with the rubber soles of our gym shoes acting as brakes. On the last fifty feet we lost traction on the wet, slippery, surface and ended up in a heap. What the surveillance team had forgotten to tell me was that the pipe ended up in the acrid slurry of a pig sty . . . I seemed fated to spend my drug raids up to my eyes in shit! This time it proved unnecessary to smash down doors or break through windows as they had been left unlocked for us.It did seem that we had been expected!

Need it be said that this was my first proper raid with this squad and my luck was running true to form! Father Sam was grinning happily. He didn't really give a hoot about there being no drugs, he'd done what he had not been able to do since he was a kid, certainly not since he'd been a respectable priest. He'd dressed up in scruffy clothes and gym shoes, gone out in the pouring rain on a pitch dark night, slid suicidally down 200 feet of pipe from the top of a cliff in the company of a bunch of officially sanctioned maniacs, landed on top of a disgruntled Scottish Presbyterian lying on his back in a pig sty and buried him further into a foot of rancid pig shit, then

101

watched him flattened further by the rest of his own squad. What a night!

We slogged our way up the track to the cars, to a message that I had become a father earlier in the evening. We drove directly to the hospital and went up to the maternity section only to be stopped by a determined Sister who was not about to have her hygienically sterile nursery polluted, however joyful the occasion. We were forcefully told to 'Get that shit off you before you come in here!' We reeked of pig manure, but quickly cleaning up as best we could, barely to the Sister's satisfaction, we went to see the baby. The Sister's eyes bulged when Sam turned back his dark jacket and revealed a clerical collar. He asked me if I objected to him blessing the baby and I said of course not but reminded him that I was a Protestant and didn't that matter? Sam shrugged, smiled, said that it wasn't the baby's fault, as he blessed my first son, Iain! There can't be too many new-born babies around who have been blessed by a priest who has just come from sliding down a 200 foot pipe into a pig sty!

Eight

BUFFALOES AND BEASTIES

Hong Kong can not exist without imported food. All the available fifty square miles of agricultural land in the Colony could barely provide enough food to feed a tenth of its population. Food imports pour in daily from every source in the world, primarily from mainland China and other South-East Asian countries. Water buffaloes are imported by sea for the fresh meat market, many of them as deck cargo on ships from Cambodia. The animal protection societies have been responsible for great improvements in travelling conditions for these animals but they still experience stress through being removed from their normal environment in the paddy fields and villages. The animals were unloaded at Kennedy Town near the abattoir, under tight security to prevent theft or escape. At one time there was quite a bit of publicity about a new security system that totally precluded any possibility of any animal ever escaping. Naturally, by the immutable certainty of Murphy's Law, one promptly did, a water buffalo!

It would be misleading to think of these animals in terms of European domestic cattle, such as Jerseys or Friesians, these are massively strong beasts used for hard draught work, ploughing paddy fields, hauling timber, and any other task requiring strength and weight. An average water buffalo stands up to six feet high, some bulls seven feet, weighs about 1900 pounds, over three-quarters of a ton, and has huge flattened horns that sweep round their head, in some instances for twelve feet or more with up to six feet between the tips. They are generally well looked after, usually by youngsters who take them for their daily bath after work, and see to it that they have plenty of fodder.

A cargo of water buffaloes arrived from Cambodia after a particularly tough voyage. The animals that survived were particularly stressed, and difficult to handle, but unloading was successfully completed. What happened next – exactly – was never completely made clear, as the stevedores blamed the abattoir people, and the abattoir people blamed the stevedores, but what is undeniable is that one did escape, and went on a panic-stricken rampage through Hong Kong, one of the world's most crowded urban environments.

The water buffalo that escaped was a big one, and remarkably fast, considering his long voyage cooped up aboard ship. The police were not informed of the escape by anyone at Kennedy Town, and knew nothing about it until '999' calls began pouring into the Radio Control Room in HK Island Police HQ. The first caller was suspected of making a hoax call, when she reported a water buffalo charging along one of the busiest streets in Hong Kong, and was practically in tears by the time she convinced the Duty Controller!

But, very soon, the '999' call board was jammed with buffalo reports, and ambulances were rushing all over the place picking up the casualties left behind by his passage. He had rampaged through the main business area in Central District by the time Emergency Unit (EU) was informed, and one of our patrol cars spotted him, and followed him, as he headed east at a trot, along Hennessy Road in Wanchai District. The nature of Hong Kong's roads packed with nose to tail vehicles, and pavements packed with pedestrians, meant that people could not get out of the buffalo's way even if they saw him through the crowds.

I first saw him as a result of seeing a tiny Chinese woman suddenly floating up in the air to the third floor window of a store before she fell back to the pavement with an awful thud. The air was filled with screams and human bodies flying in all directions as the terrified buffalo tossed them out of his way with seemingly casual flicks of his huge horns. People were also being pushed through store windows, and knocked over and trampled as he passed, some by the animal some by other panic-stricken humans.

By means of my car radio I called other EU cars to the area and we began to herd the buffalo off the main street like a team of motorised collie dogs. I wanted the terrified beast away from the crowds and headed towards the Wanchai waterfront where there was a big British American Tobacco Company godown with a huge, windowless, blank wall and a big unloading area. Even more important was the fact that there were rarely any people there, as people are not encouraged to loiter near tobacco, or alcohol, godowns anywhere in South-East Asia. My orderly, a qualified marksman, was with me in the car and we had two M1 carbines with us. Another of my EU cars was on the way with Sergeant-Major Chan Chor-choi aboard with his Winchester hunting rifle. The car crews did a great job herding the buffalo with a minimum of contact. Time after time he tried to dodge off down a side street but each time he was brought back on course. He was eventually shepherded into the unloading area and went trotting along parallel to the blank wall, still heading east. My orderly and I fired at him simultaneously aiming at the 'kill' zones. He stopped, stood still for a brief moment, then slumped down on to the ground. I went over and made sure he was dead with two more shots. All of the policemen present were silent, we felt sorry for the poor beast but at least he'd had a run for his money.

The cost to the people of Hong Kong was high, in personal injury, and general damage. Over a hundred people injured, at least one person dead, hundreds of thousands of dollars worth of broken windows, and dented motor cars! Sergeant-Major Chan arrived with his heavy calibre hunting rifle just too late to deal with the animal, but agreed that we had to take the opportunity to shoot the poor animal in the only place available where the public were not at any risk. A very bad tempered member of the abattoir staff arrived with a humane killer and proceeded to shoot the dead Buffalo again 'just in case'. The death of the buffalo ended the incident, the people could go about their business in safety, and that, we thought in our innocence, was that!

Oh no it wasn't! Criticism of our action began immediately. Some unnamed senior officers apparently complained 'privately' that the M1 carbine ammunition was too light to have killed the animal humanely but the humane societies refused to rise to the bait. They recognised the danger to the public represented by a panic stricken, three-quarter ton buffalo running amok in streets crowded with people. There followed a suggestion, attributed to an unknown source in the abattoir, that the buffalo had, in fact, been killed by the fellow who arrived with a humane killer some ten minutes after the animal died. Unfortunately, for the anonymous informant, another member of their staff told the Chinese newspaper reporters that the buffalo had two of our bullets in its heart when the carcass was dressed at the abattoir. In any case Chinese Press men had already been, checked the animal dead, taken photographs, taken quick quotes from police and civilians and gone to their newsrooms, before the arrival of the man from Kennedy Town. My own District Commander was satisfied with our action and said so. The Chinese population were satisfied too; any complaints they made were to do with why it took so long to stop the beast in the only way possible! And the reason for the carping criticism inside the police force? God knows why, that is just the way it was at that time.

In many ways the Chinese people are much cleverer than western Europeans where food is concerned. If at all possible, the Chinese housewife, or houseman, will always buy fresh food in preference to anything in cans, or frozen, or filled with artificial preservatives. When they do buy preserved foodstuffs, they always buy those preserved, dried, or pickled, in the traditional Chinese style with salt, soy, and fresh ginger, or dried in the sun. Completely fresh food is purchased twice a day for the two main meals of the day, one at about noon and the other at about six o'clock in the evening.

As a consequence of this pattern of domestic buying, nearly every residential area in the Colony has an open market packed with stalls and hawkers, busily selling every imaginable foodstuff in an absolute frenzy of activity twice a day. The Chinese housewife is a very demanding customer, money is not easily earned in Hong Kong and no sensible person parts with it with no guarantee of quality in return. In any case, they don't believe in verbal guarantees anyway. Every item bought is felt, sniffed, and closely examined before being accepted, and all accompanied by a noisy exchange with the seller loudly proclaiming the value and virtues of his products, against the disparaging comments of the purchaser. It is a lovely, animated, game to which everyone knows the rules. Ducks, geese, and fish, are supplied live to specially licensed shops and sold live to the housewives, who are possibly better 'first glance' judges of the condition of their purchase than many fully qualified veterinarians.

The organisational chain of supply to provide for the needs of a demanding, and critical, consumer market of some 3 million people was a long one, dependent on critical timing to get the goods to market when the housewives were there to buy. The top prices were paid only for fresh food of the highest quality, a pound of vegetables could lose half their value between noon and six in the evening. The whole thing started with the farmers, many of them walking long distances to wholesalers' collecting points in the early dawn, with back-breaking loads of fresh produce in two huge baskets slung from a bamboo pole on their shoulders.

Some, who were wealthy enough to own bicycles, could be encountered on village tracks, pushing their bicycles along with one or two fat pigs secured to the machine in long pig baskets, with their legs hanging down though the rattan, like plump aircraft preparing to land. Ducks and other fowl were transported in large, circular, communal baskets, with their heads and necks sticking out, looking around like tourists sightseeing in a rattan bus.

One day my friend, John, and I were responsible for, accidentally, putting a slight dent in the delicately balanced supply system. John was, almost typically, ex-Royal Air Force – always immaculately dressed, neat RAF moustache – perhaps even dapper. Anyone who had seen British movies about the wartime RAF would immediately have picked him out as an airman. He also loved motor cars. We were living in the same officers quarters in Tsim Sha Tsui when John bought a second-hand Riley two-seater, drop head, sports coupé. It was an absolutely beautiful machine guaranteed to turn heads anywhere. It was fast, smooth, and elegant, but it was not really a car for a crowded urban environment.

In the whole of the colony the longest stretch of straight, uncrowded road was the two and a half miles or so, between Kam Tin and Yuen Long in the New Territories, and we decided to go there to try her out. Spending the day travelling up the eastern route via Tai Po and Fanling and returning by Castle Peak and Tsuen Wan.

By Hong Kong Traffic legislation a vehicle being used on the road had to have an 'audible warning system', a car horn, and the horn on the Riley was out of order, so we, law-abidingly, took along an old Bombay bus horn I had. This magnificent instrument had been mounted on an old Bombay bus for over thirty years and it worked very efficiently. It was like a long herald's trumpet that had been curled into the shape of a bugle, with a flared mouth resembling a blunderbuss muzzle at one end, and had a huge rubber bulb at the other. When the bulb was pressed sharply an indescribable noise issued from the mouth, a mixture of sound that trembled thunderously between the mating call of a herd of randy bull elephants and the dying wail of a soprano sea monster! The sheer volume of sound produced, was stunning, as it had needed to be in Bombay. I wish I'd left the damn thing at home.

Most of roads in the New Territories were still mainly single track with passing bays and, provided that slow moving traffic pulled over, reasonable journey times could be achieved. Truck drivers with heavily overloaded trucks, festooned with illegal passengers, would usually pull over and let you past. The curse of the road system was the Chinese private car owner, his car packed to the gills with the whole family, including grand parents, out for a day of sight seeing and eating. These gentlemen seemed to be universally of the opinion that the money they had paid for their Road Fund Licence did not just give them the right to drive on the road, they reckoned they'd bought the freehold! They would drive up the middle of the road at about twenty-five miles per hour, gossiping unceasingly, turning round to make sure their back passengers could hear their glittering comments, never looking in the rear view mirrors, rarely looking through the front windscreen, wobbling all over the place, and ignoring every passing bay. They were mobile pains in the neck.

It was a hot day when we set off for Yuen Long with the sun beating down on us as we sat in comfort, with the top down,in the luxury of the Riley's red leather cockpit. With the heavy traffic moving slowly, the heat of the sun, and the happy enjoyment of a day off, we stopped off, from time to time, to enjoy an ice cold bottle of Hong Kong's favourite San Miguel beer, at licensed oases strategically situated by the roadside for the refreshment of weary travellers.

We discovered that the Bombay bus horn was amazingly effective at clearing the road. It may have been racial Chinese memories of pursuit by enraged dragons, or peckish sabre toothed water buffaloes, whatever the reason, whenever we sounded the horn, even the most obdurate of truck drivers rapidly pulled into the first passing bay available, and craned out of their cab windows to try to see, with bulging eyes, what the hell had made the terrifying racket that had startled them enough to send them to cover. We then drove past waving graciously, and smiling our thanks. On a couple of occasions the private car drivers were so startled out of their day dreaming progress, by the Bombay bellow, they swerved violently enough to allow John to accelerate smoothly past. We enjoyed a quick lunch in Yuen Long then whipped up and down the almost empty straight stretch of road a few times at high speed, a rare treat indeed, with the wind through our hair and the countryside flashing past.

Then we set out for Castle Peak. We drove quietly along enjoying the view from the almost empty road which was raised above the fish ponds and paddy fields on either side as a protection from flooding. There was a bicyclist far ahead, slowly pedalling along with an improbable, and unstable, load of six round baskets of ducks fastened to his rear carrier. We were busy chatting about Bombay, one of my favourite Eastern cities, and were not really paying much attention to the cyclist, and as I reached the punch line of my story I sounded the bus horn, not realising how close we were to him.

The poor man nearly had a heart attack, swerved, and with his legs still moving up and down in measured strokes, rode solemnly down the banking at the side of the road into a large fishpond. He could be seen for a moment, like a one man submarine equipped with a conning tower of full of surprised ducks, his face showing absolute amazement, then he disappeared under the water. We stopped and ran back, arriving in time to see him standing up to his neck in the pond, obviously much shaken but unhurt, releasing his baskets and pulling them to the side.

He asked me what the hell had caused the terrifying noise, like a hundred angry devils, and I explained about the offending bus horn, giving a quick demonstration. He had a fit of the giggles and said that would give him something to tell them in the village, then waved us off, refusing any compensation for his unexpected dip. We last saw him standing on the road, hands on his hips, dripping pond water all over the tarmac and laughing fit to burst. Odd people Hakka duck farmers; nice people, but odd!

There was a corollary to this incident. Having been summoned to my Superintendent's office to explain this conduct, which was deemed to be unsuitable from a junior officer, I almost caused his elderly Chief Clerk to have a coronary, by sounding the horn, too enthusiastically, at my boss's request. I was ordered to dispose of it, immediately. Later, after a good party one night, I gave the Bombay bus horn to a rickshaw driver. Whose first aural victim, incidentally, was my censorious Superintendent. It goes to prove that there is a God!

At one time I was appointed as Senior Court Inspector of the Hong Kong Island Magistrates' Courts, working under the Chief Court Inspector, a man with an unrivalled, encyclopedic, knowledge of the law. Each Magistracy had its own group of permanent magistrates, part of the Hong Kong legal establishment, but all of whom, daily, passed totally impartial, and unbiased, justice on the people appearing before them. One of the magistrates was Mr Timothy van Rees, a fair, stocky, strongly built Welshman, who looked more like a rugby player than a magistrate. He'd been in the Army, and was a member of the Hong Kong Regiment, our Territorials, and was a keen outdoor man spending much of the little spare time he had, walking, in the mountains in the New Territories, accompanied by his Jack Russell terrier, Toby.

When the Cultural Revolution burst upon us, Mr van Rees's court became the setting for many of the mass trials of Communist trouble-makers arrested for communal offences such as riot, and unlawful assembly. Because the vast majority of Hong Kong's workers had no sympathy for the awful excesses of the Red Guards, they refused to take part in politically inspired strikes, and voted with their feet

109

by going to work. The Communists tried to frighten them off by appearing in mobs at work places, but the workers still got through, aided by police action. The mob members who refused to disperse were frequently rounded up and arrested, and most of them appeared before Mr van Rees.

He was a wonderful choice for these trials as the defendants would always put on a performance from the dock, but he never lost his judicial calm. Speeches, slogans, shouts, insults, for the benefit of the left-wing press. Quotations from their *Little Red Books* of the 'Thoughts of Mao Tse-tung' yelled out from time to time during the proceedings. All designed to make Mr van Rees lose his temper so that they could claim bias, but it never worked. His decent good nature and respect for the law even impressed some of the left-wing reporters. His judgments were always balanced, and the sentences he awarded were always fair. He never convicted anyone unless the evidence against them was absolutely and clearly beyond the shadow of any doubt. He infuriated the more hard line leftists by being so patently fair, just, and open minded.

His little Jack Russell dog Toby became quite famous and much liked by everyone. He had great character, was completely well behaved and friendly with everyone, and he went everywhere with his master. On a side table Mr van Rees had two trays for papers, one marked 'In' the other 'Out'. At the beginning of business Toby would curl himself up and go to sleep. Exactly at tea break time he would wake up, shake himself discreetly, but loudly enough for us hear, stroll across the table and sit in the 'Out' tray looking expectant. We would then have a break from the heat and fug of the courtroom, to the relief of everyone, including prisoners, and resume after ten minutes or so. Toby similarly signalled lunch-time, and afternoon break, and was always looked for by school children visiting the Court as part of their civics study courses.

No Communist could ever justifiably accuse Mr van Rees of unfairness or unreasonableness, and many of them secretly admired him, perhaps comparing his justice to the farcical show trials, like Roman games, performed in football stadiums in China followed by death sentences immediately carried out! In any case, many of the Communists brought in for Public Order offences had deliberately courted arrest, as they preferred to be safely and comfortably tucked up in Stanley prison as 'heroic compatriots unjustly detained by the Imperialist-Capitalists', rather than chancing getting hurt in the streets.

One day there was a rush of Communist sympathisers into the Court buildings through an unguarded doorway and they rampaged about until we brought things under control. Some were arrested and some made their getaway. We found that Toby was gone and it was suspected that the Communists had taken him. We were later told that Toby had been hanged as an example to the 'White Skinned Pigs', the Europeans. They had actually hanged a small, friendly, pet dog! What an incredible victory for the toiling masses of international Marxism!

'Buster' was as different from Toby as any dog could be. Before taking over as OC Emergency Unit in Hong Kong I was sent back to the Police Tactical Unit at Fanling in the New Territories, to be brought up to date on the latest in Riot control. The Unit was Commanded by Mr Peter Godber, a brave, very tough man, and his Chief Instructor was my old friend Les Guyatt. The work was hard, the riots were many, and we were much in the troubles on the frontier when twenty-five policemen were killed in action. But we also had some time for fun.

Les had a long standing friendship with George and his family. George was the Customs man at Smugglers Pass and, like Les and all the other Frontier men, very much an individualist. Among other things, they shared a partiality for Gilbert and Sullivan, music played loudly on an electric gramophone, and washed down by quantities of Johnny Walker Black Label Whisky, but only after sunset and off duty!

George was the proud owner of 'Buster', the toughest, brindle, Staffordshire bull terrier in the universe, or at least, the Hong Kong bit. Buster was a charming dog, well known at every butcher's shop and restaurant in Fanling, various Police Officers' messes, in people's homes, with children, accepting all sorts of indignities from them with a wagging tail . . . but he was a terror to, cats, other dogs, snakes, and buffaloes. He never initiated any attacks on buffaloes, that was generally attested to by all the Hakka farmers, but they seemed to like having a go at him from time to time, and they usually came off second best. George was a very decent and honourable man and he was always willing to pay reasonable compensation if he thought that Buster had been in the wrong, and no farmer ever had cause to complain of unfair dealings.

He was noticed one day as he passed through Fanling in his usual fashion, stomping along like a canine cowboy, heavily muscled shoulders moving, powerful body shining with health, tail straight out behind him, giving a gentle wag to acquaintances, and graciously accepting pats from friendly children . . . just another day. There was

111

a phone call later, Buster had reportedly tangled with a village elder's buffalo bull, without provocation, and killed it, and the elder was demanding damages. Upon investigation the report was proved to be true but only to the extent that Buster had most assuredly killed the buffalo, but only after the buffalo had attacked him. Unfortunately for the owner a telephone linesman repairing a cable had seen the whole thing and was loud in his admiration for Buster.

George was a decent, quick thinking, man, but not a sucker, and he promptly agreed to settle the damages for the loss of the buffalo. In return for paying the damages, George asked for, and received, a receipt from the owner, acknowledging receipt of a sum, in excess of the beast's market value, for 'one dead water buffalo'. This made the carcass George's and he promptly had it hauled off to the butcher for dressing out, much to the dismay of the former owner who had reckoned to do just that himself and make a nice double profit.

A barbecue was arranged among some well established fishponds, with the buffalo as the main course, and the attendance was over-whelming. From the sale of tickets George not only recouped his original outlay, he had a nice profit left over which he gave to local charity. A bulging Buster, who had eaten far too many tit-bits offered by his fans, was given three rousing cheers by all present, including the original owner of the beast.

It was later suggested, but never proved, that part of the attraction of the barbecue was the fact that George, a keen and expert fisherman, and Les, no fisherman at all, had a fishing contest laid on. Whichever of them caught the most fish out of the fish pond in a given time, won the contest and, gambling being illegal, their own small private wager. For the others attending there was no more chance of laying bets than could be found at any similar occasion on, say, Epsom Downs.

The rules were simple, whoever had the most fish was the winner. George set up his chair, his rod, his keep net, and started fishing right away, continuing to do so until the five minutes before 'time' signalling the end of the contest. Les, on the other hand, stuck his rod over the water then ignored it, sitting chatting, smoking, taking Top Mill snuff, and the occasional cold beer. George eventually pointed out that there were barely two minutes to go until the contest ended, that he had ten fish for each one of Les's, and invited him to concede defeat.

Les admitted modestly that things looked bad for him, reached into his bait bag, and tossed some unidentifiable small object into the middle of the pond. There was a loud bang and a fountain of water shot up into the sky like a giant water spout, soaking the spectators, who were then bombarded by uncountable scores of falling fish. Les then sat smugly while he was awarded victory by acclamation. All the fish were paid for and sent off to poor families and charities. And, in the midst of the death and terror going on all around, a damn good day was enjoyed by all . . . except the buffalo and the fish!

Hong Kong has a strange way of bringing 'experts' down to earth. Snakes are part of everyday life for Hakka Farmers in the New Territories. The Hakka farming girls especially come into frequent contact with them as they use sickles to cut grass on the hillsides as fodder for their cattle. One of the tourist sights of Hong Kong is rows of Hakka women bent over on the hill slopes cutting grass, wearing big rice straw hats with a black cloth fringe, and tightly plaited rice straw wrist protectors. Any snake surprised in the grass and striking at the arm usually ends up pumping his poison into the wrist guards. All of the Hakkas understand the risks of snakes, from childhood, and deal with them promptly and sensibly.

There was a bungalow with a garden near Tai Po Gau pier, in which lived a nice European family. One day their Hakka gardener, Mr Wong, told them that he had found a nest of cobras in a bank at the foot of the garden and he warned them to be careful until he had dealt with the snakes. The Europeans were decently concerned for the gardeners safety and told him to leave the snakes alone as they would get the government snake expert, a highly qualified Briton, to come and deal with them. Mr Wong did as he was told, and the expert duly arrived. Wong pointed out where the snake's nest was and waited to watch.

As the expert walked over to deal with the troublesome snakes with modern western technology, his foot went through the soil and he fell down into the pit. The female cobra and her brood of a dozen young, all delivered a full injection of venom. The expert was extricated and evacuated by helicopter to hospital, where his life was saved by modern technology and expert care. He later had to spend a long time in an iron lung, but, happily, survived. Wong used Hakka technology, a bamboo pole, killed the lot, and kept the female cobra for snake soup!

Nine

'ALL THE KING'S MEN . . .'

The Hong Kong Police Force became the Royal Hong Kong Police Force after the magnificent loyalty to the Crown and devotion to duty shown by all ranks during the terrible times of the Cultural Revolution. Out of the 200 or so Pakistanis, handful of Portuguese, and more than 6000 Hong Kong Chinese men and women officers, in the force at that time, only two were generally known to have defected in favour of the Communists, despite a terrible toll in death and injury. Many foreign correspondents found this difficult to understand, especially the Americans with their Republican background. In their minds, it seemed, that such loyalty to a distant Sovereign Lady, and a handful of barely 400 European officers, just did not add up.

With the exception of American old China hands like the respected journalist Dave Rhodes, they were equally puzzled by the fact that the whole of the Colony with its teeming millions of Chinese was run by fewer than a thousand Europeans, mainly from Britain, the British Commonwealth and the Republic of Ireland. One unbelieving reporter from Boston, Massachusetts, found it almost impossible to believe that Her Majesty's Chief Justice in Hong Kong, Sir Michael Hogan, was from the Emerald Isle!

The answer to the riddle is really quite simple, although it results from many complex issues. Right from its early beginnings, British rule, was orderly, efficient, and never tyrannical. British justice in Hong Kong, even when occasionally insensitively applied, still gave a more impartial and fairer deal, than anything else available in the Far East, and the people were satisfied with what they had.

From the Liberation of Hong Kong by Admiral Harcourt at the end of the Japanese terror, the most visible evidence of the government was the smartly uniformed, well disciplined, policemen and women on patrol. The average member of the public's official contact with a policeman was more than likely being pulled up by a Traffic Policemen for a ticking off, than anything else. Crime rates, per head of population, were not only lower than most other crowded areas in the East, they were much better than in most western countries. Between

114

the Triad riots of 1956 and the early beginnings of the Communist troubles in 1966, crimes per million of population were one tenth the American rate for known murders, half for known rapes, one quarter for aggravated assaults, one tenth for burglary, one tenth for robbery and one quarter for forgery. Drunkenness was negligible and usually only involved Europeans, it is rare to see a Chinese drunk. Larcenies were about equal with the USA. In general the figures compared favourably with America and Britain, and the percentage of known crime genuinely cleared up by the Hong Kong Police was far better than either of the other countries, and they did not have approximately half a million Triad society members, at least 10 000 of them involved in crime, to deal with! It was only in respect of narcotic drug abuse that the Colony looked bad when compared with other countries, and led to many unfounded accusations that this was entirely due to police corruption. When the Chinese Communists took power in China, the country's hundreds of thousands of drug addicts faced the stark choice of labour camps, being shot in the head, or bunking off over the border into Hong Kong. Those who could do so went to Hong Kong. The government was faced with an instant influx of thousands of hardened drug addicts, many of them hooked on heroin, and the police force just didn't stand a chance.

Every police force has to deal with a vast range of law enforcement duties, from seeing school kids across the road, to major riots, and, with the best will in the world, the Hong Kong Police could only devote a limited percentage of its limited manpower to dealing with drugs, and in this their successes, and failures, bear reasonable comparison with anyone else.

The Royal Hong Kong Police Force was, and is, made up of more than 94 per cent Hong Kong Chinese of all ranks, with a civilian administrative staff of interpreters and clerks numbering about 1500. Less than 6 per cent are non-Chinese. Thirty years or so ago the top fifty highest ranks were almost exclusively held by British officers, but the invisible race barrier has long been breached. For the good Chinese officers, such as Henry Fong Yick-fai, and Willy Chan Wai-man, who were among the first to break through to 'Gazetted' Rank, Assistant Superintendent of Police, the cases of ASP John Tsang Chao-ko, who was deported as an alleged spy for Communist China, and Superintendent Wong Wing-yin who was similarly deported as an alleged Nationalist agent, represented a set-back but not a defeat. By their own excellence they demonstrated the fact that they had at least as much right to higher rank as any European, and, in my personal experience, a damn sight more justifiable right than many who were later understandably promptly kicked out of newly Independent African States, and jumped up to high rank with indecent haste after being sent from London as constabulary refugees to Hong Kong!

With few exceptions, most people started their Hong Kong Police careers at the Police Training School in Aberdeen. This remarkable place could take in a young farming boy with paddy field mud still on his feet, and within six months turn out a smart, disciplined, police officer who could hold his own with anybody anywhere. The various Commandants and Instructors at the PTS were outstanding, practical, policemen, not academics, who understood men and who delivered what was needed for Hong Kong, sound practical coppers with an excellent grounding in law, and an appreciation of the value of sound common sense in dealing with their employers, the public. Examination results counted, but were not, as today, so fanatically sought as to bar a good man from being accepted, and letting a well-educated idiot get through. Even European officers left the school with a sound basic grounding in Cantonese language, and a knowledge of Chinese creeds and customs. Later, most of the ex-Africans remained content with their sole knowledge of Swahili, presumably on the old English principle that it is all right to shout at foreigners in any language, as long as you shout loudly enough.

Even in tasks that might have been expected to test their racial loyalties the Hong Kong Chinese policemen never wavered. For example, dealing with riots. To the best of my knowledge no peaceful demonstration, or gathering, of members of the public in Hong Kong has ever been harshly dealt with by the police. The orders laid down for a graduated progress of the use of force by the police is drilled, drilled, and drilled again, into everyone in the force who has attended the Police Training School, and the Police Tactical unit in Fanling. This makes a great difference between the way the police, and any Army unit, may tackle the same situation. The police are essentially members of the public they are dealing with, civilians with extra powers granted to them by the people, through the law. When dealing with a riot, they really just want people to go home and cool off. Soldiers are basically trained to kill their country's enemies.

In Hong Kong, riot control by policemen always started with warnings that they were an unlawful assembly, broadcast in the common local dialects, and English, with loud-hailers and large banners held high before the crowd with the message in Chinese characters and

English, 'Disperse or we will use force'. The first degree of force used would be a charge by officers with riot batons. After the charge there was a pause long enough for the crowd to begin to disperse. If this failed, or if the mob became more disorderly, the next warning was 'Disperse or we use tear gas'. When gas was used it was put into the crowd either as hand thrown gas grenades, or was fired as gas shells from Federal Gas Guns in such a way as either to skitter along the ground to the front of the crowd, or high in the air to their left or right. Next, in very serious circumstances, was 'Disperse or we fire'.

Any commander giving that order had to bear in mind that he might not only have to answer for his actions to his superiors, but also to a totally impartial and unbiased Court of Law! The firing of riot shotguns, or carbines, was always very strictly controlled by Company and Platoon Commanders, and the target was always the knees, or legs, of those at the front of the crowd. People in a moving swirling crowd did, at times get killed, but, except to save lives from unlawful killing, police officers never shot to kill, and their whole firearms training reinforced that principle.

As soon as any action had ended, and order restored, Riot Company First Aid men immediately attended to any injured people, and ambulances were called for. The intention was always the same, to restore public order in the shortest reasonable time with the minimum amount of force used.

Children were frequently taken into crowds by political riot organisers to try to get propaganda out of their injury, but the propaganda didn't work in Hong Kong because the population knew that the police would never deliberately hurt a child. Control was always exercised over the officers involved. Even the smallest unit used, the half column of four men, would always have at least a senior constable in command. Individual officers were never allowed to charge about on their own, like cowboys, as may be seen in TV news reports from some countries.

But even some TV reports may be treated with suspicion by Hong Kong people. On one occasion some TV reporters from America arrived at Shek Kip Mei Resettlement Estate too late for the action, as the police had just managed to clear the area of rioters after five hours of action. The TV men had arrived with plenty of Hong Kong dollar coins in their pockets and threw them around on the ground. Kids swarmed out from their houses and fought to pick them up, this drew in some adults, and eventually the TV men had a nice shot of fighting to send home for prime time viewing over the hamburgers and French fries. It took police nearly an hour to sort things out and restore peace. The regular American reporters of the Hong Kong Foreign Correspondents Club were furious at what had happened, and we heard that the offending people were dealt with quite severely by their peers. There were no official complaints received of the, rumoured, thick ears given to them by the police.

Every order given and every action taken in dispersing a riot was recorded contemporaneously in an action diary and that was submitted for scrutiny after every action. It must be emphasised that Riot Companies were never sent to use force against any peaceful crowd in Hong Kong, and force was never used until all means of persuasion had failed. The people knew it, and the constables, who were of the people knew it. That was what the puzzled foreigners could not understand!

The Hong Kong Police were always a well armed police force, one of the best armed in the world, not because anyone particularly wanted it that way, but because that was the way it had to be to protect the public. In dealing with pirates, and post-war gangs of armed Nationalist refugees in the New Territories, RAF aircraft were available from RAF Kai Tak, at police request, for reconnaissance, close support or air strikes. Later helicopters were supplied for training police to abseil down ropes on to the roofs of skyscrapers. Marine Police Launches were armed for dealing with armed pirates and smugglers, but no police launch ever opened fire on any unarmed vessel not displaying hostile intent.

There were a few armoured cars attached to the Emergency Units, but it was rare for them to be deployed against any crowd. In 1956 at the height of the battle of Sham Shui Po police station they were deployed effectively to assist the beleaguered defenders, but that was a rare occasion. My own experiences with them were probably more common, two in particular.

Emergency Unit Hong Kong had a particular responsibility right on our doorstep, in the presence in Central District of the main banking, financial, and diamond dealing, centre in the Colony. The two most important banks in particular, The Hong Kong and Shanghai Banking Corporation, the Government's Bankers, and The Bank of China, representative of the Chinese People's Government State Bank. Each of these organisations had huge banking halls with dozens of cashiers' windows working away busily all day serving typically Hong Kong sized crowds of customers. It was feared, during the troubles of the cultural revolution, that Triad gangs might try to carry out armed robberies in these banks, in the one pretending to be Communists, in the other pretending to be Nationalists.

It was arranged with the bank at local level, for us to carry out some exercises designed to make sure that all of the EU men were familiar with the areas outside the banks, and the banking hall of the Hong Kong and Shanghai. In the event of a fast moving hold up, such familiarisation might be crucial in saving human lives and that was the banker's main concern. We ended the familiarisation period with a set piece exercise, including one with the armoured cars being commanded by a European officer. He was a very keen and enthusiastic chap and had found a little known side street route that would take him in record time into position on a steep slip road opposite the bank's busiest main door, ready to move down and stop in the main road where any robbers might have been expected to make their getaway. On the day of the exercise we began immediately after the official close of banking business.

Everything went very well and I listened with great interest on the command radio network as the lumbering armoured car made remarkable speed to its final position on the slip road. Interest changed to concern when the commander's triumphant 'Arrived in position' message was followed in rapid succession by 'Sorry, the brakes have failed', 'We are rolling down the slip road and can't stop', 'We are crossing the main road, no accidents', 'We are approaching the bank door' then an awful silence followed by 'We are now inside the bank, Which do you want first, the good news or the bad news, Sir?' without waiting for a reply 'The good news is that no one has been injured in any way. The bad news is that we rather dented their nice new door!'

On arrival at the scene shortly after I could see the armoured car parked discreetly outside the bank at the side of the road. On entering the bank, the beautifully decorated bronze cast doors, sporting a huge dent in them, could be noticed! Inside stood the flustered looking commander in deep conversation with senior bank officials, who were, in my opinion, showing amazing good humour at my arrival considering the fact that, as the whole stupid exercise had been arranged by me off my own bat, I was personally responsible for an expensively battered new door. My only hope was that they would let me pay the cost of repairs by monthly instalments over, perhaps, two hundred years!

The bank men explained their apparent good humour. They had been on the gallery above the, thankfully, empty banking hall with their Chairman awaiting the denouement of the exercise. The main door had suddenly burst open and the armoured car came in then trundled its way across the marble floor with the commander standing upright in horror stricken paralysis in the open turret. It stopped dead in front of the window of a cashier who had been working away busily at his rattling abacus. He looked up directly into the muzzle of the monstrous armoured car's Browning machine gun, gave an oriental version of 'Eek', and fainted.

The Chairman had, allegedly, merely commented that it had been a valuable exercise, well worth while, then gone. Both the car commander and I were relieved, not just by the fact that we had, serendipitously, established a new way of getting in fast if robbers were inside, but also because we had both been thinking about how long it could take to pay for the door on a policeman's salary!

It may be bias, because of my personal high regard for the Hong Kong Chinese, and my personal view that the Hong Kong policemen are the best turned out and smartest in the world, but I do not know of any policemen anywhere else who, are as relentlessly pursued and photographed by tourists as the ordinary Hong Kong police constable on patrol. None more so than the traffic policemen, who control the seething mass of converging traffic at Hong Kong's busiest traffic junction at the foot of Garden Road and Queen's Road in the City of Victoria. Standing on a Traffic Pagoda, rising like an island wreathed in carbon monoxide fumes, by Police Standing Orders, reviving themselves every fifteen minutes with deep breaths of bottled oxygen. Wearing brilliantly white sleeves and gloves, they would give clear, unmistakable directions with firm and direct signals, then spin with balletic grace to face the alternate lane and continue without a break in rhythm.

On patrol one day I noticed a European lady standing on the pavement near the Hong Kong Hilton Hotel watching the constable who was directing traffic, and filming him with a movie camera. Half an hour later on my return she was still in the same place so I stopped to see if she needed any assistance. She was an American, who was involved in theatre dance in California, and she told me that she had been filming two different traffic men on the pagoda because they were so graceful, so commanding, and so relaxed she wanted her students to see how it was done!

At one time every photograph of a traffic man was virtually a free advertisement for the British Triumph motor cycle company as the force was equipped with their excellent machines, and the men liked them. At one time, it is said, it became virtually impossible to buy Triumphs from Britain as the company had no time to bother with such small orders as a few hundred bikes for Hong Kong, they were too busy with the American market. The very next day, the story goes, a member of the Japanese Trade Commission informed Police HQ that a Japanese motor cycle would arrive by the Japanese airline, JAL for the police to try on approval, without commitment. The following day the motor cycle arrived, at Kai Tak airport in Hong Kong Police colours, with radios tuned to the Hong Kong Police networks ready to go on trials, just as soon the JAL ground staff filled it with petrol, which they promptly did. This may be just another example of Hong Kong's penchant for apocryphal stories, but it fits with the attitude of some British manufacturers at the time, and the Hong Kong Police Traffic Branch was completely re-equipped with Japanese Bikes!

The Hong Kong Chinese officers of the Royal Hong Kong Police Force have my whole-hearted admiration for the magnificent way they go about their duties. Their incredible loyalty, to the death for too many, to their Queen to whom they have sworn their oath of office puts many in Britain, including some who sit in Parliament as Members, to shame.

Ten

THE CRACK IN THE
INSCRUTABLE SCREEN

In its earliest days the Triad Society was a patriotic Chinese secret society whose members were bound by oaths of blood brotherhood and were pledged to overthrow the hated Ching dynasty of the conquering Manchurian foreigners and restore the Chinese Ming.

The word Triad was coined by the British from the sacred emblem of the society, a triangle in which the three sides represent the three basic powers, Heaven, Earth, and Man. It was easier for foreigners to refer to them as Triads rather than by their colloquial names in Hong Kong, Tin Tei Wui (Heaven and Earth Association), Sam Hop Wui (Three United Association [the Triad symbol's three sides]), and Hung Mun (Hung Sect). In Hong Kong they are generally just referred to as Hak Sh'e Wui or Black Society Association, which gives some idea of how they are regarded by decent people – evil and sinister – not mystic and patriotic.

The real Triad or Hung Society is believed to have the largest membership of any secret society in the world. In Hong Kong alone in the late 1950s there were an estimated 500 000 members in a population of just over 3 000 000 people. But many were totally inactive and joined simply out of fear and for their own protection.

The Triads have reputedly, existed since AD 386 and are associated in some accounts with the ancient White Lotus society. Its true rites have been linked with mystery rites over 1500 years old, the oldest known to man. It has also been spoken of in its more modern form as evolving from the destruction of the Shao Lin monastery of warrior monks during the reign of the Ching Emperor Yung Cheng (1723-1736), but few hard facts are known. What is known for certain of the past is the Triads professed loyalty to the ousted Chinese Ming dynasty. The last of the known political, as contrasted to criminal, Triads was probably Chung Wo Tong who supported Dr Sun Yat-sen's Republican party until the successful revolution in 1911. Most of the other Triads were by that time already criminal organisations involved in murders, robberies, assaults, prostitution, gambling, and drugs, all for their private profit.

122

As with all other criminal elements, Hong Kong received more than its fair share of Triad gangsters, who fled from certain execution or labour camps when the communists conquered China in 1949. In the colony their activities have always been entirely criminal, perpetually engaged in pimping, procuring for prostitution, extortion, drug trafficking, acting as strong-arm men, nothing is too low or depraved for them as long as they get paid. There was one very senior Triad man who was a very big drug trafficker and lived in a big villa, with a Mercedes car, and plenty of mistresses, aping the movie Mafia man. He irritated some of his Triad colleagues with ill-considered arrogance and ended up floating in the Lamma Channel wrapped up in clear plastic, the same kind of plastic in which measures of heroin were sold to addicts. Not nice people to tangle with if they are annoyed, but somebody obviously had an oriental sense of graveyard humour!

It took the Double Tenth riots of 1956 to get the Hong Kong legal people moving to curb the Triads. No one would ever testify in open court against a Triad man, suicide with a blunt razor would make more sense. One witness did, reputedly, testify against a senior Triad man in a fit of jealousy over a woman. They caught up with him in San Paolo in Brazil eighteen months later and took him to pieces, slowly.

Special laws and special courts such as are now employed in Ulster were used to break the Triad leadership and they were dispersed by deportation after detention. Although this helped to break up the bigger organisations it created dozens of different alleged Triads, all playing on the same fears for extortion and other rackets, but unable to organise really big trouble. Hong Kong came under some criticism from some of the American and other civil liberty people, some of them even softer in the head than the heart, and many Triads decided that the USA was the place for them. They found the American legal system so full of loopholes, they loved it. They are now major drug traffickers in the States, fighting with Hispanic, Black,and other gangs, even the Mafia, for control with much success, of certain areas.

The Americans are a puzzle to the Triads, who reckon they take more care of criminal's civil rights than innocent people's. However, they are not complaining, and allegedly give enthusiastic support to campaigns in America directed against the Diplock Courts used against terrorists in Northern Ireland, similar to the type of Courts used, successfully, to break up their Triad organisations in Hong Kong! It may be that the Americans will eventually discover that draconian methods must sometimes be used if they wish government to control certain areas of public life rather than gangsters.

Some of the Triad men in Hong Kong assumed grandiose nicknames in an attempt to make themselves known in their own criminal circles and identifiable to the victims of their petty graft and extortion, names such as 'Big Muscle Chan', 'Chief of the Fighting Irons', one, so help me, was known as 'Ferocious Chicken'! The Hong Kong Chinese people have a tremendous knack of giving nicknames to people that can be horribly descriptive of their nature, character, and appearance, and once given they can never be lost. Mine ranged from the unpleasant 'Battered Eye Devil', to 'Poison Eye Dragon', to 'One Eyed Dragon'.

One senior officer had a long and very successful career bearing the nickname 'Flying Shit House Seat', because in his early days he did not understand as much Cantonese as he thought he did, and did not comprehend a station coolie's warning during the inspection of an old police station, that the ground he was walking towards was the site of an old cesspit, at least, not until he fell through the termite-riddled wooden cover up to his waist in its contents! To give him his due the rank and file appreciated his grimly humorous comment that he was 'in it again'.

The rank and file, in the main, disliked the ex-African officers, save one, who liked football, was fair-minded in his dealings with them, and treated them like human beings. They were extremely frank in stating, privately, how much they could understand the African people kicking those particular whites out of the African colonies just as soon as they had the chance, and they invariably referred to them as 'redundant game wardens'!

One who was particularly disliked was known as 'Crocodile Spit' because of a totally unfounded rumour that he had gone to a river to wash his face once and a crocodile grabbed him to eat him, but he was such a horrible man the crocodile was sick, and threw up, so the man made his escape.

The much tattooed Les Guyatt, was very much liked and admired by the rank and file, who frequently shortened his nickname to an affectionate, 'Uncle Dragon.'

One wickedly mischievous officer was called 'Monkey' after the Monkey God who constantly caused turmoil in Heaven.

A very slim and lightly built officer from northern England who was very much liked for his decent good nature, was horribly embarrassed one day when the Hakka lady hawker he had reluctantly arrested for obstructing the main ferry pier, refused to move her two baskets of vegetables slung on her bamboo carrying pole and invited him to shift them himself. He had ducked under the pole and strained to lift the baskets to no avail. He heaved and strained until red in the face, with sweat pouring off him, in front of a highly amused crowd. The Hakka lady took pity on him, picked up her baskets and trotted off with them up a slope to the police station. He was known thereafter as the 'Honourable Striver After Mobility.'

A very smooth Home Counties, promotion-hunting, type, who was only friendly to his colleagues faces and stabbed them in the back at the first opportunity, was known as the 'Poison Fish' after a particular fish caught in the Far East that can sometimes be safely eaten, and at others paralyses and kills the eater.

One of the most damning and insulting nicknames was given to a particular well-built, well-muscled, European officer, who had a yellow streak which he kept hidden well enough to gain fairly rapid promotion, he was called 'Limp Penis'!

The rank and file could be harsh critics but were generally good judges of character.

It may come as a shock, for those who have seen the world famous Chater Building, with its hundreds of circular windows, shown on television, and referred to erroneously as, 'The Mansion with Ten Thousand Eyes', to know that it is called, by the locals, 'The Mansion of Ten Thousand Arseholes'! Even the most expensive Public Relations exercise bites the dust, in the face of the Hong Kong public's earthy sense of what is appropriate!

Eleven

FIRE, FLOOD, AND FOUL PLAY!

In Chinese mythology the Chinese Gods display all of the attributes of humankind. One of them is undoubtedly a sense of humour.

I was very happy as Sub-Divisional Inspector of Aberdeen, a beautiful area on the south west side of Hong Kong Island with a good hard-working population mainly engaged in fishing, farming, preserving ginger, boat building, and pottery, well supplied with open hills, beaches, and the sea. After a year and a half in the post it was widely assumed that I would remain there until going on Home Leave, for which my passage was actually reserved with P & O, naturally, as my departure was due in eleven months. One day a very senior officer visited my station and I was informed that I was to be posted immediately to a police station in Kowloon as SDI with the rank of Senior Inspector.

It appeared that for some, undisclosed, reason it had been decided at a high level that the station should undergo an almost complete change of personnel with immediate effect. The police station was Mongkok, in Kowloon, the place with the stilt huts in the typhoon shelter where we had made our nightmare drug raid in the Marine Police Drug Squad, to the embarrassment of the officer who was the Sub-Divisional Inspector at that time. It was a tiny three square mile patch of land with a resident population estimated at 500 000 people, some 60 000 more inhabitants than present day Edinburgh!

With 166 666 people per square mile it was one of the most overcrowded pieces of real estate in the world and one of the most difficult to police. If I had wished to do so it would have undoubtedly been possible for me to avoid leaving Aberdeen with its nice people and lovely environment for an overcrowded warren in Kowloon but only a fool would have turned down the opportunity for promotion in an organisation where competition for advancement was fierce and the standards set by the Chinese officers were dazzling.

The old Mongkok police station was set at the side of Nathan Road, Kowloon's main thoroughfare, by a number of major road junctions. It was wreathed day and night in vehicle exhaust fumes and experienced comparative quiet for about one hour a day between three and four o'clock in the morning. Fortunately there were no living quarters available in the station and accommodation was secured in the Marine Police HQ some three miles down the road which had gardens and peace and quiet. The whole station was built like a late Victorian fort and had been besieged many times by mobs of attackers, most recently in 1956 when it had been defended by policemen, assisted by station coolies, manning the walls and gun towers firing at the attackers like a scene out of some Foreign Legion movie. My first day in Mongkok was educational. The outgoing SDI was a Chinese officer who looked at the end of his tether. Normally Chinese men look younger than their British counterparts, but this poor fellow looked a hundred years old, careworn, and exhausted. It was obvious, as we used to say as boys, that his 'string had run out'. We had only been allowed twenty-four hours for hand over in contrast to the customary week or more but, fortunately for me, my predecessor had very efficiently arranged things so that all the inspections and checks of the station funds, arms, stores, case exhibits, records and other minutiae were completed in less then ten hours. When we had finished he still looked awful but he looked as though an intolerable weight had been removed from his shoulders. He went with me for a Chinese dinner at my invitation and I learned more from him during that meal than from any official source in the next eleven months. He did not generally drink but I introduced him to Remy Martin Fine Cognac and he liked it. It also relaxed him, and by the time we reached the shark's fin soup dish he was talking freely about his time as SDI of Mongkok.

Even in the early to mid 1950s Mongkok was still basically a place where the only high-rise, high rent, buildings tended to be built along Nathan road. Most of the people still lived in pre-war tenement blocks five or six floors high, with many still in old three floor buildings, and more living in huts including the stilt-huts in the typhoon shelter. As the population began to soar with thousands of refugees arriving, coupled with a high-birth rate of one baby born every five minutes, buildings soared too. Anything less than twenty storeys high, packed with tiny, expensive flats, was an economic nonsense. The demand for business and residential accommodation was so frantic that people were moving into buildings still under construction! Bearing in mind the fact that about 40 000 people were sleeping on the streets and even living in typhoon drains, the haste to move in to a proper house is understandable.

Mongkok's population doubled, trebled, and kept rising as three-storey buildings containing maybe 400 to 500 people were knocked down and replaced by ten, fifteen, later twenty, storey buildings each containing thousands of people packed into scores of flats maximising every available inch of space. The prices of flats were sky high, at the time the highest in the world per square foot of space. For a small three bedroom flat that might have cost in the region of £6000 in any British City, a Hong Kong buyer would have to pay at least £30 000. So in order to pay the huge prices demanded most of the flat buyers had to keep one room for their own families and rent off the other rooms to whole families in order to pay off the developers.

Despite the boom in population, requests for more police officers in Mongkok police station were either denied for various reasons, or a derisory number of extra men were allocated. The total number of policemen available in the station at the time of our changeover was ninety. For a similar population anywhere in Scotland or England, the smallest acceptable establishment of police officers would have been 318 men, three and a half times the number in Mongkok!

In later encounters with some senior officers, when they gossiped about the alleged sins of omission and commission in Mongkok, I rather blotted my copy book by pointing out that my predecessor had been lucky if, on any given day, he had enough men available for duty to cover four out of the sixteen beats in the sub-division! On an average day twelve men would be on their standard one day off; at least four men would be having a day off in lieu of extra duties as no overtime was paid in the HKP; four would be on annual leave; one would be on sick leave; six would be attending court for a full day Monday to Friday; and at least three would be on detached or training duties leaving a total of sixty men for three shifts over twenty-four hours. But that was not the end of the attrition of beat men. Of the twenty men available for duty on any eight hour shift, one was the Duty Officer in the report room with one assistant Duty Officer and one Report Room Constable plus three other constables for cell guard, station guard and escort duties, one on duty in the Armoury, and three drivers, leaving ten men available for beats. But, of the ten men available, one would be an Inspector on general duties covering everything from supervision, to drug, gambling, or prostitution raids, visiting licensed premises and preparing reports, at least four would be NCOs on supervisory and relief duties, leaving a grand total of five constables pounding sixteen beats, each of them armed with a pistol, six rounds of ammunition and a truncheon, presumably protecting 125 000 members of the population! Chinese Supermen! My predecessor's worn out appearance was truly understandable.

At the end of the first week in my new post I was exhausted, as every day had been filled with what seemed like twenty-six hours of work. Crimes, fires, 'conferences', training, transfers of men out and in, patrols by day and night so that new men could see me out and about and I could see them, learning the layout of my new 'patch', gaining an understanding of the politics and internal rivalries of this police district new to me, and mountains of paper work and reports.

Late one evening I had just arrived home and settled into a hot bath for a long soak when the telephone rang. It was the Duty Officer reporting that a large fire had broken out in the Tai Kok Tsui area in Mongkok. The fire had started in a cotton mill in a place known to the locals as the 'Triangle'. It had gained this name as one side was formed by a large cotton mill, another by a big oil store, the third by a timber yard, all surrounded at no great distance by houses full of thousands of people. When I arrived at the scene I was still damp from the bath! The cotton mill was well ablaze, flames were visible in the oil store, and smoke was beginning to rise from the timber yard. I called in the beat men and the few reserves I had and asked for more men from Emergency Unit Kowloon. They could only supply a few as they were already committed at another large fire. We managed to seal the area off and began warning people to be ready to evacuate their homes. Hong Kong Chinese will not leave their hard gained homes until their shirt tails are alight!

We had done all we could and the rest was up to the Fire Service. Flames shot up higher and higher all around us accompanied by ominous bangs as containers of oil, paint, and other flammable materials exploded. Huge sprays of sparks and burning material rose and were carried by heat thermals on to the nearby houses where they were promptly doused with buckets of water by the anxious residents. I stood and looked at the scene before me. I had been promoted and had been in Mongkok for one week and the bloody place was burning down before my eyes! The Senior Fire Officer could see my face and read my thoughts and he told me not to worry as they were getting it all under control. He just grinned when my doubts were expressed somewhat forcefully. However, it was soon obvious that the firemen had done their work well, as scores of hoses and swarms of firemen visibly got the various fires under control and billows of smoke demonstrated that the flames were being doused.

THE ONE-EYED DRAGON

I began to cheer up and think that things were improving and I might still have a subdivision to run the next day when my duty Inspector came from the radio car to report that one of my constables had been reported through the '999' service as lying murdered in Tung Choi Street not far from the rear of the police station. Having a man murdered on duty was bad enough, what was worse was that he had only recently arrived in Mongkok from the Police Training School and, because of our manpower shortage, was on his first beat patrol by himself after only a week on duty under supervision by an NCO!

The Inspector was left in charge at the fire scene and my driver performed miracles getting me to the murder scene in minutes. It was a great relief on arrival to see the constable, covered from head to foot in blood and looking very shaken, standing talking to one of our CID men. In reply to my concerned questions about the blood he replied ,'Oh its not mine sir, its theirs' and he pointed up the steep flight of stairs leading up to the first floor of one of Mongkok's few remaining old buildings.

I shone my torch up the dark stairs and could see huge dark smears of blood on the walls and ceiling all the way down from an open door at the top of the stairs. My next worry was if he had shot some people but I could see his pistol still in the holster, obviously unused. The constable was sent off to hospital for a checkup as he had fallen head over heals down the stairs and was obviously very shaken and looked concussed.

We went up the stairs and through the open door. Inside what had been a very large, old fashioned Chinese style family home was an illegal clothes factory with dozens of sewing machines, twenty-five Chinese girls and four men. Built above the working area was what is known in Hong Kong as a 'cock loft', an additional floor fitted into a high room, like an attic, built as extra accommodation. In this instance the cock loft was solidly built, fairly sound proofed, and contained an amazing bed sitting room containing a huge bed designed like Hollywood's idea of a harem bed, and a bathroom with a luxurious bathtub big enough for more than one person!

In its style and decoration, dim lamps, silks, and rosewood, the place truly fitted the description 'passion parlour' it reeked of sensuality and sex. A flight of steps led down from the cock loft to a large open reception room floored with beautifully made Chinese floor tiles, this was separated from the working area by a teakwood partition with sliding glass windows which were opened to allow a breeze through.

The tile floor was slippery with congealing blood; blood was splashed on the walls, the partition and the ceiling. Everywhere there were skid marks, hand marks, impressions of a blood-stained human figure, on the doorframe distinct impressions of desperately grasping hands. On the tile floor were two dead bodies horribly slashed and torn with numerous cuts and gaping wounds, by them lay a butchers knife and a large pair of tailor's shears each bearing blood stains and fragments of flesh. One body was that of what had been a voluptuously attractive Chinese woman in her late twenties, full bodied and dressed in the remains of a blood-stained negligee that could have left little to the imagination. The other was that of a young Chinese man, barely in his twenties. He had been a handsome lad, rather in the style of the wimpish poets of the English Romantic era in dress and appearance, with long hair swept back from a good forehead and fine features with a babyish mouth. He had been trying to grow a moustache, without success. We were given the bizarre, yet commonplace, story by a succession of excited teenage seamstresses revelling in their participation in an 'event'.

The woman was a Madam Wong, described as the number one concubine of the rich owner of the business. She had, it was alleged, been bought by a businessman as a child and used as a 'Mui Tsai' servant girl until puberty, when she began to show her latent beauty, at which time she was promptly deflowered and promoted to junior mistress. Unfortunately for her she never became pregnant, and so never had a boy child, the essential instrument of security necessary in such liaisons. Because she was so beautiful and, it was reported with much nudging and giggling, an absolute genius in the art of bed satisfaction, she had been given the money to start the business with her benefactor as a, more giggling, 'sleeping' partner . . . if only occasionally these days. Madam Wong had shown an unexpected flair for design and for running the business. She had also been successful in negotiating sales of her products in America, so things boomed and the money poured in.

The young man, Lee, had been employed to do accounts and look after the important paper work related to the Certificates of Origin essential for the American market. He was a very serious minded young man, described by the girls as a 'cherry' boy, a virgin, who soon fell romantically heart and soul in love with his experienced employer and enthusiastically 'gave up his cherry' to her at the first opportunity! It was obvious that Madam Wong enjoyed his youthful passion to the full and may even have played along with

131

his romanticism but only for the pillow games, she enjoyed him in bed but she was not in love with him.

It was noticed by the workers that on the infrequent visits of Madam's partner, Lee became highly agitated and upset if they went up into the cock loft room, so much so that he would leave the works and remain absent for some hours. The affair went on for some months and it became known that Lee wanted Madam Wong to run away with him to Indonesia and get married. It might have been better in the long run if the lady had just bluntly told him that the only service she wanted from him was the service he gave her in bed, not the wedding kind, but she didn't. Maybe she did not want to hurt his feelings, whatever the reason no one will ever know now. Lee had quit his job and had not been seen by the other workers until that evening. He had telephoned earlier and spoken to Madam Wong.

Later he had arrived at the works looking excited and had gone up the stairs to the room door where the workers could hear him telling her that he had arranged for them to go to his relatives in Indonesia where she would be free of the 'horrible old man' forever and would be his respected wife. By this stage of the game no one was working as they were all listening avidly to this real life soap opera. Madam Wong said something to the effect that she had never given him any reason to believe that she would go to Indonesia or anywhere else with him, nor had she indicated any intention of giving up the profitable business she had built up by her own efforts just to throw it away for a casual flirtation.

No one was able to recount the full course of the events that followed but they suddenly saw Wong and Lee in the reception room. Lee had a butcher's knife in his hand with which he was attacking Madam Wong in a frenzy. The woman had picked up a pair of tailor's shears and was defending herself. The fight was short and ferocious and the witnesses described in vivid detail how the weapons plunged into flesh, how blood spurted and sprayed about, how the pair struggled and fell and rose up again hacking and slashing at each other, the shock view through the negligée of the woman's almost naked body covered in wounds and blood, until both slumped to the floor either dead or dying.

When the detective asked why no one had tried to intervene he received the answer, usually accompanied by a shrug of the shoulders, given in Hong Kong to cover all situations 'M'Gwaan Ngoh Seegon' 'None of my business'!

My question about the constable's part in all this, sent them all into fits of the giggles, which went incongruously with the background of blood and bodies.

Their story about the constable made the 'Scene of Crime' specialists, who had just arrived, look even more old fashioned, grumpy, and cynical than they usually do. Every policeman of every rank has it drummed into him that he must not touch anything, move anything, disturb anything, stand on anything, or even think about it, at any scene of crime until the forensic science men have given them permission to do so. Despite this, the forensic men are all firmly convinced that even the most innocent of actions at a scene are carried out as part of a police conspiracy to mess up their efforts and give them ulcers.

The constable had been proudly patrolling along Tung Choi Street keenly looking out for criminals delighted to be out on his own as a living representation of the 'Law'. It is known that he was not thinking at that time about a particular training session he had participated in at the Police Training School, entitled 'Do's and Don'ts at a Scene of Crime'. He heard a woman's voice shouting 'Help! Murder!' from the top of the stairs and he immediately ran up making quite a lot of noise with his brand new, smooth soled, police issue boots. He skidded on the landing and went into the reception room.

Here the witnesses take over the sequence of events as the constable arrived. He erupted through the door from the landing on to the blood covered tiled floor, which was as slippery as smooth ice, skidded across the floor on his smooth soled boots with his arms waving frantically like a novice ice skater, he half-tripped half-fell over both bodies leaving beautiful impressions of his boot soles on them both and somehow getting blood on his hands at the same time, he collided with a wall leaving behind impressions in blood of both his hands, he rebounded from the wall with some force and fell over both corpses again, (at this stage he was making what was described as whimpering sounds) he rolled across the floor getting covered in blood and, with some force, smashed into another wall which he seemed to be trying to climb but as his hands scrabbled at the wall his feet were skidding wildly on the tiles like a cartoon cat, he managed to get partially upright and skidded his way round to the wall he had not yet assaulted but he bounced off it and tripped over the corpses yet again, this time his luck was really out, he banged head on into the door frame and ricocheted off down the stairs out of view of the fascinated onlookers, the evidence of his passage downwards was the sound of his body hitting things and his pained reactions to the impacts.

It was estimated later that the unfortunate constable had been in the room barely a minute, and in that time he had touched, kicked, banged into, stood on, head-butted, scrabbled on, leaned on, and pushed at, just about every surface in the place, he had also trampled over the deceased at least three times. If they had not been so obviously stabbed, and if there had not been over twenty completely independent witnesses to the stabbings, it might quite reasonably have been suspected that my constable had kicked them to death!

The Officer-in-Charge of the Scene of Crime squad, was deeply affected by the witnesses' account of events and he completed up his part of the proceedings quite quickly and left, after all how could mere forensic people follow such an act? One of his men later assured me that they had found three clear imprints of the constable's boot soles between four and six feet above the floor. He may have been pulling my leg but if what he said was true then the constable must have been airborne!

My District Commander had to be given an immediate report so I made it short and accurate, within reason. He was informed that the constable was not dead but had fallen down stairs. That it was a murder case but that the murderer and victim were both dead, the victim killing the murderer in self defence.

I had to give him the full story in private the following day and he listened to me in silence, obviously torn between horror at the terrible account of the murder, and sheer disbelief when I told him in some detail of the constable's brief visit to the scene. He inquired about a Coroner's Inquest and whether the Constable would be able to give evidence, and I had to tell him that the constable could not remember ever seeing the corpses. His only recollections of the scene of the crime were of being unable to keep on his feet, painful collisions with the floor and walls, hurtling down the stairs, and unconsciousness as he hit the pavement. It was obvious that the District Commander was under the influence of a strong emotional, shoulder-heaving problem, as he agreed with me that the constable had best be left out of the inquest. In the event the Inquest was quite straightforward, bringing in verdicts of murder and justifiable homicide. As for the constable he had to live with being given a Chinese nickname related to Sonja Henie the famous ice skating star!

One of the main problems when taking over a police station as a new SDI is ensuring continuity of its good aspects, and rectifying errors that may have taken root. This is a reasonably straightforward matter when the place has been well run but far more difficult when, for a variety of reasons, things have been allowed to get out of hand. It is even more difficult when most of the original senior staff have gone in a virtual mass transfer, and some personnel are awaiting trial on corruption charges. Morale was low, more than half of the rank and file did not know each other or their beats as they were new to the subdivision, rumours of events in the station had reached the public so the men had 'lost face', the new sergeants and corporals were having to learn the area and its problems in a great hurry while concurrently getting to know their constables and their officers. Morale can never be restored until discipline and well understood routines are restored, so Mongkok had a bumpy ride for a time.

Something as simple as official meal breaks during a 'stand-by in station' can demonstrate lack of discipline. In the labyrinth of back streets behind Mongkok police station there were scores of cooked food stalls, known as 'poor men's nightclubs' providing cheap and delicious meals representative of the whole of China's fabulous cuisine. Inside the police station was a canteen serving canteen meals representative of the whole of the world's 'canteen' cuisine. Anyone who has eaten canteen food anywhere will appreciate the fact that the men preferred to eat at the cooked food stalls. However, this was not permitted, the men were required to eat in the station while on duty or on reserve and 'stand-by'.

The reasons for this are quite simply that police officers might use their authority corruptly to obtain meals without paying, and they would also be absent from the station if urgently needed to turn out for an emergency. The rules that no one could leave the station without permission were very strictly enforced, and after one or two examples had been set by disciplinary proceedings, everyone knew it! It was not fully realised just how deeply the enforcement of discipline had settled into the constable's consciousness until a typhoon hit us.

Most of the typhoons that affect Hong Kong begin fairly quietly off the coast of the Philippine Islands and then make a well-charted and reasonably leisurely progress north to arrive on the South China coast somewhere near the Colony. This gives time for everyone to batten down the hatches and sit out the bad weather until the typhoon moves away and dissipates. Now and again a 'rogue' typhoon springs up,

135

seemingly out of nowhere, charges at the Colony, batters it about, then disappears.

One such typhoon hit the Colony not long after I arrived in Mongkok, with typhoon warnings from the meteorological department indicating ever-increasing wind strengths and speed of approach, succeeding each other with startling frequency. It was a big one, it was approaching fast, and it was going to hit us hard with wind speeds estimated at over 130 miles per hour.

We were very concerned as Mongkok was full of high rise construction sites festooned with bamboo scaffolding. In Tai Kok Tsui we had hundreds of wooden buildings, timber yards, oil stores and other businesses. On every flat bit of roof space in the subdivision we had rooftop schools and uncounted hundreds of wooden huts containing whole families. In the typhoon shelter were the stilt-huts and ever-increasing numbers of small craft from sampans to big ocean-going junks. We even had to evict quickly squatters who had taken up residence in the huge typhoon drains that discharged into the harbour in our area!

To their credit every one of the Mongkok men, including those on sick leave, reported in for duty well before the storm struck us, and we began our typhoon procedures, well pleased with their response to our first emergency, and the evidence this gave of good morale. By late morning Nathan Road, the busiest road in the Colony, was empty of all traffic even pedestrians. Our men had worked like Trojans on every duty allotted to them, such as seeing that building sites were made as secure as possible, checking that schoolchildren had been sent home, ensuring that dangerous goods at wharves and stores were all safely secured, checking street signs, supervising crowds of passengers at the ferry piers, railway station and bus terminii making last minute attempts to get home. As typhoon signal number ten went up everyone had orders to return to the police station, battling their way back through winds already gusting over 100 miles an hour.

Before finally closing the main door of the station I went outside accompanied by one of my Inspectors and looked around the eerily empty main road, as we did so we saw a private car being driven down the middle of the road by a grinning Chinese man who was obviously very pleased with himself. What he did not seem to have seen following him was a huge sheet of corrugated steel flying towards the back of his car like an aerofoil, borne along at tremendous speed by the typhoon wind. We tried to warn the driver with hand signals but he just grinned wider and made a rude gesture at us. As he was

136

passing us he turned his head and, at the very last minute, must have seen the corrugated sheet approaching his rear window end on, like a letter being put into a post box, he ducked down and the metal sheet entered his back window with fragments of glass flying everywhere, sailed straight through the car out through the front window and disappeared down the road. The car had come to a stop about 200 yards from us and we ran to it to help the driver. He was gone, the only evidence of his presence being a few blood spots on the upholstery. He was one of the luckiest men alive as, had he not turned his head towards us and seen the flying object approaching, he would surely have been beheaded as efficiently as with a guillotine.

That day and the following night was one of great damage and injury for Mongkok. Many people had to be evacuated to safety by my men, not just as a result of wind damage but also because the waterfront area was flooded by the highest tide ever recorded. Our officers performed unrecognised feats of heroism getting men women and children under cover at great danger to themselves. Unrecognised because they did not bother to report it or talk about it until well after the event.

The first report of the flooding was received as one of the corporals on mobile patrol had left his patrol Land Rover to check that a hut was safe and disappeared into six feet of water where there should have been a concrete path. As he swam to safety he realised that the area was being covered with rapidly rising water. Other cars were sent to the scene, whose crews quickly established the extent of flooding and promptly evacuated everyone in the area, despite their protests. If they had not done so hundreds of people could have drowned that night, disorientated and thrown about bodily by the screaming wind, unseen and unnoticed in the dark and torrential rain. Some boats sank in the typhoon shelter but again our men managed to rescue the survivors.

By about three o'clock in the morning the typhoon had reached a stage of mind-numbing fury. All of our personnel were back in the police station as no one could survive outside. Even our Land Rovers, the most stable four wheel drive vehicles in the world, were in danger of being blown over. Everyone was tired out, so I gave instructions that, except for a skeleton staff in the Report Room to receive messages and reports, all personnel were to go to the barrack rooms to get some sleep while they could. Two of the best barrack rooms were modern buildings like Army huts at the rear of the station compound in the shelter of the back wall and when I took a brief look around later, all that could be seen were bunks filled with heavily sleeping men. They had gone out like lights as soon as they lay down.

To our disbelief the typhoon seemed to gain strength rather than diminish as the night wore on. Nathan Road was impassable, completely blocked by fallen scaffolding, signs, bits of wooden huts and all the other detritus deposited by the winds. At four o'clock in the morning the officers and senior NCOs were in my office where, to a background of tremendous noise from outside, we were planning our priorities of action to be taken when the wind let up. Someone hammered on the office door and was told to come in. A constable entered soaking from head to toe, barefoot, and dressed only in a pair of soggy underpants. He looked like a wet Yorkshire terrier. He marched sharply across the office, his bare feet slapping wetly on the floor, halted, drew himself up to attention in front of my desk and reported in a loud official voice 'It are raining in the barrack room, Sir!' When I did not immediately respond, as I was trying to work out why he looked as he did and what the hell he was on about, he repeated in a louder voice with a hint of desperation in it, 'It are truly raining in the bloody barrack room, please come look see, Sir!'

We immediately went into the compound with him and could see why it was raining in the barrack room, the whole roof had gone, blown away by the typhoon. I was concerned that some of the men might have been injured and we hurried over to ascertain how much damage had been done and if there were any injured.

When we went into the room I was astonished to see that the men were still sitting in their bunks in the torrential rain. Thankfully no one was injured, God knows how not, as the roof was completely gone. With their soaking blankets pulled around them, they looked like a flock of miserable rice birds in a rain storm. The barrack room was evacuated at once and the men were quickly supplied with dry clothes, blankets, and hot tea. Much else was going on at the time so a Chinese Inspector, Mr Lam, obtained the facts.

All of the constables had climbed into their bunks and had fallen fast asleep. At about half-past three they were awakened by a particularly powerful gust of wind, followed by the noise of the roof parting company with the rest of the barrack hut and the rain pouring in. Because they had been ordered to go to the barrack hut and turn in, it logically followed that to leave the barrack hut was disobedience of orders, and they all knew how hot I was on people disobeying orders. There then followed a bizarre Chinese game, similar to a game played by children in Scotland years ago, 'stone, scissors, paper', scissors cut paper, stone breaks scissors, paper wraps around stone. The object of this exercise however was to select a messenger to report to the SDI that the barrack room roof had gone, and take any consequences! The poor fellow who had dripped water all over my office floor had been the unfortunate loser. Inspector Lam reported all this to me giving me much to think about.

The typhoon eventually moved into Kwangdung Province and blew itself out. We were then frantically busy dealing with the aftermath in Mongkok including criminals who thought it was an opportune time to indulge in some looting, getting Nathan Road cleared for traffic, guarding damaged buildings and homes until the owners were able to get themselves organised, and the sad task of gathering up bodies for examination and identification.

It was late on the evening of the second day before we could return to normal duty routines and the off duty men could go home to see that their own families were all right. Inspector Lam and I had a quiet drink and relaxed a bit. We discussed the events of the preceding thirty-six hours and agreed that the men had done their duty well, a fact that had been recognised by the District Commander with a well earned 'Well done' message. I told Mr Lam that I felt we had managed to get the discipline message over to everyone and, without becoming slack, we could ease up a bit. As I was saying this the memory of the poor constables sitting miserably in the rain made my face feel warm with guilt, discipline is essential in any force but taking it to that extent was stupid and excessive and the stupidity was mine!

The Mongkok public recognised the excellent work that had been done by the men during the typhoon. Saving lives at risk of their own, investigating every report of missing people even malicious false reports, evacuating people in danger without fuss or waste of time, protecting property, and just generally being good coppers. Our men had regained their 'face', morale soared, and a sensible level of discipline was all that was required.

It is difficult for people who live in countries outside Asia to appreciate the true meaning of the huge population figures they may hear or read about. Even the actuality of the crowds they may glimpse in a short film clip on their television news programmes, is not quite 'real' as they are merely figures on film. The reality of the crowds of human beings thronging every space in Hong Kong can only be likened to the reality elsewhere of intense fog, or heavily falling snow. An American friend once commented that while she admired our Chinese policemen for their smartness, courtesy, and good English, she had never known policemen anywhere else in the world who were so 'damned keen on keeping you moving along'. The reason for this is simple, a group of people in Hong Kong looking at anything, or nothing, can almost certainly be the nucleus of a crowd that may take hours to disperse.

There used to be a pillar box for letter collection on the pavement outside Kowloon Police Headquarters, at the junction of Prince Edward Road and Nathan Road, one of the most critical road junctions in Hong Kong. Anything other than briefest obstruction here could create a 'gridlock' that could tie up the whole of Kowloon's traffic for hours. Kowloon is a peninsula and Nathan Road is its transport spine, anything that affects the spine paralyses the whole peninsula.

One fine breezy day, just before noon, a postman opened the pillar box to collect the letters from inside. He had the bottom of his mailbag resting on the pavement and was putting the letters into its open end inside the pillar box. One or two letters slipped out on to the pavement and were played with by the breeze, fluttering along the ground for a yard or two. The postman tried to catch them and dropped a few more letters in his haste. They, in turn, blew along the pavement, and the poor man, by now flustered, tried even more desperately to catch them all. Passers by tried to help him, but one of them accidentally stepped on the end of the mailbag pulling it out of the postman's hand and tipping more letters on the ground. More people became involved, most of them laughing good humouredly and joking with the, by now, almost demented postman who could see his job disappearing with the letters. Hong Kong Chinese people usually like to have their lunch at midday so the ranks of the letter hunters were quickly swelled by numerous people on their way to lunch. The crowd was further reinforced by curious passers-by, anxious to see what was going on. Within minutes the road junction was totally blocked and lunch-hour traffic had come to a complete halt throughout Kowloon. With the tail back of traffic to the vehicle ferry piers, it became difficult for cars and trucks from Hong Kong Island to disembark from the ferries. This caused hold ups at the piers in Hong Kong Island and traffic jams began to develop there.

All of the Mongkok men, Traffic Branch Kowloon, spare men from Emergency Unit Kowloon, even Headquarters' staff blinking in the unaccustomed sunlight, and every other policeman available, worked and sweated, cursed and swore, for more than two hours to get the traffic untangled before they got things moving again. No one will ever know how much that gridlock cost before it was cleared. We do know that the postman doggedly picked up all of the dropped letters, looked surprised at the massed ranks of people and traffic resulting from his butter-fingered handling of the Royal Mail, and slipped quietly off to the main post office for a hard earned cup of tea. The pillar box was moved later and re-sited in a less critical location!

This proved good training for the Mongkok personnel as we had a similar performance just two junctions down Nathan Road, at Argyle Street, a few days after the letter incident. Argyle Street leads down to a busy ferry terminal in Tai Kok Tsui and is an excellent site for banks. There were three banks right by the junction with Nathan road and four of five more nearby. Again it all started at lunch-time, the busiest time of the day. Two Communist banks in Sham Shui Po, to the north of Mongkok, went bust during the morning's trading. The news spread like wildfire through the Chinese population who are always, understandably, alert for bank collapses. It was unfortunate that the identities of the failed banks were not also spread as, being unnamed, everyone assumed it was their bank.

A rush began on the Chinese banks in Mongkok, especially those at the Argyle Street junction. We were at the scene very quickly and a pattern quickly became apparent. People went into the Chinese banks and drew out all their money, or as much as they could get. They then ran across the main road ignoring the traffic and instantly deposited it the Hong Kong and Shanghai Bank because everybody knew it was so big and efficient it could never go bust.

One of the banks that was being drained of cash, was a first class, non-Communist Chinese bank, that was in no danger of collapsing, in fact it was one of the best managed banks anywhere in the Far East but it was being tarred with the same brush as the banks in Sham Shui Po. The bank was rapidly running out of cash, as any bank would in such circumstances, and the owners appealed to the Hong Kong and Shanghai Bank Chairman at once for a temporary supply of cash, with repayment guaranteed by their very sound investments. This was agreed instantly.

We assisted them physically, by controlling the anxious crowds withdrawing their money from one lot of banks, and seeing them safely over the main road to the other bank, where they deposited it. At the same time, vehicles from Mongkok were being loaded in the basement of the Hong Kong and Shanghai Bank with the money just deposited, which they then took across the road to the Chinese bank where it was unloaded and paid out again to people who then took it back across the road . . . and so it went on all day. By the time the panic cooled down in the evening we calculated that the same money must have been paid out, paid in, taken for a short drive, then paid out, and in again, at least twenty times. It was an interesting lesson in economics, there was no more actual cash in the banks at the end of the day than at the beginning, but everyone was content and the bank rush was over!

The rest of my time in Mongkok was just ordinary police work, Hong Kong style. The occasional Triad fight over drugs or prostitution; ordinary robberies and assaults; drugs, gambling, prostitution. Regular arguments with some senior officers, so divorced from operational police work that they thought it sinister that a gambling school, or discreet brothel, could go undetected on the eighteenth floor of an apartment block.

On one occasion being quite properly scolded by my very decent District Commander for losing my temper with a Very Senior Officer, who was grumbling about undetected gambling schools, for suggesting to him that we should only recruit bloody supermen with x-ray eyes able to see through high rise blocks of apartments. As with many other SDIs in rapidly developing high-rise areas, I became fed up to the back teeth with pen-pushing policemen in air-conditioned offices complaining about events occurring twenty floors above the heads of the men on the beat without their knowledge and, by implication, without the knowledge of the SDI.

One day, in a fit of irritation, I submitted a plausible paper, full of statistics, for a system of 'vertical policing' in high rise building complexes, which was promptly rejected. It was not surprising, we would have needed at least 400 men in Mongkok alone just to provide 60 per cent coverage, but it made the point and we noticed a reduction in the level of criticism about high rise vice offences. At a convention I attended later, American police officers told me they would never have tolerated such criticisms, as high rises are almost impossible to cover without a legion of informers.

My relief took over four weeks before I was due to board the P & O Line ship the *Oronsay* for the trip home on leave. I was able to hand over a reasonably efficient police station, old, noisy, and cramped as it was, and some of the best and hardest working men in the Police Force. On one front I had failed completely. Our Force Headquarters' bureaucrats still reckoned that ninety men and women police officers were quite sufficient to provide all the necessary police services needed by some 500 000 citizens. It was, in a sorry sort of way, quite a backhanded compliment that somewhere in our labyrinthian hierarchy it was seriously thought that one lone Hong Kong Chinese Police Constable, quietly pounding his beat in Mongkok, was enough to protect the lives and property of an average of 125 000 people, living like human battery hens stacked twenty and more storeys high in their expensive roosts!

Twelve

MONEY, MONEY . . . MONEY!

Events in Hong Kong are constantly monitored very closely by economists and financial experts all over the world. The brief collapse of the Colony as an entrepôt, at the time of the Korean War, and the American inspired embargo of trade with China, was rapidly followed by a recovery of a new style Hong Kong buzzing with activity as a manufacturing and financial centre. The Stock Exchange, Banking and Financial Services, handled with keen entrepreneurial flair by the Hong Kong Chinese and their European colleagues, brought millions into the colony in invisible earnings, and was a force to be reckoned with in the international money markets. Even during the time of the cultural revolution and the excesses of the Communists, ordinary people retained confidence in the Treasury and in the Hong Kong Banks.

Hong Kong has generally been very fortunate in its succession of Financial Secretaries never more so than during the troubles of the 1960s. The Financial Secretary foresaw an attempt to start a run on the banks, as part of a Communist plan to disrupt financial stability and confidence in the Colony as a trustworthy business centre. Any sensible Chinese knows from China's past history that the collapse of banking institutions always hurts the small depositors more than the big shots who always get forewarning. Historically, the rich in China invariably switched their money elsewhere, 'purely by coincidence', before a bank went broke and the small people were always the ones who were wiped out financially! Consequently, even a rumour that a Bank was in trouble was enough to start panic withdrawals of funds from that bank guaranteeing that the prophecy was fulfilled. No bank can keep more than a fraction of its deposits in ready cash, if it did it would not be able to make the profits necessary to pay interest to depositors or earnings to shareholders.

The local Communists were not doing very well with their terrorism so they decided to trigger a run on the banks by broadcasting rumours of impending bank collapses. Their campaign began quite well for them, with swarms of fearful depositors besieging the banks and withdrawing their funds in cash but it fizzled out in a matter of days leaving the leftists once more with egg on their faces. They were defeated by the Financial Secretary's foresight and forward planning. They had also provided the Emergency Unit with the opportunity to protect three of the world's biggest movements of gold and money since the Second World War!

Arrangements had been made secretly with the British government to hold £50 million in cash on immediate call for shipment to Hong Kong via Britain's major airline BOAC, now British Airways.

Other secret arrangements had been made with the Treasury's printers in UK to do a print run of Hong Kong currency to the amount of HK$4000 million, this money to be shipped in total secrecy aboard one of the P & O lines very fast, high security, cargo ships. Coincidentally with these preparations there happened to be a gold shipment valued at £45 million due for Macao via Hong Kong.

EUHKI were to be responsible for the £50 million, only after it arrived in the Island en route to the vaults in the Hong Kong and Shanghai Banking Corporation, the Government's official bankers. Our EU trucks with our drivers and guards were not to be our responsibility while they were at Kai Tak Airport being loaded with cases of money, nor were they under our control until after they had crossed the harbour by ferry and landed in the Island.

However, in respect of the $4 billion, in Hong Kong currency, we were to be responsible for it from the time the P & O ship arrived at the pier in Kowloon, to the time it arrived in the bank vaults. Our responsibility for the Macao gold was limited solely, to its arrival and movements in the island.

A few days previously, almost at the end of an ordinary, and boring, session of the Legislative and Executive Council, a minor administrative amendment had been made to the Finance Act that had the effect of making British Pounds Sterling legal tender in Hong Kong. The BOAC cargo meant that even if every bank depositor in Hong Kong asked simultaneously for their deposits in cash, the Treasury, and through them the banks, could pay out in legal tender! It was brilliantly done.

Within an hour of the first bank rumours being started by the Communists, a call was made to London and the £50 million, equal to approximately HK$800 million, was immediately loaded into the BOAC aeroplane and on its way to Hong Kong. Knowledge of this was strictly restricted on a 'need to know' basis. In the island it was limited to the District Commander Mr Clough, his Deputy

Peter Moore, Superintendent Rik Darkin, myself, and the justifiably trusted Corporal Charles NG, and the Emergency Unit's part in the operation was planned carefully and in detail. There was every need for strict secrecy as the British currency was exchangeable anywhere in the world without question. If either crooks or Communists heard about it they would move heaven and earth to steal it regardless of loss of life.

We received the code word informing us that the aeroplane had landed and immediately put our plans into operation. Our officers and men were quickly briefed and took up their positions near the ferry landing, to escort the trucks as soon as they left the ferry ramps and their Kowloon escorts. There had been only one small last minute addition made by me to the original plan. I utilised some old friendships made with the ferry people when I had been in Marine Police and they allowed some of my men to travel in plain clothes in the wheelhouses of the ferries 'operationally testing some portable radios recently supplied for police use'!

Frankly, I hate lethal surprises and I wanted to be certain that nothing happened in the ferries between the Jordan Road pier in Kowloon and the Connaught Road pier in the Island. My 'testers' kept us well informed, in code, that all was well as the ten trucks, some from my unit, some from Kowloon, began making their way across the harbour, each carrying some £5 million equal to HK$80 million.

The Hong Kong Island truck crews had just been ordered to go to Kai Tak and report in to the Airport Police, they were not told why, just that further instructions would be given to them there. According to the overall plan, the money would be checked into the trucks directly from the aircraft in sealed wooden cases, under the supervision of senior representatives of the various authorities involved. The truck crews would not be told what they were carrying but they would be instructed to proceed to the Hong Kong and Shanghai Bank Headquarters, Main Branch, where they would receive further orders. All simple and straightforward.

There is no direct Chinese equivalent for 'Murphy's Law' but there should be, because it was fully operational at Kai Tak Airport that particular day! What the experts had overlooked was the fact that the trucks could not all assemble at the security unloading bay simultaneously, there was not enough space. So the trucks waited in a reserve area and were directed out to the aircraft, individually, as a loaded truck drove off.

This was a very time consuming process and the hours began to extend far beyond the original estimates. By the time Corporal Lee, the NCO in charge of one of our trucks, was called forward for loading it was already early evening, and the officials in charge of the operation were obviously much harassed. Lee was told peremptorily to go to the Hong Kong and Shanghai Bank Main Office. He asked for the instruction to be repeated and was told to get a bloody move on and go to the Hong Kong and Shanghai Bank Main Office where he would be given further instructions. He did as he was told. He went to the Hong Kong and Shanghai Bank Main Office near the Peninsula Hotel in Tsim Sha Tsui in Kowloon! He had not been told to go to the Bank Headquarters Main Office in Hong Kong.

When the truck arrived at the bank it had been closed for over an hour but, as he had been told he would receive further orders there, he waited, and waited, and waited. No one came and he and his crew were hungry as they had not eaten for over six hours.

The bank was only 100 yards from the back gate of Tsim Sha Tsui police station so, leaving one of the men behind in case a messenger arrived in their absence the corporal and the remaining men went up into the police station and, parking the truck in the compound, they all enjoyed a good meal in the canteen, then relieved the look-out at the bank so he could eat too. During this meal break, to which they were entitled, the truck with its £5 million, HK$80 million, cargo sat in the compound unguarded!

The corporal eventually telephoned us to ask what he was supposed to be doing and to double check that where he was, was where he was supposed to be! I was pleased to hear from him as we had noticed that he and his £5 million were at least absent, if not completely missing, and we were not sure if he had been hijacked or tempted to emigrate on voluntary retirement! He was directed to go immediately to the Jordan Road Ferry, cross over to Connaught Road and go to the Hong Kong and Shanghai Bank Headquarters Main Office where he would meet Inspector Wong. This he did and after his cargo was unloaded he reported to me with his crew.

When I told him that he had been guarding a load of HK$80 million, in Sterling, he went an interesting shade of pale green; and the driver nearly had a fit trying to remember if he had taken the ignition key with him when he went to the canteen. Secrecy is all very well and much needed at times but it is bloody stupid to be so secret that the chaps who are doing a secret job know so little about what they are doing for security reasons they could inadvertently cock the whole thing up.

147

Every man was given special training for our next cash escort and fully briefed just before departure. After briefing no man was allowed to leave his platoon for any reason until we were deployed in position and in action. It was a beautifully timed delivery of HK$4000 million aboard a P & O ship. Timed to arrive before the Communists could launch any campaign designed to create mistrust in the Pound Sterling previously delivered.

The ship was one of P & O's superb modern cargo ships constructed with special high value security holds. These so-called 'holds' were in fact huge armoured vaults, built like the security vaults in Fort Knox. They normally contained high value goods such as expensive watches and clocks, furs, jewellery, alcohol such as whisky or cognac, anything easily disposed of for cash through the criminal black market. In the ship we were to board, only the Captain and Chief Officer knew that the cases in their main vault marked 'Glenlivet of Glenlivet', 'Linkwood', and 'Glenmorangie' did not contain priceless specimens of Scotland's gift to human society, beautiful malt whisky, only hundreds of millions of Hong Kong Dollars! No one on board even suspected that they were carrying the equivalent of £250 million in cash! The beauty of the plan was that everybody and his dog knows that the value of Scotch malt whisky per drop of liquid ecstasy is the highest 'value added' of any drink produced anywhere, so no one raised an eyebrow at the security imposed when the cargo was loaded in London. It was nicely done. We were waiting with one platoon with curious Customs and Excise men in their launch when the 'Pando' sailed into the Immigration anchorage near Kai Tak runway. The Customs men were equally curious at the presence of one of their most senior officers but nobody asked any questions.

We remained out of sight until the Pando had dropped anchor and then swarmed quickly up her gangway. All of my EU men were wearing gym shoes in place of their usual boots, and quickly went to their positions which they knew from their rigorous and, to them, puzzling special training. My entry to the bridge to meet the Captain caused quite a stir as I was accompanied by my best squad who were armed with sub-machine-guns and M1 carbines, and my radio operator with a portable radio netted in to the EU radio network. They quickly took up their pre-rehearsed positions around the bridge and wireless office. We also met up with some of my men who had boarded the ship in plain clothes with the pilot. As arranged with Immigration the Captain immediately hoisted anchor and headed in for the pier the ship had been allocated at Tsim Sha Tsui. The

Customs men discovered why their senior officer was aboard when they invited the Chief Officer to open the security vault, they were told to their amazement, to leave it alone.

As we moved down the harbour two sea-going seventy footer Marine Police launches took up station to either side of us with their gun crews at action stations and harbour launches fell in ahead and behind. Flying over the harbour in long sweeps was a helicopter from the Royal Hong Kong Auxiliary Air Force with one of my Inspectors aboard as observer. The Captain took the Pando alongside with the easy skill expected of P & O. There was a difference between this berthing and those usually seen, as the pier was completely secured by my white helmeted, heavily armed, men. Two huge cargo junks came alongside, with my men on board in ready prepared gun positions. The junks were owned by a well trusted member of Hong Kong's harbour junk community. As we went alongside I went down to the vault to see it opened. More of my men had, by now, come aboard and taken up positions between the vault, and the hatch, which had been quickly opened, and on board the junks alongside.

Orders had been given by the Captain that no one, except the Chief Officer, was to enter the vault area until further notice. One of the engineer officers, either, had not been told, or like all sea-going engineers, decided that engineering tasks came first. Whatever the reason, a bulkhead door suddenly swung open and a man in overalls with his face covered in black streaks like commando camouflage was seen stepping over the watertight sill. He only got one foot on the deck and froze in sheer terror looking straight into the muzzles of two Sterling sub-machine-guns. All he could see, he told me afterwards, were the muzzles, the eyes of my men glaring down the sights, and their fingers on the triggers, he was sure he was a dead man.

It was quickly established who he was and he was sharply told to go. He was so shaken by what had happened he could not even explain to his curious shipmates what was going on, all he could tell them was to keep out of the way of the swarm of homicidal maniacs wearing white helmets if they valued their lives. They did!

The puzzled looking First Officer spoke to me as I stood by a Treasury officer who was checking the cases being unloaded into the junks. He could tell by my speech that I was a Scot, and he said that he knew the Scots could be cranky about their favourite liquor but that he had never seen such security over the stuff in all his time at sea, 'What the hell is going on?' he asked. Before I could say anything the Treasury man, also a Scot, answered him in a broad

Scots accent and advised him not to ask 'It's better ye dinnie ken laddie!' As he walked away we could hear him muttering something about bloody Scotsmen taking over the world and too much haggis eating affecting the brain! He was really miffed.

The Pando men did a superb job and the cases were unloaded in no time. It seemed that the whole crew from the Captain down were watching as we set off across the harbour escorted by marine police launches and the helicopter, to unload near police headquarters. Our arrival caused quite a stir and we could see faces at all the windows in HQ. Police bureaucracy came to a standstill for at least two hours, no doubt to the benefit of Hong Kong as a whole and the police force in particular.

The unloading zone was the helicopter landing pad, usually just a large empty area of concrete stretching back from the sea wall. As planned, a code word over the radio had sent a convoy off from EU comprising two armoured cars, trucks and jeeps loaded with over a hundred EU men in battle gear. They arrived at the pad and took up positions as we were a hundred yards from the sea wall.As we tied up alongside a convoy of civilian lorries arrived each guarded by armed policemen and escorted by police Land Rovers.

The unloading was completed in record time and truck after truck sped off to the Hong Kong and Shanghai Bank, some two miles away, escorted by an EU vehicle. All side roads were sealed off by traffic police, all buildings on the route had policemen checking and watching them, the whole area was swarming with CID men, the helicopter came and went above the operation at low altitude. It caused quite a stir! The operation went off without a hitch, and the happy bankers and Treasury people unbent enough to suggest that it was 'Quite well done . . . quite.' We wrapped things up, Traffic got all the traffic going, and we all went back to the Unit happy that all had gone off without any disasters.

Then the complaints rolled in. Too much noise (the helicopter); a waste of manpower (the police); unnecessary disruption of traffic without warning (we should have told every crook in Hong Kong why?); too many guns on display (EU should have been armed with Ken Dodd tickling sticks?); unnecessary display of force (from an arrogant Britisher who, despite warning, tried to barge his way past an EU man at the helicopter pad to see what was going on and got an M1 carbine muzzle stuck enthusiastically up his nose!): a waste of taxpayers money (taxpayers? money? in Hong Kong?).

We had moved one of the world's biggest ever shipments of money without a hitch from a ship, across one of the world's busiest harbours to a bank and finished the job in three hours. The Financial Secretary's plan had worked and his foresight was justified. When the news 'leaked' out, the Communist-inspired run on the banks was stopped dead and confidence in Hong Kong was reinforced in the colony and abroad. My EU men had done their usual good job. Neat but not gaudy!

The escort of the £45 million of gold for Macao was an anti climax. It arrived in secret. We escorted it, in secret. It was loaded in the ferry, in secret. It was secretly guarded, by Hong Kong and Macao policemen in plain clothes, across the Pearl River Estuary to the Portuguese Colony and safely delivered to its destination.

Thirteen

SHIP TO SHORE

It is typical in police work, that there is a counterpoint to all events. There was a bar in Lockhart Road, in Wanchai, owned by a Ghanaian, which was very popular with the sailors from the US Seventh Fleet, especially black sailors.

Shortly after midnight one night, a call came from radio control reporting a riot in the bar and asking for EU to go to the scene. My car was not far away and we arrived first. Lockhart Road is always ablaze with neon signs, and full of people enjoying themselves. This night was not noticeably different, except outside the Ghana bar. Some of the bar's huge decorated windows had been smashed, a chair or two lay on the pavement, together with some San Miguel beer bottles, the bar girls were clustered round the bar front chattering like excited magpies and pretending to be scared, there were a number of well-lumped American sailors being helped away by their friends, presumably for first aid treatment as they were all displaying the stigmata of a first division, super league, Wanchai bar brawl; bleeding noses, puffy lips, recently created gaps in their teeth, rapidly swelling half-closed eyes, muted groans, painfully muttered promises of unlikely revenge, and the occasional plaintive 'but I didn't do nothing'.

We entered the bar ready for the Third World War, or at least to do combat with a platoon of paratroops. The interior looked as the interiors of bars look in cowboy movies after the good guys and the bad guys have redecorated it by fighting – it was a shambles! Broken mirrors, broken glass, broken bottles, broken tables, broken seats, in fact there did not seem to be anything left to break. The bar had been famous for its boast that it could serve any of the world's alcoholic drinks on request and had displayed scores of varicoloured bottles on the bar shelves to prove it. The shelves were gone, and lying unconscious on the floor in a jumble of shelf debris and bottles was an American sailor, his basically white uniform turned technicolour by the spilled contents of the bottles. He was the only American we saw that night who had a smile on his face!

Walking across the deep carpet was quite an experience because it crunched under foot! In this landscape of utter desolation stood two completely still and silent figures. One was the tallest, broadest, strongest, most muscular looking man any of us had ever seen, a black American sailor standing with his hands clasped on the top of his head. The other was one of our men, the shortest, thinnest, tiniest corporal in the Hong Police, a good policeman and an immensely intelligent, precise, studious, Stage 8 English speaker. We looked at the corporal then at the huge sailor and then back at the corporal, we were *very* impressed. I would not have tackled him on my own for a King's ransom! The sailor smiled and asked for permission to lower his hands promising no further trouble, permission was granted, gravely, by the corporal. The events of the 'Battle of the Ghana Bar', as finally reconstructed, were interesting. Earlier in the evening the American, 'Smith', had gone to the bar for a drink. He liked the place and had stayed on for the remainder of the evening quietly enjoying himself, chatting and flirting with the girls, and drinking rather more than he was accustomed to as he was very keen on physical fitness .

The bar gradually filled up with more sailors as the evening progressed and the noise level increased. A group of very noisy sailors from the same ship as Smith came into the bar including, unfortunately, a few who had an undisclosed grudge against him. They saw him and, made brave with booze, they unwisely began to abuse and insult him. His quiet dignity and lack of reaction to their provocation annoyed the loud mouthed drunks who redoubled their efforts, to such foul-mouthed effect that the bar keeper suggested they take their business elsewhere, as he did so Smith's girl companion arrived at the bar to get a drink, just in time to be involved in a scuffle accompanied by the sound of breaking glass. Smith went to her assistance and all hell broke loose with everybody seeming to take punches at everybody else, and a classic general punch up ensued. The bar girls had taken to the street in a well practised retreat yelling for the police, just as the redoubtable corporal was passing by. What happened next is best recorded as reported by witnesses.

Smith had disposed of all those foolish enough to attack him by means of ordinary boxing and simple scrapping tactics. He stood alone in the middle of the dance floor surrounded by recumbent sailors nursing their lumps, drawn up to his full impressive height an imposing sight bristling with rage and indignation, his fists up, bellowing 'Come on you goddamn sons of bitches! Who's next?!'

In came the corporal who barely came up to Smith's chest and,

153

before the awed gaze of onlookers peering through the shattered windows, he introduced himself to the furious sailor. 'I am a corporal in the Hong Kong Police and I have been informed that you are responsible for the damage here and for various assaults' before he could say anything else Smith growled 'You bet your sweet ass boy!' Reportedly the corporal's mouth was seen to tighten in disapproval and he again addressed Smith 'In that case I am now placing you under arrest and I caution you that anything you say will be taken down and may be given in evidence . . .' Smith, still in a rage, interrupted him shouting 'See here boy, I'm the Karate Champion of the Seventh Fleet and I can cut you in half with my bare hand.'

Observers swore that they did not see the corporal move but suddenly they noticed that he was standing grim-faced in the 'ready to fire' position with his pistol trained on Smith.

'Sailor,' he said, 'this is a Colt Police revolver containing six rounds of .38 police positive service ammunition. I am an expert pistol shot, as I am sure you are an expert in Karate. Please tell me, can you cut a moving bullet in half with your bare hand?'

Smith looked at him closely in some surprise and said 'Holy shit you really mean it don't you boy, you will shoot me' and slowly raised his hands on to his head.

'Second,' said the corporal firmly 'I am not a boy, I am a mature man with a family. I understand that your people in the southern part of America are offended by being addressed insultingly as 'boy', why then should you so address me? You may call me corporal, copper, whatever you like within reason, but not, please, boy'! Then, we arrived!

We took him to the US Navy Shore Patrol Office at the Fenwick Street pier. Under the Visiting Forces Acts which apply to all armed forces visiting foreign countries, it is almost impossible to bring servicemen to trial in civil courts save in the most extraordinary and serious cases. They are usually dealt with by their own service tribunals, and in case anyone thinks this is a soft option it should be pointed out that it is truly easier for a camel to pass through the eye of a needle than for a visiting serviceman to get away with disgracing his service and his country in a foreign land! This is certainly so in the case of the American armed forces where the Tribunal Boards contain lower rankers as well as officers, with a senior officer as President of the Board. The sentences passed by a service tribunal are invariably far tougher than any that would be imposed by civil court, and sentences are very likely as the whole tribunal is comprised of long service men who already know all the excuses, ploys, half-truths, and downright damn lies that any optimistic accused person can put to them. They had probably tried them out themselves twenty years before with an equal lack of success! A great advantage of the administration of the Act is that matters are dealt with immediately, without the delays inherent in civil trials, so claims for compensation are settled at once.

Smith had promised to behave himself but still seemed surprised that we did not handcuff him as was apparently customary in the USA. Our explanation that (a) he seemed an honest chap and had given his word not to escape, (b) the British are not too keen on handcuffing people unless absolutely necessary and (c) that we didn't think our Hong Kong handcuffs would fit him, brought a smile from him, and a nod of his head at the corporal with the comment 'and (d) he'd probably drop me before I got ten yards anyway Huh?' The corporal had undoubtedly made quite an impression on Seaman Smith but none of us, including the corporal, could work out how?

The Shore Patrol office was full of burly American patrolmen equipped with stout truncheons who all obviously recognised our prisoner as we escorted him in and regarded him with cautious respect. The harassed Shore Patrol Officer bemusedly wondered that, as they were busy giving First Aid to half of the Fleet, and as most of the injured seemed to have run afoul of Smith, and as some of them were at least as big as Smith, he was dammed if he could understand – with an apologetic look at the corporal – how in the F..k a half-pint size oriental could have F...ingwell arrested him single F...ing handed!

The big sailor explained 'Those assholes were full of booze and bull. This guy,' pointing at the corporal 'was full of guts and was going to arrest me no matter what. I could see it in his eyes, I could see it in the set of his body . . . hell man I could smell it oozing out of him. He'd have shot me dead!' Everyone regarded the corporal with awed respect, no doubt a good yarn was born that night to circulate through the Navy for years to come, the tale of the tiny, Chinese, Hong Kong Police David and the giant American Navy Goliath.

In the car back to Emergency Unit, the corporal was asked if he would have fired his pistol if Smith had attacked him. He replied instantly that he would, as he truly believed the American had the capability to kill him, and other people, with his bare hands and that would have put his use of the pistol into the 'permitted' category as laid down in the police force *Guide to the Use of Firearms* but, he added, he would have shot him in the knees as he felt that Smith had been more sinned against than sinning, and he sat back in his seat, small, quiet, fair-minded, determined, courageous, a damn good policeman and a credit to his Force.

We heard later through the Shore Patrol that at Smith's court martial in the Philippines the corporal's very fair statement, including a detailed report obtained from the bar keeper and bar girls of much of the vile abuse directed at him, had saved the sailor from any serious penalty as the Court judged that although he had been severely provoked he had responded primarily in self-defence! The sailors responsible for starting the punch up were each made to pay a proportional share of the compensation given to the bar owner.

Weeks after the event, the corporal came into the EU main office and showed me a big post card, of pictures of Hawaii. It was addressed to 'The Tough Little Cop from the Ghana Bar' c/o US Shore Patrol, Hong Kong, and was from Smith, it bore the simple message 'Thanks. Wish you were here.' He was a stolid and very serious man, the corporal, and that was the only time I ever saw him smile . . . briefly!

Immediately after dawn one morning a very smart, new, Danish ship sailed proudly into Hong Kong harbour on her maiden voyage, via the western approaches rather than the more commonly used Lei U Mun Pass entrance. The Captain had quite sensibly come that way as, in addition to the general cargo he had stowed in his holds for consignees in the Colony, he was also carrying a huge drum of heavy duty BICC electric cable, secured on a massive spindle on his after deck. This was for the Hong Kong Electric Company and was to be unloaded by a floating, heavy-lift crane on to a barge, for towing to the site of the new power station under construction in Aberdeen. Securing to a buoy in the western end of the harbour near Belcher Bay would help to reduce the distance for the final tow to about six miles, and would reduce the chances of causing any obstruction in the main harbour. The crew had begun the preparations for unloading on her long approach up the West Lamma Channel and as she approached the harbour limits they had finished the very noisy task of opening up the newly designed steel hatch covers and were able to look about them as the marvellous view of Hong Kong was revealed before them. The ship was secured to her buoy, the cargo lighters clustered around her up forward, and the barge for the drum of cable went to secure aft to receive it. The drum was there but the cable was gone!

Every harbour has its harbour thieves, and very skilled thieves they usually are, but no one had ever heard of hundreds of feet

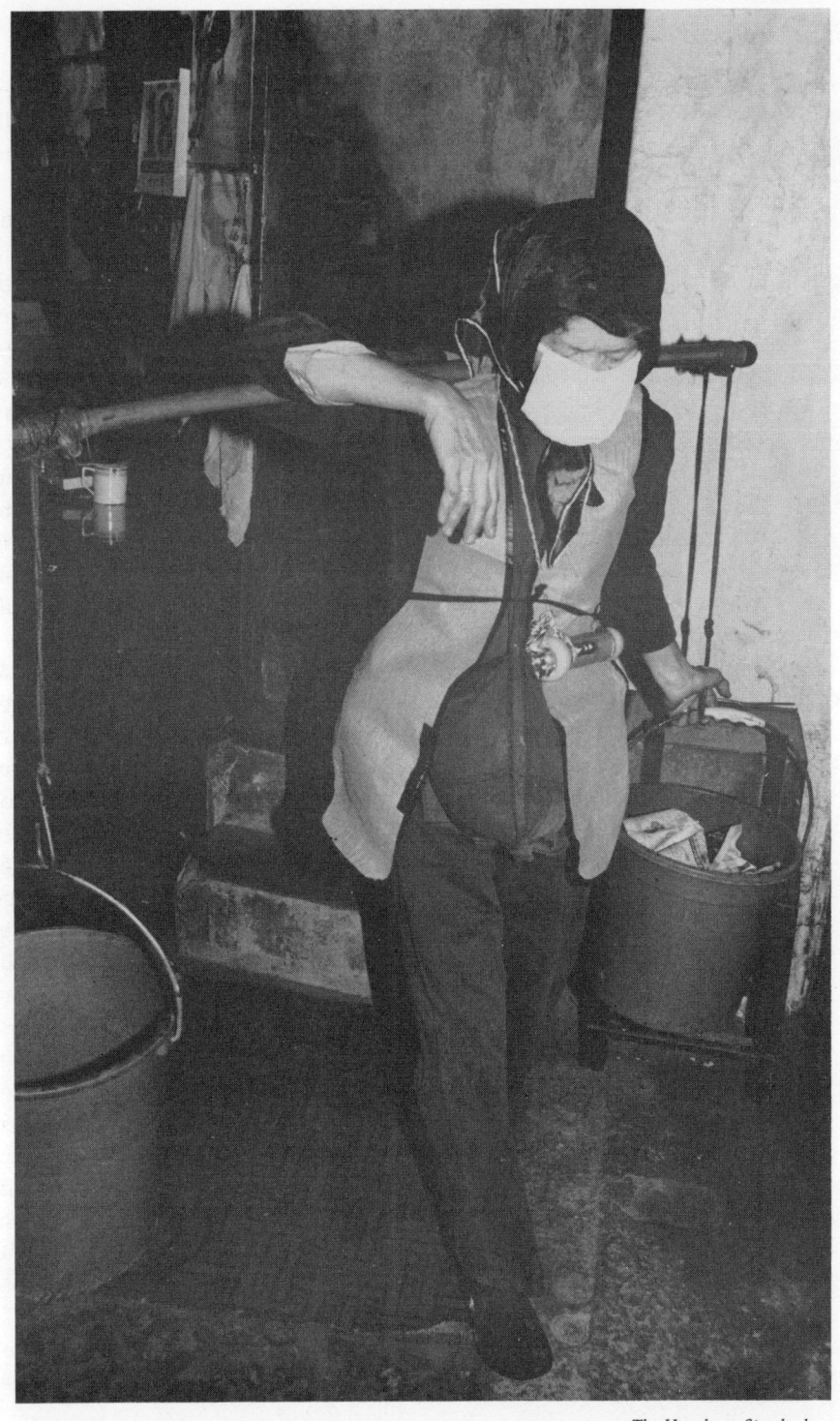

The Hongkong Standard

A "night-soil" woman – a formidable ally.

The Hongkong Standard

Top. Police Ballistics Officer, Norman Hill (right) and Vic Moss working to defuse a home-made bomb. Bottom. When things go wrong . . . Hill is led away in agony having had his right hand blown off in an explosion.

of thick cable being stolen without anybody noticing. After all, it was not the kind of loot that could be tucked in a sack or a bag, or wound round the waist under a coat. The Divisional Detective Inspector of the Marine Division, himself, had difficulty in believing the first report, checking his calendar to ensure that the date was not April Fool's Day. Even the patrol launch Commanders queried the message, relayed to all police vessels to be on the look out for a thief escaping with hundreds of feet of electric cable!

The investigation revealed that during the voyage a cover had been secured around the drum to protect the cable from the weather. This cover had been securely lashed with ropes threaded through eyelets, as laces are secured through lace holes in a shoe, and the drum had then been turned until the lashings were facing downwards, to prevent rain or spray from getting in. The lashings were undone and the cover removed on the final approach to Hong Kong.

It was first, somewhat wildly, theorised that the cable might somehow have broken loose in bad weather, worked its way out through the lashings and gone overboard without being noticed. That was loudly and profanely denied by the crewmen who had removed the cover the previous night, who pointed out that even in the dark, working under deck lights, they would have noticed something was amiss if a flaming great cable they had carted all the way from Britain had somehow gone adrift!

Eventually, through questioning the crew, it was established that the ship had slowed down between the Communist island of Ling Ting and the beginning of the West Lamma Channel in order to enter harbour at the previously arranged time. If the cable had been stolen, that appeared to have been the only opportunity the thieves had for carrying out the theft, but how on earth had it been done, and why steal a cable that could not be sold on the open market?

The DDI was certain that there was a more simple explanation, and he proved himself right. He made a visit to Macao some time later, accompanied by detectives. The Macao Police have always had a close relationship with their colleagues in Hong Kong.

The story was quite a simple one. A Kwangdung Province boat, licensed to fish in Hong Kong waters, had been getting ready to shoot its nets to the south of the West Lamma Channel. They had seen the Danish ship slow almost to a halt and went over to her to see what was going on. The crew were all busy working on deck, all of them seemingly up for'rd making a tremendous din . Two of the fishermen swarmed aboard, up the unattended boarding ladder which was hanging over the side for the Pilot, and they looked about for anything worth stealing.

Their attention was drawn to the drum, nearly fifteen feet high, and they could see that the cable had copper in the core. They pulled out the end of the cable, released the braking blocks on the drum, and payed out the cable through the stern hawse pipe to the fishing boat waiting below. They then slid down the cable to the boat and secured its end to a line from the boats stern. They then sailed off to Macao towing the cable, hanging down in the sea, behind them. With the amount of noise on deck nobody on board the ship heard the drum turning, and because everyone was working up forward, no one saw the cable going.

They arrived in Macao the following night and anchored close to the shore. Once they had found their customer they stayed on the foreshore with the cable stretched out under the sea, pulling it ashore a bit at a time, cutting it in two-foot lengths and delivering them to the buyer, who weighed them and paid on delivery of each load.

When they were sent to Stanley prison for their crime they were grinning, the cells were warm, dry, and comfortable, the prison uniforms were better than their commune issue Mao suits, the food was good, they had hot showers, the work was easy, and the guards were OK. Even prison beat the hell out of fishing for a living!

Just over a month later the Divisional Detective Inspector nearly threw a fit. Somebody had stolen the underwater telegraph cable between Hong Kong and the Philippines, or at least a mile-long chunk of it. He only recovered his composure when it was discovered that the cable had been cut outside Colony waters, and he could properly say 'M'Gwaan ngoh Seegon' , 'None of my business.'

One night there was a serious incident in the Jardine's Bazaar area of Wanchai which resulted in a fire, death, and injuries to a number of people. At first it was not certain whether it was the work of Communists or Triads but there had been reports of suspicious-looking people leaving the scene as police sirens were heard approaching. Emergency Unit were not directly involved in the case which was being handled by CID but they asked us to carry out a sweep through the myriad back alleys and scavenging lanes that provided good cover for anyone wishing to leave the area unobtrusively.

Search patterns, rendezvous points and recall signals were quickly worked out and allocated and thirty of us fanned out and plunged into the smelly back alleys of Wanchai. Everyone was alert and well aware, after the number of policemen who had been killed and injured in recent months, that quick reflexes could mean the difference between life and death.

In a particularly dark and filthy scavenging lane, to the rear of some small shops, I heard the sound of a furtive movement behind me and swung round with my revolver at the ready. Piled against the wall there was a heap of old cardboard boxes covered in indescribable dirt and from them I could see a spookily shapeless figure rising making strange mewing sounds.

In Cantonese and English I said I was police and gave a challenge. In English and in a quavering voice came the reply 'Oh Gawd where the hell am I an' what's happening?' I switched on my torch and saw in its bright beam a naked European standing with his hands up in the attitude of surrender, revealed in all his manly glory, well perhaps grimily pathetic and limp rather than glorious!

On enquiry it was established that he was a sailor from a Royal Navy ship who had come ashore some eight hours earlier to celebrate his birthday. He could vaguely remember the early part of the evening but the latter part was a blank. While he was talking it slowly dawned on him that he was completely, definitively, utterly, bare-bummed, stark-naked. He did not even have his socks on, like all the naked men did in old fashioned pornographic films presumably to cover up their indecently dirty feet, all he had on was his hair and tattoos.

He was the principal character in every Jolly Jack Tar's least favourite private nightmare, in a dark alleyway in a foreign port, stark-bollock naked, no uniform, no pay book, no identity disc, suffering from the initial stages of a cosmic thundering hangover, wanting to be sick, dying for a pee, and some shadowy figure in a police uniform pointing a gun at him . . . God!

My revolver was stowed away and it was all I could do to keep a fit of the giggles at bay. The poor chap was a naval cliché in the flesh. With bits of cardboard clutched round his nether regions for the sake of decency, I led him cautiously out to the road at the end of the alley where my driver and radio operator were waiting for me in my command Land Rover.

It was unfortunate for Jolly Jack that, just then ,it was tea break time for the night shift girls in the laundry about fifty yards down the road,. They were all sitting in the street chatting, drinking tea and smoking the cigarettes forbidden inside the laundry.

Our appearance made their day, or at least the appearance of my naval companion, who promptly had a fit of nerves and lost his cardboard at the sight of some forty young women looking at him. It was the reverse situation, to that of a similar group of sailors, who would look at a pretty girl passing, with mock lechery and making obviously rude, bawdy, and personal remarks about her private anatomy. He fell into the Land Rover a distraught and shattered man to a chorus of wolf whistles and catcalls from the girls. Even we policemen looked at him with interest, as it was the first time we had ever seen anyone blush all over from head to toe.

At the British Shore Patrol office in HMS *Tamar*, the Royal Navy's land base and dockyard, we obtained a blanket to cover him as we handed him over to the Naval Provost Marshal's staff.

Such is the resilience of the British matelot, he was already perking up as he enjoyed a cup of tea in the Patrol office, while details of his adventure were being recorded. I ruined his whole run ashore by advising him to see his ship's doctor as soon as possible as the whores in the shack on the roof of the building where I found him, and where he had undoubtedly been a customer, were known drug addicts and were also notorious for handing out doses of venereal disease.

Like all drug addict prostitutes, male or female, they sold sex to buy fixes of drugs and did not give a damn about getting or giving sexually transmitted diseases. They already had the monkey of addiction on their backs why should they care about a tingle in their genitals?

Fourteen

WHEN IT HITS
THE FAN . . .

The Chinese cultural revolution, as it affected Hong Kong, caused much change in the official thinking in Police Headquarters. In the post-mortem following the Double Tenth riots of 1956, it had become apparent, even to the most hide bound senior officers, that the clumsy and outmoded sixty-four man, eight section, platoons of bygone days were totally useless in modern Hong Kong. It had also dawned on them that civilian drivers could not be expected to stand firm in the face of armed mobs. There were many stories from 1956, similar to ours at Tai Hang Tung Resettlement Estate, where drivers dropped the policemen off, then disappeared without warning. As a result the Police Training Contingent (PTC) was set up in an old army camp near the Railway Station at Fanling in the New Territories and new Riot Control systems were hammered out, with my old friend Les Guyatt as Chief Instructor. A new slimmed down platoon was created, of four sections plus Headquarters section drivers, and guards. Fast, compact, well armed, very flexible, and sensibly structured so that no one section could ever again be sent into the kind of situation that we had faced, in 1956, without appropriate armament. Rioting mobs kill people, whether armed or unarmed. Force ideas changed and it became policy that everyone, would be rotated through a six month attachment to PTC in the course of their career, so that eventually everybody would have a sound knowledge of the new riot procedures.

The troubles in Hong Kong ten years later differed again from 1956. That had been short, sharp, and vicious. This was going to be a long haul, and it was obvious that men could only be kept in front-line riot work for a reasonable time before being relieved, or employed, at least for a time, on less demanding duties. The courses at PTC, now renamed the Police Tactical Unit, PTU, were shortened to two months, and more people were as a consequence, trained in the skills needed for riot work in a third of the time previously taken. From the more intellectual legal circles of the Magistrates Courts I was transferred to the hurly burly of PTU to be greeted by a smiling

Les Guyatt, and a disgustingly healthy looking P.T. person, who obviously disapproved of the girth of my waistline gained by my sedentary court work. Senior Superintendent Peter Godber was the Commandant. He was tough, demanding, and much admired. It was widely known among more junior officers, and the rank and file in the police force, that when the Communists had first begun their campaign, a hundred and more had occupied the pavement of Garden Road at the side of the Hong Kong Hilton Hotel. Some of the more jumpy senior people wanted Peter Godber to use his PTU men to disperse them as Garden Road leads up to the Government House, the main government offices, and the US Consulate General. Godber, with his authority as Commander in the Field, held on coolly. He also got the world's media to hang on and watch. Under growing pressure from headquarters to do something he still waited, and his patience paid off. At a given signal the untouched and healthy Communists took bandages out of their pockets, which were made up to look as though covered in blood, clapped them to their heads and lay on the pavement groaning and crying that they had been assaulted by the police in the course of a peaceful demonstration. They did not know that the whole performance had been filmed by TV news cameramen and that it would be shown around the world, revealing them for what they were, liars and cheats. They were later cleared from the area at Godber's orders and this was done with an absolute minimum use of force. Godber's coolness and operational common sense gained the Hong Kong government, and the British Foreign Office, a propaganda coup that gained them the moral high ground, internationally, at the start of a long and horrible time of blood and death. It also, according to the bamboo telegraph, gained Godber the deadly enmity of some of the ex-African 'Game Wardens' who had been urging early action and criticising him for taking so long to act. We trusted him to act wisely under fire, which was more than could be said for many far senior to him in rank!

We formed up 'Alpha' Company under the command of Superintendent Vic Moss, a former Sergeant-Major in the British Army, who had fought in the Far East. I was Company second-in-command. We had three riot platoons, and a good bunch of platoon officers, and after a quick and intensive period of training we were thrown into the fray in Kowloon, where the men in action were approaching exhaustion. On our first deployment we went to the relief of tired units in Sham Shui Po in northern Kowloon and, quite by chance and good luck, hit at the right time, clearing every junction of the main Nathan Road for its whole two mile and more length in one great sweep, all the way down to Tsim Sha Tsui. Then we were involved in a variety of skirmishes, with rioting groups into which the main mob had broken up, vicious little back street fights, that gradually dwindled down and finally handed over the ground we had won to fresh units and we went off to rest. It was a good start for Vic Moss's Company.

One day we heard, through some CID friends, that there were rumours of a plan by some Communist school teachers, to have some of their young schoolchildren, kids between eight and ten years old, swarm out from a road-banking on to a main road in front of vehicles carrying some very important people, as part of a campaign to embarrass the British authorities. If we stopped them by using policemen we would be filmed as big bully cops in riot gear harassing little, crying, schoolchildren. If we did nothing, we had to bear in mind the fate of the two famous comedians who had annoyed the Communists and stopped in their car at a junction near their home for some kids to cross the road, only to be attacked by Communists who filled their car with petrol bombs and burned them to death. We had to do something but what? The information was so damn vague it had not even been up the chain of command. My Company Commander, Vic Moss, and I had become quite friendly since first forming up the Company. He was a quiet and steady man and I trusted and respected him. He had a bit of heart trouble but, as far as his Company was concerned, that was his business nobody else's, although we kept an eye on him because he was a very hard worker. I asked him if I could have a bit of time off, in civilian clothes, to go and see some friends of mine. However, I would take a portable radio with me, and my driver and orderly could park the Land Rover near my position, and call me on the radio if we went on immediate stand by. Vic was puzzled but he trusted me enough to agree. We drove off to Yaumati at one o'clock in the morning and I met some old lady friends and treated them to a cup of tea and some sweetmeats at a favourite food stall I had known for a long time.

Some eight years before I had been posted to Yaumati on my first operational duties as a land officer. As the 'new boy' I had ended up doing an awful lot of night duties but I didn't mind as it was an amazing place late at night, and there was a whole breed of night people that one never saw during the daytime. The whole area was transformed in the dark from a dirty squalid maze of old Chinese tenements built higgledy piggledy all over the place, to a quite exotic oriental scene that would have done credit to the old Fu Manchu movies. Most of the area was 'Out of Bounds' to British troops as it was full of Chinese brothels, but that didn't stop them from going in when they had been drinking.

It was here that I had first met the 'Sisters of the Night', the night-soil ladies, all Hakkas from the New Territories, and all grandmothers! The old Chinese tenements had no connection to the sewage system. Every house had its own dry toilet, and each household paid for the ladies to empty their toilets and take the contents away. Each of the ladies had two large containers which they carried, on bamboo poles over their shoulders, to a large human-slurry tanker into which it was emptied by two crew men. The women then went off to collect more, and so on throughout the night. By nine o'clock in the morning they had usually finished their area and driven off to dispose of the load. In those days much of it went into settling ponds in the New Territories, to be used on paddy fields three years or so later.

From them I learned that in the old days, when the wealthy mansion owners in the Peak district still had dry toilets, the manure from the Europeans fetched a higher price from the rice growers as they reckoned it was 'stronger for the paddy' as the white devils ate better and consumed more meat than Chinese! As somebody might say 'Not a lot of people know that'. Then again they might just have been pulling my leg!

A friendship had sprung up between us because I did not look down on them as most people did, and I frequently joined them at the stall where they took their tea break, and had a cup of tea and chat with them. They were fascinated when I told them about old Edinburgh, and how people in the High Street used to shout 'Gardy loo' as they threw their slops into the centre of the street. When they heard how some of the tenements in the Edinburgh and Glasgow of my youth, still had dry toilets, or one flush toilet and a tap for each floor of four or more flats,they were astonished, all of them thought that all of the British lived in similar luxury in the home country as that which they enjoyed in Hong Kong. It had not dawned on them that we had poor people who could not afford even one servant!

They were tough ladies, and it was a well known fact that anyone who annoyed them would immediately get a container's horrific contents emptied over their heads, whoever they were. No one in their right minds stood in their way when they shuffled down the street; no one, not even Triad men. There were blood curdling whispers that some cocky Triad members had once tried to squeeze some of the ladies for money and had disappeared into the slurry tanker never to be seen again. It was undoubtedly untrue as I just could not see these kind grandmotherly types doing such a thing. Then again . . .?

One night, on patrol on my own, I was in real trouble with a gang of drunken British soldiers. I could have shot them, but that did not recommend itself to me as they were being stupidly beer-brave and showing off, but men have been killed in such situations. My night soil ladies had seen what was going on and arrived at the trot, like a most improbable 4th US Cavalry, carrying their buckets of noisesome ammunition which they promptly tipped over the soldiers' heads. They then beat the hell out of them with their bamboo carrying poles, scolding them fiercely for misbehaving, until they fled. It was the only occasion, that I know of, where the British Army has retreated covered in human excrement, and being beaten with bamboo poles by a squad of Chinese grannies! It would be a reasonable bet that the battle of the night-soil ladies never got into their Regimental records!

So it was very pleasant for me to spend some time with the ladies talking over old times and the cultural revolution, of which they strongly disapproved. After making some strictly private, and unofficial, arrangements for the next day, they went back to their necessary, but unpleasant, job and I went back to mine.

By half past nine the following morning Alpha Company were officially out on an exercise, gaining local knowledge of the area. We were in a position, tucked away not far from the school where the demonstration was supposed to happen. Vic and I were looking at the scene through binoculars when we saw the slurry lorry trundling slowly along towards us. Well back down the road were the official cars carrying the VIPs. My fingers were crossed and Vic was looking at me with a 'What kind of nice mess have you gotten me into now, Stanley?' look.

As the slurry tanker swept slowly past the banking in front of the school, its discharge valve seemed to spring an accidental leak and, despite the efforts of two of the ladies who seemed to be trying to rectify matters, a horrible, stinking, sheet of urine and excrement sprayed all over the bank. We could see the figures of children and adults, who had been well concealed, suddenly spring up and run for the school as fast as they could. Vic grinned and I relaxed. The official cars swept past without hindrance, and carried on up the road. That night the ladies had a slap up meal laid on for them at the cooked food stall, with thanks from an anonymous admirer!

In the days following we had some remarkable experiences. We were ordered in to the Kowloon Walled City on a number of duties, one of which was to check a school. This school was quite a well run place providing a good standard of education for mainly poor students, but information had been received in HQ that there was some suspicious activity going on there. I led a platoon up to the premises and we quickly broke open a door and made our way inside.

The day was very hot and there were a number of well dressed students, about seventeen or eighteen years old, sitting round a table as we entered, whose clothes were marked with sweat. They also had sweat on their faces which is very unusual for Chinese people, especially young people. The atmosphere in the room was stifling hot, all of the windows were shut and the ceiling fans were not in operation.

One of my men went to the switch box near the door and went to switch the fans on but I yelled at him to leave them alone, why I don't know, maybe just a copper's hunch, but I had noticed the seated students looked scared as the constable reached for the fan switch. We checked carefully and saw some wires leading off into the ceiling panels. I sent for Norman Hill, our overworked Bomb and Ballistics officer. He could be very grim and stern-faced at times, which is not surprising as one false move, or accidental spark, could kill or maim him at any time, but with us he was always so damned cheerful, and full of life, that the constables used to grin when he turned up. But he took his work very seriously and never allowed others to be in danger through any fault of his.

I had kept the students where they were until Norman arrived, but we questioned them without any result. They claimed they had just arrived to see if there were any classes and were merely chatting idly when we burst in.

Norman ordered everyone out of the room while he went to work and I sent my men off with the students, to hold them for further questioning, remaining to give Norman a hand, but only of the fetching and carrying kind. He worked quickly but safely and very soon showed me the sticks of dynamite that had been wired up to the ceiling fans.

It had obviously been a carefully planned death trap for the police but the would-be killers had messed up their timing and had passed in the false information too early. What was supposed to happen was that the police would enter the empty school to start a search, and switch on the ceiling fans because of the heat. The amount of explosives in the ceiling would, Norman calculated, have destroyed the school, the floors above and below, possibly killed at least twenty of more policemen and, God knows how many, innocent civilians!

Norman and I went down in the lift together, him carrying the explosives, and me operating the lift, and standing as far from him as is possible in a four foot square space. Which, as he pointed out, was pretty damn silly as, if the dynamite went off, we'd probably have been blown clean out of the roof of the building and into orbit.

My men, and the students, were ordered to watch as Norman took the explosives to an empty building site and, after we had warned people nearby, detonated them. The students looked horrified at the blast, and my men looked very thoughtful. The students had to be released later as there was no evidence of wrong-doing on their part.

That, in its own way, was a valid and, we hoped for the youngster's sake, thought-provoking, demonstration of the great difference between our system of justice and the kangaroo courts operated by the Communists!

We were sent for a break at Kwun Tong police station after a particularly busy time all over Kowloon. At the very top of the priority list for men involved in riot control, is a shower to wash tear gas out of the hair and off the body, clean clothes, a meal, and sleep, in that order.

We had barely had our showers when we were called out again to Sham Shui Po, where trouble had broken out. We arrived to the usual scenes of fast-moving riot chaos. Our men set-to energetically in the, by now very familiar, business of clearing the streets. All the time we were in action we had orderlies and other sharp-eyed men watching doorways, rooftops, and alleyways for ambushes and snipers. One of our men spotted what he thought was a group of armed men passing behind a block of buildings and reported it. When things had quietened down we went to Sham Shui Po police station and reported to the CID commander what the constable had seen. It fitted in with some information he had already received and it was immediately arranged for him and his men to carry out a raid, with us providing cover for them.

The place to be raided was a shipyard, a nest of pro-Communist sympathisers that had, apparently, been described in some left-wing British publications, as an example of enlightened employment in vile capitalist Hong Kong, recommending that other yards should be compelled to follow their working practices.

167

We went to the shipyard and had it sealed off before anyone knew what was happening. As the CID went in, accompanied by some of our men, we came under sporadic attack from groups emerging from, and disappearing into, nearby alleys, but they presented our battle-hardened men with no real difficulties.

A very good search by the CID men turned up a large cache of weapons, obviously made in the yard's workshops. There was all the usual stuff, fighting knives, short stabbing swords, Chinese fighting irons, but, chillingly, they also found copies of Sten gun barrels and parts.

The Sten gun was the basic, automatic, and single shot, weapon of the European Resistance movements during the Second World War, cheap and easy to produce. The CID took some men away for questioning. After finishing with the scene of crime we went off to try again to have a shower, change our clothes, eat, and sleep, and, just for once we made it!

On one occasion we were deployed in Kowloon on a fairly easy duty, seeing that the bus crews were not being intimidated by Communist bullies, and that the ferry terminals were operating normally, as the leftists had been trying to disrupt the essential transport services. We were directed, by radio, to go to a minor incident in Kowloon City Division where, what was described as a group 'scuffle', was taking place between coolies.

We arrived at the location, and found that it was near the main slaughterhouse, and the 'scuffle' was a full scale riot involving hundreds of slaughterhouse coolies armed with all the wickedly sharp implements of their trade. There were bodies all over the place some of bleeding groaning men, others lying still and bloodstained on the ground. Some Divisional men were already tackling the mob, but they were vastly outnumbered.

We quickly debussed and got into action, much to the relief of the local men. The weaponry the coolies had armed themselves with was quite horrifying to see, and it made everyone realise how horrible ancient battles must have been in reality, not on a bloodless movie screen, as men hacked and tore at each other with axes, knives, and swords. The screams, and curses, and yells, and smells, of hate, fear, and blood.

We gradually broke them up and began driving them back into the slaughterhouse where most of them helpfully barricaded themselves in. This made it easy for the local men to keep them there while we set off to round up others who had fled in all directions as we tackled them with tear gas and baton shells.

168

It is a fact that dealing with riots demands both a quick, keen, sense of place and tactics. It also requires concentration if the policemen are to succeed in imposing the official will on mobs of people who always outnumber them by hundreds to one. This can result in fragmenting mobs being driven in a desired direction without the police noticing their immediate surroundings, and this was brought home to us in this incident.

A large, well-armed group of coolies, including two who were suspected of murder, was very successfully herded into a dead end street that led into a large, well-fenced yard. They ran in and began to try to set up defences but the platoon, led by Inspector Ted Stevenson, kept them off balance by sustaining his attack while they were simultaneously advised by loud hailer to surrender. Some did and stood with their hands up until led away. Gas and baton shells were being fired at groups all over the place gradually whittling down their numbers as more and more of them gave up.

Action came to a sudden stop when a terrified looking man with bulging eyes, suddenly appeared from a seemingly empty office building, and shrieked 'Stop! Stop shooting! You'll blow up the whole of f...ing Kowloon you f...ing idiots!'

In the heat of the action no one had really noticed that they were in the gasometer compound of the Gas Company, and that every gasometer was filled to its full height with enough explosive gas to produce a memorable bang! He almost fainted when one constable let off a baton round at some men actually standing high up on the metal stairs winding up around one of the gasometers.

The coolies suddenly realised where they were, and lost their appetite for riot and murder. Against a background clatter of dropped, and thrown away, weapons they began surrendering. The two wanted men were found drowned in the water inside one of the gasometers about a week later.

Not long after this, Alpha company came to the end of the tour of duty at PTU, and we disbanded to return to our different districts. We had a farewell party but, in view of the violent death still going on in China, and all around us,it was a subdued group of 150 or so men who quietly enjoyed the well-earned celebration. As always happens at these sort of 'do's' somebody started the 'do you remember?' conversation.

In view of some of the truly hair-raising things we had been involved in, it was surprising that the two best remembered things were the horror stricken face, and trembling voice, of the boss of the gasometer yard, and the callous disregard for people's lives shown by the people who wired up the bombs to the school fans.

We said a respectful farewell to Vic Moss, a super Commander and a fine man. Throughout the whole of our action filled time he led from the front. Even when exhausted he never lost his temper, and he was never unfair. He and his family had, years before, defended Tsuen Wan police station when it was heavily attacked, and had beaten off the attackers until relief came. He never took risks with his men for his own glory, and he did all this with a tube in his heart, and a selection of pills which we constantly had to remind him to take. There are not too many like him about, and we all thought the world of him.

Ted Stevenson went to the frontier where he served happily until he had a leg blown off bravely going into a minefield to rescue a little girl. He was given a well-deserved medal for that, and later, fitted with an artificial leg, served in Special branch. My posting, some eight weeks later, was in Command of Emergency Unit Hong Kong Island.

Fifteen

'BROTHERS UNDER THE SKIN . . .'

My tour as Emergency Unit Commander, began with an intensive retraining schedule for all the men in the unit, passing on all that I had recently learned in the Police Tactical Unit. To their credit, everyone buckled down to the work. It was indicative of their common sense, that they accepted the fact that small units of trained, and disciplined, men can keep control, and stay alive, even when dealing with huge mobs on the rampage. It was my great good fortune that the administration NCO at EU Hong Kong Island, was Corporal 2771, Charles Ng Chueng-chung, the man to whom this book is dedicated. Charles is a quiet family man, a first class policeman, and one of the bravest men I have ever known. We had been recruits at the Police Training School, and involved in the Double Tenth Riots, at the same time but had not served together since then.

The first duty given to the EU, after a week of intensive training, was to open up part of the Western District, which had become a virtual no-go area under the control of leftists. Constables patrolling on their own, could hardly be expected to deal with groups of cargo coolies lying in ambush, armed with wickedly sharp coolie hooks used for manhandling sacks of rice, or slaughterhouse coolies with incredibly sharp knives. One constable had already been ripped to death , others injured, and no one had been brought to justice for the crimes. As with most divisional commanders in Hong Kong, the Divisional Superintendent of Western was lucky if he had enough men on duty to cover one beat out of every two during any shift. Yet the prolonged absence of the ordinary beat patrol constable is a signal to the general public that all is not well, and that the powers that be, are not fully in control. Such a dangerous perception of government impotence, cannot be allowed to take root in any civilised society, without anarchy prevailing, certainly not in Hong Kong.

The Western District of Hong Kong Island is a fascinating maze of godowns, shipping agents, cargo forwarders, and long dark open-fronted shops trading in everything but it is not the easiest place to police. In many ways its waterfront is like a living history lesson of

171

early colonial Hong Kong. Wing Lok Wharf, Macao Ferry Pier, West Point Wharf, China Merchants' Steam Navigation Company Wharf, Belcher's Cape, Slaughterhouse Landing, Kennedy Town, a roll call of essential points of access, stretching westwards from Central area to the Sulphur Channel that separates Hong Kong Island from Green Island and signals the western limits of the harbour.

Except during typhoons this is possibly the busiest, noisiest, dustiest, most exotic, place in the whole Colony as far as visitors are concerned. Much of Hong Kong's essential food supplies from China, about £25 million worth a year, has traditionally arrived here from Canton ninety miles to the north west. Brought in long rows of huge river barges towed down the Pearl River by steam-powered tugs crewed skilfully by sturdy Chinese girls. Everything imaginable is loaded and unloaded here, from people using Macao ferries to buffaloes and pigs destined for the kitchens of the Colony via the abattoir in Kennedy town. Sea-going junks, river boats, and coastal traders, are secured by bow or stern in long bobbing rows, connected to the land by pairs of one-way system gangplanks swaying and bouncing under the feet of sweating, cursing, half-naked coolies, burdened individually with huge loads on their shoulders gripped by gleaming coolie hooks, or working in pairs with some massive weight slung between them from a stout bamboo pole.

Coolies are not generally paid by the hour but by the amount of cargo they shift, so they never waste time. There is a ground-covering coolie 'shuffle' halfway between a walk and a trot and, as with the night-soil women, when they shuffle along laden down, uttering their peculiar warning cry, everybody gets out of their way. The consequences for failing to do so are most unpleasant as coolies are, understandably, very short-tempered people. It was this area and these people who had been diverted from their normal 'live and let live' philosophy of existence by the leftists.

The Western District Magistrates Courts were in session when the Court building came under attack from a very large crowd apparently intent on freeing some Communist prisoners who were on trial inside. The men from Western Police Station were already at full stretch and none available to deal with incident. As a matter of fact they barely had enough men to guard the station, so EU were called in.

We went to the scene with one riot platoon and found the Court building completely surrounded and under siege by rioters. After warning them to disperse and giving them enough time to begin leaving the area; an opportunity they ignored, we fired baton shells and this had no effect so, after further warnings, tear gas was used, and they began to disperse slowly, yelling slogans and wiping their eyes. Although some of the gas entered the Courts' air conditioning system those inside did not complain, they were only too glad the mob were going. The Senior Magistrate who knew me well, was surprised that we were not dispersing the dawdling rioters more urgently than we seemed to be doing but he did not know that two more of my platoons plus three special squads were moving quietly and discreetly through back streets into positions near the no-go area while attention was focussed on the skirmish at the Courts.

The standard police scenario after such an incident was for the Riot Platoon to be deployed into four columns of eight men who would then do a sweep through the side streets to make sure that the rioters were dispersing and not lurking at rendezvous points to join up again as soon as the police had gone.

No one noticed that the columns engaged on the sweeps were actually just a handful of heavily armed men busily imitating four full columns. The rest of the platoon had slyly infiltrated the centre boundary of the 'no-go' area. The whole EU Company moved in on command and caught everyone by surprise. The look-outs posted on the roofs of some godown and coolie quarters to warn of the approach of police, were caught completely off guard when we moved in, and their rooftop strong points had been seized and demolished before they realised the well armed special squads were there. There was a burst of fierce street fighting and some gas was used but within thirty minutes everything was under control without the use of lethal firearms.

Few arrests were made as most of the people involved were not really bad people or criminals, just simple folk, people who worked at killingly hard physical jobs just to survive, who were easily led astray by political windbags spouting propaganda. It was rumoured afterwards that many of the would-be Red Guards had gone into the harbour, but there was no hard evidence to that effect, nor were any bodies picked up by Marine Police later. The area was heavily patrolled for some time but, as Chinese coolies have done throughout history after a fit of bad temper, everybody just got back to their ordinary business of rubbing along making a living, doing a bit of illegal gambling, some drinking, a bit of down-market whoring, and the occasional fight. There were no other 'no-go' areas established in Western, the divisional men made sure of that!

Charles NG is an outstanding man for whom I have the highest respect. Yet in saying that, I do not in any way infer that any of the other Chinese officers in the Hong Kong Police Force were any less worthy of respect and admiration. Charles first showed his remarkable qualities to me when I took him on an ill-advised visit to Shaukiwan one night.

The location of bomb factories was something that exercised many minds in the Police Force during the whole cultural revolution period. There were so many bombs, so widely scattered, on so many occasions, it was almost as though they were being made on a production line. Yet we knew they were not. This had been a matter of discussion with some CID friends one day and they had mentioned to me that they believed there might be a bomb factory somewhere in the hills above Shaukiwan, not far from the Taikoo Docks, but they had no idea where. It was no use driving around there in a Police Land Rover, so one evening, when things were quiet, I told Charles to change into plain clothes, draw a revolver from the Armoury, and come with me in my private car, just to survey the area quietly and inconspicuously, and work out some EU sweeps through the huts on the hillside. We took a portable radio with us and my second-in-command stayed in the EU office ready to call me back if anything broke, or to come if I called for back up.

We drove to Shaukiwan, then Chai Wan, and spent some time quietly reconnoîtring the area without being noticed. Some places were noted to be recommended to Superintendent Rik Darkin for possible sweeps, then we headed back into town. As we were passing the Taikoo Docks we noticed a young man pushing a bicycle with a delivery carrier on its front which seemed to contain a basket full of goods. This was unusual at that time of night even in Hong Kong, so we pulled up, identified ourselves as policemen and questioned him. He was completely uncooperative but a quick check revealed that the carrier contained bombs. It later transpired that he was a Communist student. We called for EU back up on the portable radio but received no reply; we were in a 'dead spot' for radio.

Before we could move to a better area for reception, we noticed that there was much noise and activity coming from the Dock's coolie quarters. The bomb carrier had been followed at a distance by a car driven by his friends and they had gone to their contacts among the coolies to arrange for his rescue. Approximately 2000 coolies suddenly spilled out on to the street and surrounded us.

I ordered Charles to make off up the hillside, as he was in civilian clothes he could easily disappear into the darkness, mingle with crowd if necessary, and make his way to safety. He was deeply offended and told me so in no uncertain terms. When he was reminded that he had a wife and children he told me that they would never speak to him again if he deserted me in the face of a mere thousand or so coolies, and he grinned.

We pinned our prisoner between us and the rock face of the cliff behind us, then stood back to back, with our pistols in our hand, facing the mob as it surrounded us in a semi-circle, I mentioned Custer's Last Stand to Charles, and he laughed.

As we waited for the crunch we heard the sound of sirens and a whole fleet of EU cars came tearing into sight, sirens going, blue lamps flashing, warning lights blinking, they really looked quite urgent, impressive, and businesslike. Charles had, wisely, previously told them to come looking for us if we had not reported in, within a certain time limit. The mob melted away back into their quarters, and Charles and I were overwhelmed by the genuine anxiety of the EU men.

Our prisoner was handed over to CID, who later tracked down the bomb factory, and the bombs were efficiently detonated by the ever-smiling Norman Hill.

It was not the only occasion on which Charles stood by me at great personal risk, but to me it was the most memorable. The Britisher and the brave Colonial are almost a cliché from stories of early Empire, but the reality is something quite unique. Charles became, and remains to this day, my best friend.

His daughter Elena is as my own daughter, and was my ward from the age of nine when she came to Britain to study until she qualified as a nurse. She is now a midwife in London.

Charles is quite a small man for someone from Shantung Province in north-eastern China, a place that bears some resemblance to the west of Scotland in climate, and in the type of people it produces. It is a tough place to scrape a living, but they do. The similarity between Shantung people and Scots was made quite clear to me when I told Charles I could probably get him a medal, or commendation, or promotion for his night's work in Shaukiwan. He reminded me that I had once told him how little it cost to cast a medal, and pointed out that he would earn more than that from a year's extra salary as a sergeant! He got his promotion. Years later he was awarded a well deserved Colonial Police Medal!

Training was an essential part of Emergency Unit life. Riot drill training, rescue training, pistol courses, carbine courses, riot shotgun courses, baton shell and gas shell course, grenade courses, first aid courses, lectures and briefings in law, all this in addition to normal patrols and duties. All ranks were constantly encouraged to work and study for promotion, to use their initiative on duty rather than just wait for orders, to aim actively at being the best policemen in the Force.

More than any other formation in the Police Force in my opinion, the Emergency Units gave good officers the opportunity to show positive characteristics and ability. Their beat was the whole of Hong Kong Island, patrolling independently far from the Unit and in contact most of the time only by radio. This demanded a high standard of confidence and good personal discipline, or the result could have been undisciplined, ineffective, chaos.

During my three years as Commander no one ever let the Unit down. To the contrary, they gained and upheld a good reputation for us all. So much so that we incurred the enmity of many of our fellow officers or at least some senior officers who slyly criticised us and tried to find fault, without success. No one remained in the EU more than three years before returning to ordinary police duties, and our aim was to return men who would be assets to any commander in any formation.

It may be that my typically Scottish keenness on self-improvement by education, the 'lad o' pairts' syndrome, Charles called it, occasionally led me 'over the top' in pushing my long suffering chaps for promotion.

One of my dottier ideas had to do with the toilets in the rank and file accommodation at Emergency Unit. The toilets were Chinese of the 'crouch down' not 'sit down' type, and I had noticed subconsciously that the men using them during their tea breaks and rest breaks usually took a newspaper to read when they went to the loo. The papers were undoubtedly for reading as there was always plenty of toilet paper available, after all the Chinese did invent it!

Promotion examination time was approaching, and I had some damn good men who deserved promotion even though that meant they would have to leave the unit. With a bit of research, and the repayment by friends of past favours owed, I managed to put together a fair a selection of examination questions and model answers for the preceding four years.

There then ensued, roughly, the following conversation with Charles, long accustomed to some of my wilder ploys.

'Corporal, I've got an idea about rank and file promotions!'

Cautiously 'Yes sir?'

'Have you noticed that the NCOs and PCs always take newspapers with them when they go to the toilets?'

A bewildered look followed, with a noncommittal reply .

Cautiously 'Er . . . yes sir . . . newspapers sir . . . they read them in the toilet you know, it's customary . . . er . . . don't Europeans?'

By this time Charles's face displayed complete puzzlement.

'Yes, yes, Charles but don't you see this is a marvellous way of preparing them for the promotion exams?'

At this stage Charles was looking at me as though I'd gone completely off my trolley, and his voice took on the soothing tone of a sane person talking to a barking lunatic busily eating the carpet 'P . . . preparing them for examinations in the toilet?'

'No Charles don't you see?' It was obvious he didn't from his rapidly glazing eyes.

'I've got four years of examination questions and model answers. We'll paste them on the inside of the toilet doors and they'll read them when they go to the bog. Even if they don't consciously read them, they'll probably get some ideas even by a sort of osmosis!'

His range of expressions had run out and he just sat looking me for a moment struggling to keep his face straight.

Then, thoughtfully, 'It has never been done before sir, using a loo as a training aid, it could work given the right conditions.' He did not specify what conditions he meant, but he brightened up appreciably 'and it would drive the opposition crazy trying to work out what the hell you're up to.'

By 'opposition' Charles presumably meant certain senior officers who did not care much for the EU.

He suddenly burst out laughing 'Toilet training for EU men!' The image of our tough EU men sitting bare-bummed on a row of potties, like a Communist nursery propaganda film, got to us and we both sat and roared with laughter.

We were sitting grinning at each other when my immediate superior officer, Rik Darkin a tremendous, courageous, man whom I liked, admired and trusted, came into the office and saw us imitating Cheshire cats. He immediately looked alarmed, said 'I don't want to know what the hell you are planning now,' turned round and walked out. I explained to him later what we were up to and he had a good giggle.

One of the EU platoon commanders, Inspector Wong, had reached officer rank the hard way from constable. He was another of the

177

brilliantly intelligent, small, tough, tenacious, serious, men the Force was lucky to have in its ranks. His opinion of the men's likely response to 'toilet training' was important as it would have been disastrous if the men had seen it as a loss of 'face'. He had a mild fit of hysterics at the idea but once he had got his sense of humour under control he said that he thought it a good ploy and he thought the men would too.

The copies of the past examination questions and model answers were pasted on the inside of all the toilet doors where the men could not fail to see them. There was also a small notice telling the readers that in case of difficulty, educational not functional, they were welcome to approach the Administration NCO, the long-suffering overworked Charles, or any Officer including the OC, for enlightenment.

The papers were changed weekly in the lead up to the examinations so that by examination time all of the toilet users had seen the questions and answers for the preceding four years. It also happened, quite by chance, that a rumour spread round the unit that anyone seen entering the loo with a newspaper would, purely coincidentally and nothing to do with 'proper conditions', end up doing some unpopular duty like prisoners' escorts for weeks and weeks!

Bog power worked, as EU Hong Kong gained nearly two thirds of all the rank and file promotions in Hong Kong Island that year! It also gained me a visit from two officers from the anti-corruption Branch as a result of anonymous complaints that there must have been monkey business involved to achieve such a result. They were told the whole story and were actually taken up to the toilets to view the evidence for themselves.

It was the first and only time anyone had seen A-C Branch men laughing out loud in public. It was intimated that they were laughing at the prospect of making the Anti-Corruption Branch's first full frank 'toilet inspection report' to be sent openly through official channels to embarrass and annoy certain 'anonymous' senior complainants!

Sixteen

'ONLY FIREWORKS...!'

Soon after returning to Hong Kong Island from Alpha Riot Company on the Frontier, I was posted as Officer Commanding Emergency Unit Hong Kong Island. This unit was the immediate response group of the District Commander, deployed in the event of major disaster, crime, disturbance, or any other serious emergency. At all hours of the day or night EU men were out on patrol in radio cars with enough riot and other equipment to deal with almost any situation. Certainly enough to contain a situation until reinforcements could be called in. There was always an Officer of the rank of Inspector in operational command with a sufficient number of men on duty to form up at least one fully equipped riot platoon within minutes of being ordered to do so. It was a good system, tried and tested over the years in the forcing house of fast moving Hong Kong events, and one that has now been adopted, with varying degrees of success, in other countries such as America, with their SWAT teams, and the Special Patrol Groups in the United Kingdom.

When I took command of the Emergency Unit, the madness of the Cultural Revolution was still going on. It began in China by the aging Mao Tse-tung, perhaps fearing for his own supreme position. The brutal murders, cruelty, and public humiliation, being inflicted on innocent people by his adolescent Red Guards, were a foretaste of things to come in Cambodia later, under the bloodthirsty Pol Pot and his Khmer Rouge.

Many of the leading lights of the Communist group in Hong Kong were publicly regarded as 'lychees', like the fruit, white capitalists on the inside hiding under an easily removed red coat worn on the outside. All of them noticeably lived well and enjoyed a good social life, and many of the Marxist socialist 'intellectuals', were better known for chasing pretty girls, or boys, than for any new insights they gave into the proletarian movement!

In general, they were regarded with contempt, by the Communists in China, who saw them for what they were, self-seeking manipulators, exploiting the hopes of a minority of ordinary people, out of the

179

Colony's majority, refugee population. It is against this background that the attempt to import the cultural revolution into Hong Kong must be viewed. The leadership were trying to convince Peking of their credentials as good Communists. They tried to copy the terrorism of the bullies with red books, in China, but they were consistently thwarted in their ambition to impress Peking, by the fact that the vast majority of the Chinese residents of Hong Kong refused to be cowed. On the contrary, they went about their lawful business in the face of threats, intimidation, and possible death, from bombs planted at random, by cowards, to kill the innocent.

In Kowloon two of Hong Kong's most popular Chinese comedians, who did wickedly funny satires on the more ridiculous claims of Chinese Communism, were publicly and horribly burned to death in their car by Communists using petrol bombs. If their intention was to frighten the local people by terror, it didn't work. Like the London Cockneys in the blitz the Hong Kong Chinese had the nerve, determination and courage to 'tough it out'.

They, also, had a thin blue line of well trained policemen standing between them, and the terrorists, committed to stopping the violence and restoring peace. Sir David Trench GCMG,MC, Governor of Hong Kong from 1964 to 1971, led and guided a fair and just administration that did not panic in the face of Hong Kong's longest and most sustained emergency. He was a quiet, firm, strong man who liked and respected the Chinese people and was liked, respected and trusted by the people in return. He encouraged and supported the Hong Kong Police Force and the ordinary policemen, many of whom died or were severely injured defending the people of the Colony.

It is interesting to note, in passing, that the British news media representatives, who gather in Hong Kong, like swarms of expense account vultures, at the merest whiff of a police corruption scandal, rarely took the trouble to mention the heroic deaths of police officers killed doing their duty!

Wanchai, in the Eastern District, is well known to every sailor who has been in South East Asia. It was also made universally known by the film *The World of Suzie Wong*. In normal times, Wanchai is a place of great fun and enjoyment, its crowded streets lit up brilliantly and colourfully throughout the night by the gaudy neon signs advertising its scores of excellent night clubs, some featuring world-class entertainment, bars filled with Suzie Wong look-alikes to dance with, at the cost of a glass of 'champagne' . . . usually 7-Up, excellent restaurants, dance halls with lovely dancing girls as partners at the cost of a ticket, even discreet but illegal brothels ranging from roof-top shacks to small hotels.

One evening all hell broke loose in Wanchai as the cowardly bomb planters had been very busy. Rumour had it later that some 200 bombs had been laid in the area, from motor cars, with holes cut in the floor through, which the terrorists placed their bombs by the roadside every time the cars pulled up. The pattern in which the bombs had been laid, virtually isolated the whole of the 300 000 plus population of Causeway Bay, North Point, and Shaukiwan, the easternmost part of Hong Kong Island, from access to Eastern, Central, and Western districts, and the vital road to Queen Mary Hospital. Queen Mary was the only hospital in the Island with the fully trained staff and equipment able to deal with the serious injuries caused by explosions and other violent traumas. As it was, it seemed that the bomb planting had been done deliberately, with the specific intention of preventing injured people being taken to the hospital. After all, was it not a Marxist who said, 'that the greater the terror caused the greater the victory gained'?

Emergency Unit was sent into the area to check the Wanchai roads for bombs, and the rooftops for bomb droppers. On the police radios were numerous messages about ambulances carrying injured people being prevented from going to the hospital. Bill Boyton, the Sub-Divisional Inspector of Eastern was out with his men doing what they could to curb the bombers, spot where bombs were placed, and establish alternative routes for ambulances and fire engines. He was joined by Roddy McEwan, a Scotsman and Senior Traffic Branch Inspector for the Island.

Roddy was almost typical of the expatriate Scot who can be found anywhere on earth. Hard-working, keen family man, proud of his work, and proud of his Scottish heritage. He had gone to Wanchai, we heard later, because of reports of ambulances containing injured people being prevented by bombs from getting through He had an encyclopedic knowledge of the roads in the island and was well qualified to find alternative routes if they existed. But it seems that even he could find no route that would safely by-pass the bombs.

However, in Yee Wo Street near a crucial roundabout and road interchange system, there was only one suspected bomb in the road-way, an airline bag, if it could be moved or dealt with, emergency vehicles could get through on their missions of mercy. There was no possibility of a bomb disposal officer arriving at the scene for at least an hour in which time patients could have died.

Roddy knew this and bravely decided to move the bomb to give the injured people a chance of life. Using a long piece of string he pulled the airline bag gently to the side of the road and as members of the public a safe distance away were about to applaud him for his bravery, the bomb in the bag exploded with immense force blowing his legs off and killing him.

Bill Boyton reported Roddy's death over the radio, not loudly, not excitedly, but with the most immense and deeply touching sadness. Like so many other brave Hong Kong Policemen Roddy died doing his duty but the ambulances got through!

The following day there was an unprecedented uproar in the Colony because a daily newspaper had published explicit full page photographs of Roddy's mutilated body lying at the side of the road.

Opinion was divided sharply between those who were outraged by the publication of the photograph, which must have been taken immediately after the explosion, and those who defended the right of a free Press to print and publish freely matters of genuine public interest.

The main charges levelled against the newspaper were of upsetting Roddy's family, offending against decency, outraging the feelings of 'right thinking' members of the public whoever they were, with side issues of the effect it could have upon children who might accidentally see the photograph. The secondary charge was that the Editor had printed it for its shock-horror effect just to sell more newspapers, a charge the Editor straightforwardly and indignantly denied.

Members of the Police Force were equally divided in their opinions, which was surprising as the Press are rarely friends of the Police, anywhere, in these permissive days, and it might have been expected that the Force would have been universally condemnatory. Operational officers and their men spend much time in reserve together, on 'stand-by' during times of riot, disaster, and typhoons, and commonly chat with each other much more than is usual.

Naturally the subject of the photograph came up during periods in reserve in the Emergency Unit in the days following Roddy's death. The general opinion of the men was that the Editor was absolutely right to print it in all its explicit horror. This was contrary to the general opinion of Europeans in the Colony who fulminated in the English language papers with letters usually of the 'Disgusted of . . .' variety.

The EU men explained that their attitude was basically logical. Newspapers regularly pander to the modern liberal convention, much-loved by defence lawyers, sociologists and their ilk, that everything in an offender's favour must be made public no matter how vile the crime or offence he has committed. Reams may be written on how kind he is to animals, accompanied by photographs of him, smart and neat, petting a nice pussy cat. But if one explicit photograph is printed of his wretched victim immediately after the crime, the full weight of legal and sociological fury will immediately be directed at the offending editor, and he will be accused, at the very least, of poisoning the minds of potential jurors and perverting the course of justice! The victim is at best ignored or, at worst, treated as though personally responsible for the crime.

The ordinary constables in their simple fashion put the point that the public should be allowed to see photographs of the effect of physical violence on victims and judge for themselves whether or not the penalties provided by law were suitable punishment. They questioned the right of terrorists in politically inspired crimes of violence and murder to claim justification on political grounds. As far as the constables were concerned, murder is murder, violence is violence, crime is crime, and politics is no excuse for either. They felt that if the photograph caused people to think twice about claims of political necessity then the Editor had performed a public service.

Publication of the photograph had a deep impact on all the people in the Colony and even horrified some of the cocktail circuit Marxists enough to make them rethink their sympathies. The Editor was absolutely justified in publishing. My own views are quite simple too. If the public is shown the truly horrible effects of violence – not the unrealistic bloodless nonsense of movie fights or murder scenes – there might be less publicity from the chattering classes and the 'Prisoners' Rights' industry, about the rights and comfort of convicted criminals and more public concern for the protection and promotion of the rights of their victims.

Emergency Unit Hong Kong were given the privilege of providing the Honour Guard for Roddy's funeral, and all saw for themselves the immense courage and dignity shown by his grieving widow. Mrs McEwen had lived the nightmare experienced by so many women married to policemen, firemen, lifeboat men, and all other men with a duty to save others, her husband had gone off to work as usual and a messenger with a sad message had returned. She was a very brave lady and she inspired us all in very dark and dangerous times. All terrorist bombs are confessions of weakness by the terrorists using them. Each time one explodes it demonstrates loudly to the world at large that they are incapable of achieving their ends by acceptable, civilised, reasonable, means; that they have been unable to convince a majority of the public at large of the fairness and validity of their point of view and they have, therefore, resorted to killing and maiming innocent people to compel them to obey.

Those who send letter-bombs, or plant bombs in public places to kill innocent men, women, and children, are not heroes, not freedom-fighters, not liberators, they are cowards. Politicians and media people who refer to them and their murderous activities in military terms give terrorists credibility. Whenever reporters fail to make the point that what happened was murder committed by a gang of murderers, they are terrorist collaborators; PR men for assassins!

Hong Kong had some experience of this from a slightly different angle. During the Cultural Revolution period a British Peer, a member of the House of Lords, visited the Colony, where he was given maximum security protection by the police. He was quoted in the British and foreign media as stating that the Press were exaggerating events in Hong Kong and that the so-called bombs, going off day and night, were nothing but big Chinese fireworks!

This did not go down well with the ordinary people in Hong Kong, nor the anti-terrorist forces. One well respected Chinese lady suggested that the noble Lord was so obviously full of bullshit that he would probably be improved by the insertion of a Chinese firework suppository!

Bomb-makers began making particularly terrible types of bombs designed to harm children. The majority of the Colony's children came from poor families with no money to spare for toys, so anything unusual found lying around was likely to be picked up and played with by the kids. Some bombs were made by taping packets of paper staples around an explosive core equipped with a handling fuse, then wrapping them in brightly coloured paper and scattering them around in public places, near play areas and schools.

They exploded when touched or picked up spraying out a lethal cloud of up to 400 metal staples. When these tiny pieces of metal hit anyone they did horrible damage to the human flesh and presented doctors with the almost impossible task of finding the scores of tiny individual needle like slivers of metal before they could remove them. Sometimes they were only found when severe infection began at the minute entry site of an otherwise undetectable wound. It was especially stressing for doctors that so many of their patients were children too young really to understand what had happened to them.

One little girl was hit by more than 300 staples, we heard, and it was estimated that she would need treatment for about two years or more to get them all out.

The bomb factories where all such devices were made were a top priority for the security forces and one came to our attention purely by chance.

Late one day there was a report of a tremendous explosion on the upper floor of a Communist school in Central District not far from the American Consulate General and the Colonial Secretariat. Emergency Unit were deployed to the scene and immediately cordoned off the area. It could be seen that one of the upper floors of the school had lost most of its windows and there were thin traces of smoke coming out. The first EU squad that arrived battered down the locked front doors and made their way upstairs to what had been the school laboratories where they extinguished numerous small fires with extinguishers.

The laboratories were a disaster scene with adolescent students strewn about amid the wreckage suffering from a variety of blast wounds and injuries caused by flying debris. Everywhere lay all the various components needed for bomb-making scattered about in dangerous profusion.

Lying on the floor at the end of the laboratory, where normally a teacher would have stood at the blackboard, was the bomb maker who had caused the explosion while preparing a bomb; a young lad of seventeen years. Most of his clothes had been blown off and he had suffered injuries all over his body. His face was an especially horrible sight to see, resembling a football made of minced beef topped with a singed wig. His eyes had been shattered by the explosion and looked like hard poached eggs with fluid trickling from them. His hands and arms were a mess.

One of my senior sergeants impelled by common humanity kneeled by his side and tried to give him first aid. I saw the boy push at him with his bloody arms and he said 'Do not touch me you running dog. Armed with the thoughts of Chairman Mao I feel no pain,' he then became unconscious.

Months later after much skilled and extensive medical treatment at government expense, he appeared in court charged with bomb-making for which he was sentenced to fourteen years imprisonment. His attitude of bravado in the Court did not differ from his attitude to the sergeant. My NCO had sons of his own and he commented sadly on the useless waste of a youngster's future for the benefit of an old man afraid of loss of power – Mao Tse-tung.

The Police Ballistics Officer, Norman Hill, arrived and ordered everyone out of the school as it was, in his words, 'a bang waiting to happen' with all the explosives scattered about. It says volumes for Norman's skills that ambulance personnel were able to remove all the injured and we were able to remove all of our prisoners, without the bang happening. He rendered all the explosives safe and removed them for disposal without any trouble. Norman was not so lucky a few weeks later.

One evening, bombs of a new type were found in a car-parking area, again not far from the US Consulate General. One he disarmed safely. The other was apparently equipped with a highly sophisticated booby trap device and it exploded blowing Norman's hand off. A police constable who was with him immediately used the lanyard on his police whistle as a tourniquet, and tightened and released it until he was taken to hospital. The doctors said that without the constable's quick thinking action in applying the tourniquet Norman would undoubtedly have bled to death.

Almost unbelievably he was back at work in his ballistics office within a matter of weeks at his own insistence. He could not take bombs apart with one hand in a public place but he could, and did, carry on with all the other ballistics work that was flooding in. He was rightly very much respected by police, army, and public alike.

Seventeen

COCKTAILS AND CHERRIES

An ugly Chinese girl is as rare a sight, as a chicken with teeth!

For a foreign man visiting Hong Kong, twenty or thirty years ago, of all of the views he saw, it would be a good bet that, the one he remembers best was his first sight of a small, slender, beautiful Chinese girl, strolling demurely along, dressed in a form-fitting Chinese Cheongsam made of exquisite silk, with the sides of the skirt slit to her mid-thigh! The feminine Cheongsam is uniquely Chinese, and no European woman can wear one successfully.

Outsiders, especially in Britain, have always taken a keen, if covert, interest in the sex life of Hong Kong, especially between Chinese and Europeans. In the past, in Britain, there have been intermittent public outbursts of prurience, disguised as moral outrage, at a variety of perceived breaches of 'the standards of morality (sex!) observed (in public) by all right-thinking (English public school) decent (not foreign) God-fearing (British) people!' These insular tantrums always provided much innocent amusement to Britain's more broad-minded European neighbours, especially the Latins, who were able to view, objectively, the Britishers calm acceptance of the slaughter and subjugation of thousands of people world-wide, in the name of the Christian Empire, but could be roused to a state of irrational hysteria at the mere suggestion of a bit of inter-racial nooky!

Even now, British hypocrisy is alive and well. In a country where approximately 170 000 innocent babies are aborted every year, people express horror when told of dry wells used in old Chinese villages for the disposal of unwanted girl babies. The new born baby girl would be lowered to the bottom of the well, in a straw basket and left there to die; different technology, same result!

In the old Chinese families a son was essential to the continuation of the family blood, name, and lineage, as in Europe. Where a son's status, differed, materially in China, was that only a male child could carry out the necessary religious rituals to ensure the welfare of his deceased ancestors in the afterlife. Girls married out of the family completely, usually at a financial loss because of her dowry, taking her blood and name, and exchanging her ancestral duties for those of her new family. Boys were a gain, girls a loss.

In 1878, the first eruption of British moral indignation at Hong Kong, triggered off in the Motherland, occurred when the traditional Chinese Mui Tsai custom was criticised; and condemned by officials as akin to slavery. Mui Tsai were young girls, sold by their poor parents to richer people as servants. They were oriental Cinderellas, basically household drudges. The Colony's officials were responding to complaints that the girls were being sold into prostitution in Singapore, Indonesia, and in other islands in the East. Some were even being shipped off to brothels in America and Australia, when they reached puberty and outgrew their role as skivvies. Many were, hurriedly, sold as soon as the Number 1 wife in the house noticed that her menfolk were 'eyeing-up', the formerly ignored, household menial. Through, despised, European intermediaries, a brisk trade in girls, with its own trade jargon, and differential pricing system, and agreed trade descriptions, was carried on not just from Hong Kong, but also from China. As with horse traders, complete physical descriptions were given, down to the most intimate detail. From the top of her head to the soles of her feet she would be examined and, like a horse, certified free of defects and disease before her export price was decided. Virgins fetched a premium, the younger the virgin the higher the premium. There seemed to be an insatiable market of men, who could only be satisfied when deflowering young virgins, and who would bid big money, against each other, in grotesque hymeneal auctions, for the privilege!

Morality and repugnance at what seemed virtual slavery was the basic case, put by government, to the traditionalist Chinese who defended the practice of Mui Tsai. Their reply was an oriental raspberry, and a quick response that eight out of ten of the prostitutes, working in the Colony's licensed brothels, had been sold into prostitution without their consent. Also, that the government, with its policy of licensing and inspection, was itself gaining a profit and, in effect, living on immoral earnings like a gang of gorgeously uniformed and bemedalled, colonial pimps!

This was rather unfair, as the Chinese knew that the sole reason for the licensing and inspection was to exercise some control over the brothel keepers, and the possible spread of venereal disease. But it was a, stingingly, effective riposte. It was all a waste of time, anyway, as draft laws for controlling the Mui Tsai system, sent to London for approval, were so amended and diluted, in the House

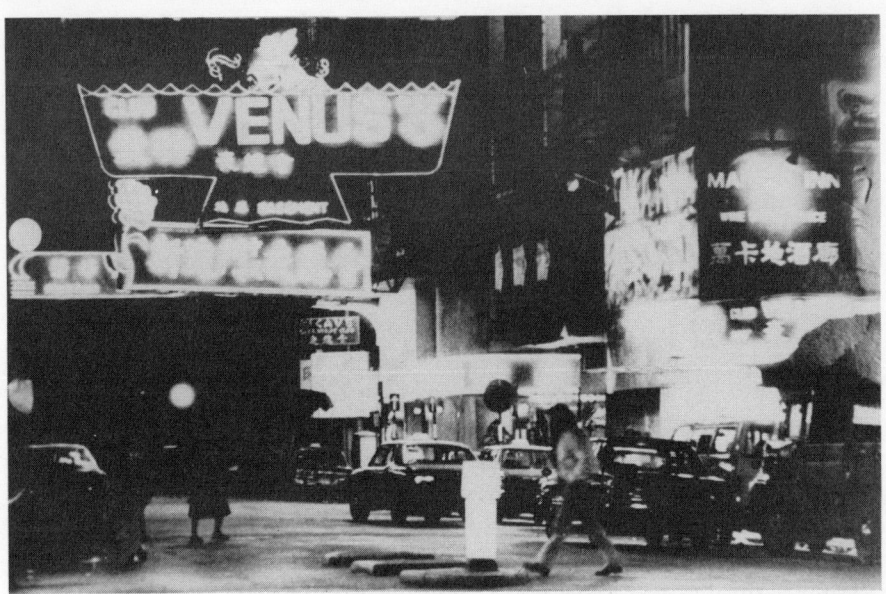

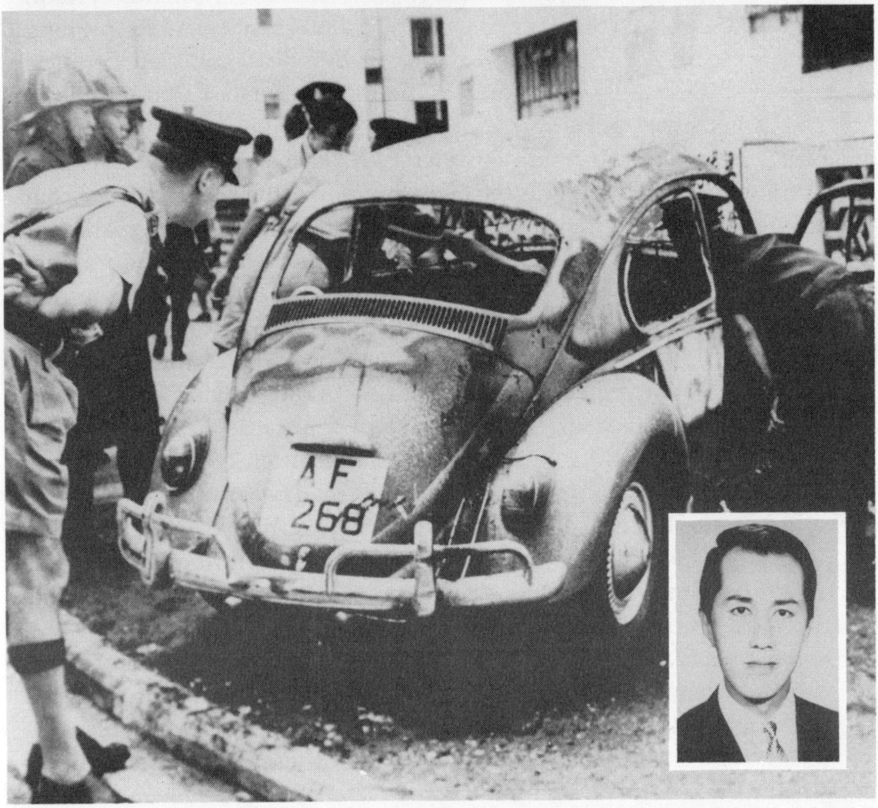

The Hongkong Standard

Top. Wanchai bars at night.
Bottom. Lam Bun, anti-communist satirist and the remains of his car in which he was burned to death.

Left. Inside Kowloon's 'Walled City', some 50 feet below ground level. Here "Ching" was kept as an eight year old sex slave. Above. "Taffy" Hunt on his way to Victoria Court flanked by two ICAC officers.

Ex-Chief Superintendent Peter Godber under ICAC escort arrivest at Court.

of Lords, they were virtually useless. There was one small victory for the girls, The Po Leung Kuk, the Society for the Protection of Virtue, was set up, and undoubtedly helped to reduce the more blatant cases of kidnapping of women and girls for prostitution.

The general attitude of white anglo-saxon society towards prostitutes is, at best, ambivalent. Prostitution would not be the flourishing business that it is, if there was no market for the merchandise on offer. In simple terms of economics, the women, and men, who offer sex in return for payment, are traders offering a service, in return for payment. Most of the world's peoples seem capable of digesting that fact; except for Britain and those countries settled by British colonists and immigrants. Certainly, the Chinese seem open minded about it, possibly on the 'none of my business', principle.

In Britain, prostitutes are generally seen, subjectively, as lazy sluts too idle to go out and get a decent job, content to lie on their backs having sex with anybody for money, while decent folk strive hard to make a living. These views might be understood in a welfare state but the Far East has no welfare states. Even in *The Constitution of the People's Republic of China* it states, in part: 'The state applies the socialist principles: He who does not work, neither shall he eat.' That just about sums up the general principles of life in the real world of the East.

Family comes first in Hong Kong life, family is central to living, family is love, welfare, social identity, security, health service, unemployment refuge, old age pension, and decent burial when the striving is over. The majority of girls in the sex for money business in Hong Kong, were not in it because they were lazy, or for their own enrichment, but because they, alone, out of their whole family, had a commodity that could be sold frequently enough, and for long enough, at a price sufficient to pay the rent, support the family, pay for education for brothers and sisters until they were qualified and in a position to take over the responsibility . . . their commodity was themselves, their youth and beauty, and their skill in entertaining and in love-making.

As Officer Commanding Bars and Brothels in Wanchai it was evident to me, that hundreds of girls worked in all the variations of giving themselves to men of all nations, for money. But even in the oldest profession there were grades of excellence and prestige, and a girl's standing could be broadly judged from her place of employment.

Hong Kong has almost certainly a greater selection of superb nightclubs, providing superb entertainment, food and wines, at reasonable prices, than any other place in the world.It is in these clubs that you are likely to see the mistresses, of rich men. Contrary to the old Chinese custom of mistresses just waiting at home to serve her lover, in Hong Kong, many of the women had a business, or were engaged in show business as an actress or singer. Some of the women were wildly successful as popular 'stars', but still maintained their original agreement with their lover. Others split up with their lovers when they achieved personal success much to the joy of the Hong Kong Chinese 'Mosquito' press, mini-tabloids devoted to sex, scandal, corruption allegations, sport, and general tittle-tattle.

One beautiful woman, Lola, who became a friend, gradually told me her story, which was typical and true. Her family had been reasonably successful, middle-class, business people in Shanghai before the Communist revolution. Her father, and mother, had been associated with the Nationalist cause, during the war with Japan, and knew that they had to escape from China or risk almost certain death, for them and their children, at the hands of the local Communists. They could not get to Taiwan, as the Communists exercised a maximum effort to prevent people from crossing to the island so, like thousands of others they set off for Hong Kong from where Lola's father was certain he could get them to Taiwan.It is only some 900 miles from Shanghai to Hong Kong, as the crow flies but can be over 2000 miles as the refugee travels, especially refugees with strong Shanghai accents. After months of travelling and hiding, paying bribes and excessive prices for food and occasional shelter, half-starved, and exhausted they arrived on the coast near Hong Kong. Having bought passage in an illegal immigrant junk with much of their last reserves of cash, they eventually ended up in a shack on a hillside in Bay View District.

Her father soon found, like many other refugee Nationalists, that Taiwan had absolutely no interest in him unless he had wealth or rich relatives, and he qualified on neither count. He was totally unqualified for any job in Hong Kong where, in any case, jobs are generally kept within the family or given to personal friends. He did get some occasional manual work, but his health eventually broke down. Lola's mother, like thousands of other hut dwellers, did piece-work at home, labouring for hours making paper flowers, sewing dresses, and other work, but the money she made barely kept them all alive.

Lola had already reached puberty and was showing the early signs of her eventual beauty when she caught the eye of a well known 'Madam', also Shanghainese, while on an errand in the market with her mother. After much discussion there and in the Madam's luxurious flat Lola was 'apprenticed' to the Madam who would become her tutor in the arts of love, her agent, and her manager. She quickly found out from the other girls that she had been lucky in being taken on by a good Mamasan, who was strict, but fair, with the girls.

Lola was a virgin and understood that her virginity would be sold and she dreaded the prospect of being deflowered, having heard hair-raising stories about the pain and blood involved in the act, but she was so grateful for the money advance that had already been given to her mother, she promised that she would be brave and not make too much fuss when the time came. She was amazed when Mamasan burst out laughing and told her that she could be as noisy, and make as much fuss as she liked, as long as she, eventually, allowed the man to penetrate her.

Mamasan explained that she had a list of special clients, all of them rich men and all unknown to each other, who were incapable of enjoying the full fruits of love-making with an experienced woman. They could only achieve a 'cloud burst', an orgasm, with a young inexperienced virgin, and the younger and more frightened the virgin girl seemed, the better they enjoyed it! In fact, she was told, with good training in the art of being 'deflowered', she could be kept in the 'timid virgin' price list for half a year! Lola proved to be an excellent actress and managed to stay in the list for a year. She only had to give up the virgin act because her breasts began to grow to an extent that would have cast doubt on her youth and inexperience. Her last client as a 'virgin', she claimed, was a highly respected member of the legal profession!

She remembered vividly the night she 'lost her cherry'. She had been well trained and knew what to expect but she still felt apprehensive as she sat in the discreetly furnished lounge of Mamasan's large flat awaiting the arrival of the man who would take her virginity.

At one stage she got up and looked at herself in a large mirror and had a fit of the giggles, she was dressed in the full school uniform of one of the most respected Missionary girls' schools in the Colony, school hat with hat band, hair in two long pigtails with neatly tied bows, a blouse type shirt and blazer worn with a gym slip dress, stockings, and sensible shoes, underneath she wore a vest and school knickers, nothing like the *femmes fatales* seen in the currently popular movies.

She was sitting down again when Mamasan brought her first client into the room. She was surprised. She had expected a much older man would be first, but this was quite a young and good looking Chinese who, she later found out, came from one of the richest families in Hong Kong. They had China tea, with Lola sitting sipping her tea as any demure Chinese maiden would, with her eyes cast down and speaking only when spoken to. Eventually Mamasan led the way to the bedroom escorting an, apparently, reluctant Lola. The bedroom was luxuriously furnished, dimly lit with expensive Chinese lamps, and the bed was a sumptuous invitation to love-making. She left them together, quietly closing the door.

All the years later, when she told me the story, Lola smiled at her memory of that night and said, how grateful she had been that Mamasan had arranged that particular young man to introduce her to the physical act of love. He had been kind and gentle, he had taken his time as he undressed her, he had lain in the bed with her accustoming her to the feel of his naked maleness touching her, kissing her 'pimple' breasts and giving her intimate caresses for the first time in her life, creating strange feelings she had never before experienced. When the time came for him to enter her the pain was sharp, sharp enough for her to respond and cry out, naturally, but not so sharp as seriously to distress her. He made love to her once more before leaving.

On a practical note, he gave the Mamasan a bonus as he had enjoyed himself. As soon as he had gone, Mamasan, and some of the other girls, burst into the room to see how Lola was, and hear all the details of her 'cherry picking'. After showering and cleaning herself up, Lola, a bit sore and feeling well introduced to love-making, joined with the others in an impromptu party incongruously like the illicit midnight feasts in English public schools for girls. Mamasan was in her own way running a school, but it was a school for professional love-makers!

In the course of that first year, Lola made ten times more money, tax free, as a reluctant 'cherry' girl than she could have as a civil servant, or a schoolteacher. After Mamasan's share had been deducted she had enough of her earnings left to buy her father and mother a small food shop. She helped her brothers and sisters through school. She was a very clever young woman and lucky with her Mamasan who helped all her sensible girls to invest wisely for what she called wrinkle time! Lola invested wisely in property and legitimate businesses, and 'retired' from Hong Kong at the age of twenty-seven! When I last saw her she was leaving for the USA to get married. A wealthy former 'business' woman, departing for a new life with a decent man, who knew all about her past, but understood about Hong Kong.

For Ching, things were quite different. Her introduction to sex came, with the cruel violence of rape, at the age of eight, when she was sold to a procurer in Kowloon Walled City. She could not even understand what was happening to her, only that a horrible, fat, greasy, old, man, was using her in a way that hurt, and hurt horribly. That became the pattern of her life day and night, week after week, interminably. She was used for oral sex, and anal sex, whatever the customer was willing to pay for; she was a sex 'thing' for sale, sometimes to two men at the same time. Any reluctance on her part to do as she was told, was met with sadistic punishment, so severe, that she would do anything for it to stop. She could not even remember faces, they were just a grunting, heaving, sweating, blur.

When she approached the age of puberty, she was given injections to retard her development, as the place she was in, catered only for the 'little girl' trade. She might have stayed where she was, until sold on to a brothel, but an unusual police sweep through the warrens of the Walled City created such confusion and panic, she managed to escape into the open, for the first time, since she had been taken to that horrible place.

She had one piece of good fortune, she came into the care of religious people who were preparing her for a new life, far from the Walled City. She was an intensely self-contained, quiet, waif-like, little person, who stilled into wary immobility whenever any man went near her. Her age could only be estimated but it was believed that she was about thirteen or fourteen years old when she escaped. She had been sold, as many as fifteen times, daily, or more for five years, for sex acts that would not be performed by animals. The good lady, who was looking after her, was a gentle soul but her voice shook with intense anger when she said to me she hoped, God forgive her, that the men who used her would roast in hell for eternity. When I hear, academically correct, psychiatric explanations, put forward in mitigation of the acts of a child molester, I think of Ching and how she froze into immobility when I walked past her, and agree with the good lady's hope that they roast in hell, and I beg no forgiveness for the thought!

Janey was a tiny Cantonese girl, with a chest like Jayne Mansfield! Her story was different, but still a typical Hong Kong story. She had been married at sixteen, and had a daughter, but her husband had been killed, as a casual worker, on a building site with non-existent building safety regulations. She was left with no money, a young daughter, and her aged mother-in-law to look after. She had no qualifications, and no chance of any job, that would pay enough to support her family, so she became a bar girl.

Chinese girls who do not speak any English can rarely get such work, as most of the business is done with visiting foreigners, but the owner of one of the biggest bars in Wanchai took one look at her enormous bust, something that had always caused her embarrassment as a Chinese girl, and took her on. She was an immediate success, especially with American sailors, and soon picked up enough English with which to get along. She was a sensible girl who looked after her money wisely, and she made very good money. As a bar girl she could cater for as many customers, or as few, as she wished. If she didn't like the looks of a man she did not have to go with him, the choice of sexual partners was hers. The bar owner's main interest was that people were encouraged to stay in the bar and pay for drinks and food. If he was lucky a customer would buy his bar girl companion a 'champagne cocktail' or two, usually a mixture of 7-Up and juice with two cherries on a toothpick added to make it look like a cocktail, good enough to convince a well-oiled big spender! If a bar girl took a customer out for a time and then returned, the police could not accuse the bar owner of any offence. Whoever a girl went out with and what they did together was their own business. Most weeks she made more money than a police constable's pay for a month. She had a wicked sense of humour, an infectious giggle, and the funniest spoken English ever heard. The Triads left her alone because she had many European friends in the police force, friends not clients, maybe because of her Jayne Mansfield look. She achieved every bar girl's dream. She met, liked, and married a nice American man and went to live in the USA with him, her daughter, and her old mother in law. The American got a bargain, she was a super woman.

There are however, Chinese women too, who go into prostitution because they are lazy, greedy, or stupid. Among the stupid must be counted those who get conned by a pimp, hooked on heroin and become prostitutes to feed their habit. I met one in my early days in the force when I was working in Tsim Sha Tsui. Hers was an almost classic story. When she was younger she was working in a restaurant as a 'Dim Sum' girl, walking around with a tray slung from her neck selling tasty dumpling appetisers. The work was quite hard with long hours, low pay, and men always trying to 'feel her up' as she passed with her tray. One young fellow came in a few times and got to know her. Before long she was sleeping with him, and not long after that he had her working as a prostitute. He introduced her to heroin and got her hooked but soon became tired of her as the heroin took its toll. She had ended up in the side streets of Tsim Sha Tsui as a street-walker. Her identity card showed her as being twenty-eight years old and I had thought that she was at least fifty. She had died of an overdose, apparently taken deliberately. Nothing glamorous about such a uselessly spent life.

Even the sailors left aboard the merchant ships on duty were not neglected by the business girls, they could have their 'bunk comforts'. Seamen calling at Hong Kong regularly, usually had steady 'girl friends' who slept with them on board, and took the occasional trip ashore with them, during the ship's stay in port for a mutually agreed fee. The fact that the love making and companionship were paid for, did not alter the fact that both enjoyed the relationship. Some of these girls eventually married their partners and escaped from Hong Kong. Other girls were one-nighters, who would ply their trade from Walla Walla water taxis. These girls were subject to be detained and questioned by Harbour Police, as some were, not just prostitutes, but also went on board ship to spy out anything that could be stolen and sold for a profit by harbour thieves, who paid them for information. Because of this, Marine Police officers had legal authority to board and inspect ships in the harbour at any time.

During one such inspection, I boarded a Dutch ship late one evening, and made my way to the cabin of the First Officer, who was in charge of the vessel, in the absence of his senior officers who were ashore. The Indonesian steward, who spoke no English, directed me to the cabin with a gesture that I took to be an invitation to enter, which I did. It was a large and comfortable cabin, typical of those provided by good Dutch shipping companies for ships' officers engaged in long trading voyages through the Indonesian archipelago and the islands. The light was dim but I could see the officer's bare white bottom going rhythmically up and down as he made love to a Chinese girl in his bunk, and I could hear their heavy breathing and impassioned love murmurs! I was preparing to make a hasty, embarrassed, retreat when the young officer, without interrupting his rhythm, grinned at me over his shoulder, invited me to have a drink in the officers' mess, told me he would be with me soon; and turned his full attention back to the pleasure in hand. He and the girl were not bothered by my intrusion on their privacy, but I was deeply mortified and red-faced. They both joined me in the saloon shortly afterwards, and I squirmed inwardly, while we chatted casually over coffee, and while I informed him that my men were checking the ship for unlawful boarders.

It was not just girls who sold their favours, there were male prostitutes too; the glamorised gigolos. As more jet aircraft went into service with the world's airlines, and Hong Kong became more popular as an exotic place for a vacation, the market for commercial sex expanded with all the other service industries in the Colony, to include foreign women. The greater freedoms being enjoyed generally by the emancipated women of the 1960s, and the invention of the 'Pill', gave them the opportunity to enjoy the sexual freedoms historically enjoyed only by men. The 'double standard' formerly applied, by which a man who screwed around was a virile character but a woman who had sex out of wedlock was a slut, bit the dust.

Rich English women had, traditionally, discreetly enjoyed the services of handsome, well-skilled, male prostitutes, in places such as Alexandria in Egypt, while on 'educational archaeological tours' of the Middle East. Many of the female visitors to Hong Kong sought similar services, and they were provided, at a price.

The most popular women, with the gigolos, were the American women who were more down to earth, and treated the event more practically, than many women of other nationalities, especially British women, who seemed to feel it necessary to get emotionally involved as a justification for the sexual act.

There was a discreet gigolo-contact service organised through staff in all the main hotels, paralleling the call girl network, through which female clients could make their requirements known. Almost all of them wanted to try out Chinese men but the choices of partners covered all the colours of the human spectrum.

One of the men involved, was crazy about oriental martial arts, and was supporting himself as a gigolo while studying Chinese martial arts in Hong Kong. One evening in the males only bar of the Mandarin Hotel, in response to a passing, and unprurient, remark of mine regarding the number of times men and women, respectively, could perform the Act. He looked up from his restorative glass of Remy Martin and said, wearily 'Never more than twice a night!'

Some of the gigolos tried various chemicals and drugs alleged to aid men to increase their staying power, or to make it possible for them to make love more frequently. Some of these preparations were simple frauds, some involved the drug cocaine, rarely seen in Hong Kong, but all had the same long-term effects, ill health or drug addiction. The clientele seemed to go away satisfied with their sexual adventures, perhaps just the fact of having had a fling, but the gigolos never lasted for long.

Despite the impression that may given that only Chinese women gave their favours for money, it is well known in the Colony that there has never been any shortage of European women available, at a price, for the enjoyment of men of Chinese, Philippino, Indian, Malay, Japanese, Korean, and other non-European races. Some of these women, like the women of Hong Kong's, unwanted, penniless, White Russian refugee community, who made it to the Colony after an epic 2000 mile journey of deprivation and occasional rape, had no other means of making money to support their families in their barren refugee camp accommodation.

Most of the others had no justifiable reason, if one was needed, for being 'call girls'. Many of them were, reputedly, the wives and daughters of men in government and military service, or working in banks and companies, earning good salaries. For the White Russian women it was sex for family survival, for the others it seemed to be sex for luxuries, from the boredom engendered by having too many servants, for kicks, to spite husbands who were having affairs with Chinese women, for money to go home with, occasionally to make up for compulsive spending and living beyond their considerable means, and sometimes because the husband was too poorly paid to live reasonably in a place as expensive as Hong Kong.

The White Russian women, traditionally, operated discreetly from places such as the Tea Lounge of the famous Peninsula Hotel in Kowloon, not far from their camp. Much credit must go to the hoteliers for turning a blind eye to their genteelly conducted negotiations in the afternoons, over tea, and biscuits, in the evenings over cocktails, with cherries in them. Any assignations arranged in the hotel were rarely ever consummated on the premises.

Other European women reputedly had an efficient contact network, which was never broken into by the police possibly because it could have been too embarrassing politically, but it was rumoured to have been organised by a female beautician who made initial contact in the course of her legitimate profession. There was at one time a quiver of excitement on the gossip circuit at the rumour that the wives of two government officials had been accidentally caught naked in a three-in-a-bed situation with a rich Indian businessman by police investigating another matter, the alleged fee of £5000 being quoted as verification, but nothing came of it. If it did happen it was carefully hushed up, but, as the cynics, European and Oriental, said . . . it would be wouldn't it! However, all of the gossips, in good standing, carefully watched the divorce announcements for months afterwards!

Scandal did not just affect the European women, there was gossip enough about a rumoured homosexual scandal that allegedly involved some of the most highly placed Europeans in the Colony, Chinese boys and young Chinese men. This was at a time when homosexual practices, especially with boys, was a serious criminal offence. Nothing was ever disclosed officially but it is to be hoped that the man generally identified as the Investigator, Taff Hunt, may someday write his own version of events.

At the time Taff was the Divisional Detective Inspector in charge of CID Wanchai; an extrovert, good at his job, but equally good at annoying prim-faced senior officers, with his down to earth, Welsh Valley's insistence on calling a spade a bloody spade. He was also guilty of the sin of being loyal to his friends.

While in the North point area, in a place much frequented late at night by actors, actresses, nightclub floor show people, courtesans, call girls, and Hong Kong's various bohemian characters, in the course of an investigation into a unrelated crime, it was said, Taff came across evidence of a homosexual organisation. Evidence that was so serious it could not be ignored. If true, it implicated Europeans of very high standing in business, government, the legal profession, even, it was said with bated breath, the police!

He, quite properly, took his initial evidence to an honest senior officer, who was, reportedly, shaken by the implications of a huge scandal such as had not been seen since the Victorian period, and he quite properly instructed Taff to follow it up. If true, this would have been horrifying news for anyone involved as Taff did his CID work, digging away stubbornly against all opposition, with the same determination as his Welsh miner forbears dug at the coal hidden in the secret ground of the valleys of Wales.

With the best will in the world, such enquiries could not be kept completely secret, and rumours began to circulate. Stories began to be told of young boys' 'cherries' being auctioned to rich Europeans, among others, at secret drinks parties, where the drinks were served by the bathed and perfumed naked Chinese boys whose virginity was to be auctioned, so that the prospective buyers could touch and examine the goods before buying. Some of the buyers were allegedly so well known that they wore silk masks or dark glasses to conceal their identity from strangers. However, they apparently seemed to know each other well. Most of the boys were said to come from very poor families who were paid more for them than for a girl, but some, it was suggested, had been accidentally separated from illegal immigrant parents trying to get into the colony, and had been picked up by touts who found them begging in markets, and sleeping rough.

Other stories painted a lurid picture of communal sexual orgies, such as the so-called Conga Circle, where a group would form a close circle, each penetrating the person in front of him while being simultaneously penetrated himself by the man behind, continuing in this fashion until all were satisfied, and tales of other orgies involving groups of men, youths, and boys, having sex together, swapping partners and roles at will.

This was all glorious grist to the gossip mill to be told in strict confidence, and with oaths of secrecy, to only a dozen or so of the raconteur's best friends, at a time! Gradually a more sinister element began to slip into the titillating tales of sexual perversion in high places. It began to be rumoured that this was not just another story of Triads providing sex for money. It was hinted that China's equivalent of the KGB was deeply involved . . . then the rumours abruptly stopped.

Later, it was widely said that Taff Hunt, had compiled a massively detailed report, buttressed with verifiable facts, that incriminated scores of the top people in the Colony, and that he had suddenly been ordered to stop his investigation and take his report, every statement, photographs, crime diaries, lists of events and addresses, any tape-recordings, everything, even a list of every officer who been involved in the case, and deliver them personally by hand to a senior officer in Police Headquarters. This certainly seemed to be so, as afterwards he resumed his normal work.

Not long after he was promoted and transferred. In fact there was quite a flurry of transfers, some with promotion and some without. People waited for the results of the investigation and the report to become known . . . and waited . . . and waited . . . and are still waiting! If all the rumours were true, and if such a report existed, it is interesting to speculate in whose safe it is lying now, if it hasn't been destroyed. Maybe Taff knows? Did he really hand over all the documents, without keeping a single copy? It stirred quite a flurry of well-concealed speculation some years later when both Taff, then a Superintendent, and the very tough Peter Godber, a Chief Superintendent, were sent to prison on corruption charges. Could there have been any connection with their well known disgust at the cover up and the so easily discovered 'evidence' presented against them at their separate corruption trials?

Chinese girls are not necessarily as obedient and compliant as many European myths suggest. Some Chinese men of experience are ready to advise you 'Better pull a tiger's tail than argue with an angry woman'.

In the Inspectors' quarters in some of the older police stations, baths were taken in what were known as Shanghai bathtubs. These tubs were like huge, thick-sided, plum pudding bowls made of painted and decorated, baked clay. The room boys would roll them into one's large bed-sitting-room and fill them up with hot water then leave you to enjoy a soak. It was said that if you were so inclined, there was plenty of room in the tub for your girl friend to join you, and enough sweet-smelling Chinese bath foam to cover you both when the hot water top-ups were delivered in response to your bell by grinning room boys.

My room was very big, with a large verandah, set three floors above ground level, looking out towards the harbour. The view was splendid on a bright day, as seen from my position, lolling at ease in the hot tub with a drink in my hand.

The outlines of the verandah made the view look like a painting, with a shaped frame made of brick and plaster, until a pair of bare feet appeared at the top of the frame, followed by a pair of rather thin legs, followed by the lower portion of a naked, obviously very male, body, then the rest of the body, dripping wet. It was my upstairs neighbour, who shall be known as Mark, hanging at the full stretch of his arms, stark naked and dripping water three floors down to the concrete below. He was a very skinny chap at the best of times, but hanging as he was, he looked like a plucked, drawn, cockerel, just out of the boiling pot.

He was very English, very polite, and well-spoken, and he said in a rather strained voice, 'I'll explain it all later but may I drop in please old chap?'

Coming from a fellow hanging in the air, naked, about seventy feet above the ground I thought that approach was really quite good.

Taking my nod as an affirmative he began swinging to and fro in order to drop on to my verandah. To have tried to help him could have proved lethal and, in any case, he had tumbled in on to the floor in an obviously exhausted but relieved heap by the time I could get out of the bath.

He was immediately given a bath towel and a brandy and, without any questions asked, offered a chair. He gulped his brandy and gratefully accepted another, while displaying extreme nervousness, jumping at every sound, looking up at the ceiling and quivering every time there was a faint noise from above, looking in general like a well qualified candidate for a five-star nervous breakdown. He took a cigarette held it in shaking fingers, took a huge drag of smoke and began, 'Y'know my girlfriend Jackie?' This was an absolutely gorgeous Shanghainese girl, sometimes seen on the stairs, who had a share in a Travel Agency. 'Well y'know she is in Singapore at present?' No I did not know, but why spoil what promised to be an interesting story, I nodded. 'Well,' he said despairingly, 'she ain't,' and he looked upwards. It did not take an Einstein to work out that the gorgeous, and notoriously short-tempered Jackie was not in the Lion City but upstairs.

It appeared that the unfortunate Mark had been enjoying a bath but not in virtuous privacy like myself, he had a female companion! The bath was hot, as was his partner, apparently, when he heard a voice that chilled his blood . . . Jacqueline's.

He told me that his life had flashed in front of his eyes as a drowning man's is supposed to do, and all he could think of was escape. Pausing only to tell his companion to bail out when she could, he had exited via the verandah, ignoring the drop, as that at least would be quick, compared to the fate he feared at the hands of an enraged Jackie.

He had got this far, when we heard footsteps approaching my door. Mark blanched, and dived into my wardrobe, which was out of the direct line of view of the door. In response to a knock, I opened the door and stood in the doorway dressed in my bath robe rubbing my wet hair with a towel as she asked me something in Shanghainese, too angry to remember to speak English, clutching the biggest pair of scissors I have ever seen in her right hand. Mark's apparent terror seemed quite understandable. She was so angry she lost patience with me and stormed off.

A few minutes later her car roared out of the compound and away. Mark fell out of my wardrobe trembling with relief, and we went up to his room, once he had been reassured that she had really left. The room was an amazing sight, we both stood in the middle of it and looked around in awe. There was nothing in it larger than one inch square in size. Clothes, uniforms, bedding, towels, belts, shirts, underwear, curtains, of the shoes only the soles remained, Jackie had done a superb and detailed demolition job. Mark sighed, then held the bath towel out, slightly, looked down at himself, and smiling commented, 'she didn't get that at least'. The rest of the stuff he could buy, but if she had got 'that'! He shuddered.

In northern Kowloon was the 'suburb' of Kowloon Tong, about the only place of its kind in the whole Colony. There were, at the time, no high rise apartments, just low buildings and mini-mansions. The buildings were low by legislation as the area was directly in one line of approach to the airport at Kai Tak. The houses were very expensive, very well designed, luxurious, and discreetly situated, each in its own little garden. On one road there arose an elaborate Indian palace of a place, on another a miniature English country house, film stars such as Bruce Lee, and other popular people from the entertainment industry made it Hong Kong's copy of Beverly Hills, except for the fact that it was flat.

Tucked quietly away at the end of one of the more secluded streets in Kowloon Tong was a long two storey building, elegantly built, and well concealed from view by a high wall topped with daggers of broken glass and barbed wire.

Access to the property was through a pair of massively strong but aesthetically decorated iron gates, set one behind the other, so that a car could enter through one set of gates but would then have to remain between the gates, like a sheep in a sheep crush, until the inner gates were opened.

Inside, the garden was tended by a female Hakka gardener and was screened by trees and shrubs with displays of flowers all the year round, many of them grown in beautiful Chinese jardinières, some almost as high as a man. The interior of the house was a decorator's dream come true, as it should have been, for the amount of money it had cost the owner to fly the famous man to Hong Kong to supervise the creation of his own design.

Unusually for Hong Kong there was even a small but functional indoor swimming pool, and a brightly tiled children's paddling pool. There were no real little children in this house though, but there were numerous stunningly beautiful women, some of whom, the Chinese girls especially, could look like ten or twelve year olds when required to do so.

Lola's 'Madam' had achieved her ambition to move from Northpoint to a private house in a select area where she would cater only for the very rich, very famous, very powerful, men who wanted their sexual needs, fantasies, and desires catered for secretly, and were prepared to pay for the privilege.

She knew that wealth and power were usually the rewards gained by men impelled by powerful drives to success, and that such men normally had powerful sex drives too. Other men who reached high positions by influence, class, or inherited wealth, frequently had sex urges that were so specialised, they needed help.

Madam's regular clientele could have filled a volume of *Who's Who* of the world's famous men. Many of the, male, world figures seen in newsreels and whose photographs regularly appeared in the London *Times*, *New York Times*, *Herald Tribune*, *Time*, *Life*, and other international publications, at one time or another, strolled into Madam's reception lounge to enjoy vintage champagne, and a superb, cigar while making their sexual requirements known, and the selection was very wide. There was a basic rule, however, any form of sado-masochism that could cause real harm to anyone was totally excluded.

The type usually asked for by upper class Englishmen was available, for example, the man wishing to be placed face down over the arm of a leather chair with his trousers pulled down, being spanked by girls dressed like middle-class Englishwomen of the 1920s and 1930s, with the difference that the girls' clothes were so arranged that the 'victim' could see their bare breasts and naked pubic region as he was being 'punished'.

The range and variety of the fantasies of the men involved were truly remarkable. The children's paddling pool with its cartoon character tiles, was used almost exclusively in sexual romps by rich American men. They played childish games in the nude with a selection of Madam's tinier girls, who could be easily provided with the necessary bathing costumes of the period, from her vast costume and props department, that could have served equally well for a small film studio.

One fantastically rich client from the Middle East, who had been educated in England as a boy, and whose official life was filled with legions of the most beautiful and compliant women in his land, came from time to time to visit his favourite girl in the house.

She was a lovely girl of mixed Chinese and Malay blood who could look plainer and primmer than a Deacon of the Free Presbyterian Church when the occasion demanded. For him she wore no make up, her beautiful long black hair was brushed flat and secured just above the neck in a tight bun. She was dressed plainly in what used to be, between the wars, almost a female school mistress's uniform, plain white blouse, with a single strand of pearls, buttoned up to the neck, a sensible skirt with pleats at the back reaching down to mid-calf, plain Lyle stockings and flat highly polished shoes secured by firmly tied laces, on her wrist a plain gold watch with Roman numerals and a brown leather strap. Only the underwear departed from the outer appearance, she wore a sensuously provocative French silk brassière and silk French knickers.

The scenario was always the same. She sat alone in a room at a tea table on which was set an English afternoon tea. He would knock at the door and she would call for him to enter, as he did so she would sit with her feet tucked primly together and her dress pulled tightly down over her knees. She served tea and went through the routine of offering sandwiches, biscuits, and cakes to her polite 'little boy' guest. Things would gradually change.

At an appropriate moment she would complain quietly that her shoe laces were too tight and her feet were hurting. He would immediately kneel on the floor, untie the shoe laces, take off her shoes and gently rub her feet. Next, the bun in her hair was undone letting in flow down her back. Then the blouse was unbuttoned leaving the pearl necklace round her neck. The skirt was removed next, followed by the Lyle stockings which were slowly rolled down her legs by the client, accompanied by intimate kisses. They kissed and caressed for a time before he removed her underwear, leaving her naked save for the string of pearls which were never removed.

She then undressed him exchanging passionate caresses all the time. He then lowered her to the carpet covered with scatter cushions and they engaged in extended and passionate love play until, at the appropriate moment, they joined together and she brought him to a climax. Sometimes they made love more than once but his departure always followed the same pattern.

When they had finished, he watched her as she dressed as she had been when he entered the room, even to the bun in her hair and the laced up shoes, and as he left he always said 'Goodbye Miss. Thank you for my tea.' Who could fail to wonder who, if anyone, made such an impression on this powerful man, when he was a lonely young boy, in a foreign land?

One of their fairly regular visitors was, allegedly, a member of the British House of Lords who was described as softly spoken, distinguished, very elegant, obviously from a high class family.

He always telephoned in advance giving the precise time of his proposed visit, so that the chosen girls would be prepared for his arrival. He always arrived on foot, late in the evening, with a small leather bag in his jacket pocket, like the make-up bags ladies used to have in their handbags. After chatting with Madam over champagne he would go to a room and change.

In the small leather case he had a set of ladies underwear, always purchased from the same company, Marks and Spencer. He would strip naked, put on the underwear, then go through a connecting door where four girls were waiting for him clad in long flowing Chinese silk robes.

In the centre of the room was a table with a thick glass top placed over a Chinese carpet and he would politely bid the girls good evening then lie on his back under the table. The girls would then slide off their robes and allow them to fall on the floor revealing that they were naked. Three of them would stand close together astride the table rubbing against each other above the client's head. The fourth would kneel on the floor with her knees either side of his hips, stroking him with her hands and, from time to time, gently rubbing him with her pelvis.

As the girls above his head began to perform their natural functions, which he needed to see, he became sexually aroused and the girl kneeling over him would remove his panties and bring him to the climax the performance was designed to achieve.

The girls liked him very much, calling him a gentleman, and saying that before leaving the house he always thanked each girl personally and gave her a cash gift which was in addition to the fee given to Madam.

These special clients represented only a fraction of her clientele who came to the house for expensive and enjoyable sex with lovely girls of all colours, races, and nationalities, from black to blond; all superbly trained and skilled in the many arts of their profession.

Madam had arrangements with trusted colleagues overseas through whom suitable foreign girls in the business could arrive in Hong Kong for a profitable working holiday and then fly home later with a nice tax-free sum of money tucked away safely through one of Madam's many International Banking contacts.

For her girls, life had nothing in common with the short horrible existence of the poor common prostitutes exploited and bullied by Triads and pimps. Madam's girls all retired in their mid-twenties with nice investment portfolios prepared for them by reputable investment bankers. Many of them had extensive and profitable holdings in property in popular areas of the USA such as California, Florida and, amusingly, in the American Virgin Islands!

THE ONE-EYED DRAGON

Madam retired from the business after a long and profitable life supplying the needs of many men. She had started at the age of eight by being kidnapped and sold into a Shanghai brothel from which she eventually escaped at the age of fourteen. She had been the mistress of a rich man until he died, when she was twenty. Then she had gone into the business herself, as a Madam, to support the children she had borne her dead lover. At the end of the war she had gone to Hong Kong. Her money had always cannily been kept safely abroad and she had the means to start up again in Northpoint.

She always trained her girls well, looked after their interests, physical and financial, and treated them firmly and fairly. She always worked the 'quality' trade not the mass market and so never attracted attention. There was never any problem with Triads, although it had been rumoured that the only one who ever tried was found floating in the Lamma Channel!

She never came to the official attention of the police, although this might have been because both government, and big business, were rumoured to make use of her services for important visitors, when appropriate, during negotiations of great value to the Colony and its prosperity.

It was her children, all married and successful in business, in the USA, who pressed her to retire and enjoy her grandchildren with them, so, like a proper Chinese grandmother, she did as she was asked.

The night before she left Hong Kong she attended a farewell party given for her. The party was attended by what was, possibly,the largest single group of beautiful women ever seen. They were Madam's girls who had flown in from all over the world, a sorority of unique sisters, all successfully living new lives, and all grateful to the little woman they knew as 'Mamasan'. It was quite a Bon voyage!

Eighteen

RIDING A TIGER!

(The problem with riding a tiger is . . .
how do you get off?)

Natural justice demands that a record be made of the names, and political parties, of all those Members of the British Parliament who voted for the racist 1981 British Nationality Act, by means of which more than 3.25 million Hong Kong citizens, born British, as subjects of Her Majesty Queen Elizabeth II, had their legitimate right of abode in the United Kingdom taken from them.

To this list should be added the names of those MPs who, by their silence, absence, or abstention, collaborated in this blatantly racist piece of legislation. The names will almost certainly be needed some time in the not too distant future so that the British public, world opinion, and future historians, will know who the guilty men are when Chinese Communism takes its toll in the 'Hong Kong Autonomous Region'.

It is truly astonishing that, barely forty years after the Nürnberg, and Tokyo, War Crimes Trials, British politicians are handing over millions of innocent Hong Kong people, British by birth but, God help them, Chinese by race, to the tender mercies of the unpredictable masters of tyranny who govern Communist China.

Vidkun Quisling of Norway, and hundreds of other Nazi sympathisers throughout Europe, were executed after the Second World War for collaborating with the Germans, some of them for betraying Jews and other people of 'non-Aryan' races. None of them, to the best of my knowledge, handed over more than 3 000 000 people in one transaction! But the British Government intends to do just that, and is trying to justify this horrifying act of betrayal, by smooth and mealy-mouthed propaganda designed to conceal its racist origins, and give the impression that Hong Kong and its people are being granted a favour.

As in the Europe of the 1930s, this propaganda contains a 'Big Lie' intended to divert attention from a troublesome truth. Again and again it has been said that our 'lease' on Hong Kong expires in 1997 and, as with any lease, the leaseholder has the legal right to have his property back! But the lease is not on Hong Kong, the lease is for the New Territories and the Islands.

Hong Kong Island and the harbour were ceded in perpetuity to Britain in 1841, and this was confirmed by the Treaty of Nanking in 1842. Stonecutters Island, and the Kowloon Peninsula as far as Boundary Street, were given into Britain's legal possession by the Convention of Peking in 1860.

Hong Kong Island, Stonecutters Island, and the Kowloon Peninsula are, by any system of law as we know it, as British as Shetland, Orkney, the Western Isles of Scotland, the Isle of Wight, Anglesey, and the Channel Isles!

Can it be argued then, without racial prejudice, that the people born and brought up as British subjects, in a British Hong Kong, transferred legally to Britain by the Chinese, have less right of abode in Britain than the people in islands transferred to Britain by Scandinavians, annexed by the Kingdom of Wessex, taken from Welshmen by conquest, or inherited by the Sovereign through a Norman dukedom?

The gentlemen of the Foreign Office, and their Masters in Parliament, will, no doubt, immediately go to Plan 'B', and say that, even if the argument given above were correct, and they will never admit that it is, Hong Kong could not exist without the New Territories, and, even if they could, they could not survive without the water and food from Mainland Communist China, deny that if you dare!

China does not donate the food and water, she sells it to Hong Kong at a good price, for payment only in foreign currency which they desperately need, if they are to modernise China's ramshackle economy.

In any case, that would be an extraordinary argument to hear from people who have been conducting an unremitting campaign to convince the people of Britain, and Hong Kong, that the men they have been dealing with in Peking are really decent chaps, neo-democrats at heart, who only have the long term interests of the people at heart, and guarantee, Scout's honour, that nothing will be changed in the Hong Kong Autonomous Region. Have these chaps in Peking said, in so many words, that they would cut off the food and water they sell to Hong Kong to starve the people there into submission?

If they have said as much, have the British Foreign Office people warned the overseas investors who have been pouring huge sums of money into joint ventures with the Chinese, supplying the essential capital for development that forty years of Communism could not earn? Have they threatened to invade?

Have they said that they would gladly lose the 30 per cent to 40 per cent of their total foreign exchange income earned through the colony, and sabotage their own 40 per cent or so, investment stake in industry, property, and financial services to have back a chunk of land representing less than 0.000025 per cent of China's land mass?

Was any attempt made to renew the lease at the very beginning of negotiations? After all, that is the basic first step when a lease is running out isn't it? If not, why not?

With all the government inspired information about how good and fair the administration of the Hong Kong Autonomous Region will be, has any thought been given to China's record in the other Autonomous Region recently in the news, Tibet?

According to some independent sources at least 1 000 000 Tibetans have been killed by their Chinese masters, hundreds of thousands of others deported to do hard labour in China, tens of thousands forcibly deprived of their land, businesses, homes, which were than handed over to mainland Chinese incomers, their temples were destroyed and their religion proscribed.

But, the British government might say, we have a written agreement, not enforceable naturally, but nevertheless signed by the Chinese. Chamberlain had a bit of paper signed by Hitler and much good that did anybody!

As this is being written more than 6000 peaceful, and patriotic, protesters, asking for a halt to corruption and nepotism, and some democratic reforms, have just been massacred in Tien Ah Min Square in Peking by their own countrymen, soldiers in the, grotesquely misnamed, People's Liberation Army. The corrupt old men who ordered this mass murder are sitting safely in luxury barely hundreds of yards from the scene of this totally unjustifiable slaughter of the idealistic innocents. The same men with whom the British Foreign Office people drink tea, as they decide the fate of millions of decent people in Hong Kong.

Meantime, in the United Kingdom, a senior Conservative politician, and a senior Labour politician discuss the massacre of Tien Ah Min Square on television. Being reasonable chaps they seem to agree that, yes it was a bit nasty, and all those idealistic, and rather dead, young men and women students lying about the place were a bit upsetting, but, after all, China is a big country to govern, and the government had to reassert its authority in its own capital, don't you know, and the British Parliament would still have to deal with the old men in power, and Hong Kong must be got rid of as quietly as possible.

Both of these men have long been highly respected politicians, one served with honour fighting Nazism in the British army, the other is Jewish, and neither seemed aware of the incongruity of the words that were coming out of their mouths!

For those with the eyes to read between the lines the message is sickeningly clear, we are hoping to do big-money business with China, and we do not want to take the risk that over 3 000 000 Hong Kong Chinese might come to Britain!

What makes it more awful and immoral, if that is possible, is that the general response from the right to the left of the British Parliamentary spectrum is so blatantly, sickeningly racist, and the racism is directed against millions of the Queen's most loyal, law-abiding, and fanatically hard-working subjects, the Hong Kong Chinese!

Who are the people that the British Parliament are so terrified might use a right of abode as a licence to come to Britain? The basic Hong Kong Chinese was either a refugee from China, or the child of a refugee. The basic creation of Hong Kong from a heap of overcrowded rocks to a world league business and financial centre was the work of these people, and a few examples of their energy and determination might cause wonder that we do not seem to want them here, officially!

One man and his father arrived one night wearing their only possessions, a pair of underpants, dripping wet from their swim from the Mainland. Within ten years they owned and ran one of the most successful textile businesses in the world, bringing millions of dollars in foreign exchange into Hong Kong, and putting millions in business into the UK. At the last reckoning all of their enterprises were estimated to be worth at least £300 million. No freeloaders on any welfare state them!

Another arrived in a snake (illegal immigrant) boat with his wife and child; laboured as a coolie for a while to get a bit of capital. Found an old tyre iron, and a broken shoe last, got a couple of boxes, bought a sharp knife and went into business in a scavenging lane, making rubber soled 'flip flop' sandals for coolies out of thrown away car tyres. He made a bit more money and went in to the leather shoe business in a rented space at the bottom of a flight of stairs in a tenement in Tsim Sha Tsui, where I first met him. Within seven years he had his own plant employing over 200 workers, and he was making quality leather products as 'own label' goods for some of the best known retailing businesses in America and Europe.

Another started off as a rickshaw coolie and went in for repairing broken rickshaws with primitive tools. He repaired abandoned broken rickshaws and rented them out. He went on to become the founder and owner of one of the colony's biggest transport groups.

Another 'jumped the wire' on the frontier when sent there in the Chinese Army; got a boat building and furniture-making business going in Aberdeen. He went into construction and built airfields all over the Far East. He ended up in business in the USA. The list is endless, and these energetic, entrepreneurial, good, people are the cause of panic in the Mother of Parliaments. What on earth are they afraid of? Are they scared that they may all come here and make this an incredibly successful country?

We recently fought a justified, but bloody, and expensive, war for the Falkland Islands, and we have spent, and are spending, millions to keep its 2000 odd inhabitants British. No reasonable person can cavil at that it is just and fair. The Falkland Islands are more than four times the size of Hong Kong and make an annual income that would just about cover the petty cash for some of the Hong Kong companies. They are a constant temptation to any tin-pot Latin American General, out for some Gringo-bashing, who can increase the costs of defending the islands, merely by sending a training aircraft out to rhubarb the air defences from a safe distance. For the price of a couple of gallons of two-star kerosene he can cost the British taxpayer thousands in jet fuel.

Why not offer the Falkland Islanders and the Hong Kong Chinese a fair and decent deal that could benefit them both. The right for British born Hong Kong Chinese to take up residence there, if they wish, with their capital, and all their immense skills in business and finance, and develop the Falklands as they could be developed.

Sir Alexander Grantham, former Governor of Hong Kong, almost single-handedly created the present prosperity of the Colony by being open-minded enough to see the entrepreneurial refugees, as an asset rather than a nuisance. Are there those in the Falklands with similar vision? The thought of a Stanley Stock Exchange serving all the smart investors of Latin America is truly mind-boggling.

The Falklands are not going to get many, if any, British immigrants. They must know that; everybody in Argentina does. As long as they continue with a tiny population, they are going to be up for grabs sooner or later, and, sooner or later, the political climate in Britain will change enough for the Falklands to be a suitable candidate for dumping! Perhaps as a result of some esoteric deal with some Latin country in the EEC?

This possibility could become remote in a multi-racial Falkland Islands, managing an economy that could be as vibrant as that of present-day Hong Kong. Any would-be Peron would not only have to face up to the British, they would also be in trouble with the independent Afro-Asian countries.

Trade could be conducted with every country in the world, and young Falkland Islanders could, for the first time, have prospects of a future in their own homeland's modern business community rather than having to seek work abroad.It is possible, it could be done, if the will existed to go about it without racist preconceptions.

What has been most puzzling about the whole 'right of abode' affair, since it began some eight years ago, has been the presumption by the British that the whole 3.25 million Hong Kong British would immediately flock to Britain. It would not be unreasonable to accept what the majority have been saying up to now . . . that they want the right so that, if everything went horribly wrong in Hong Kong, they would have an internationally recognised right to leave.

Most Hong Kong people love living in the Colony. They do not want to leave it if that course of action can be avoided; only as a last resort will they go.

The British political parties are still in thrall to the East African Asian affair, where Britain was seen as being submerged in a flood of aliens, and there were political repercussions from the grass roots. Yet those people who came are most notable now for their industry, business acumen, and generally law-abiding nature. And many who did arrive in the first rush to escape from Idi Amin, very soon moved on to other lands such as Canada and America.

In the whole of my, nearly twenty-nine years, in the service of my Sovereign and my country, it was always a matter of pride to me, and the great majority of my contemporaries, that we British had a tradition that a man's nationality, or the colour of a man's skin did not count. It was the man himself who counted. That, as is said in Scotland, 'We're a' Jock Tamson's bairns'! It would be horrible to find out now that my belief in Britain's sense of fair play was stupid, and founded on a really big lie!

Portugal, one third the size of Britain, has granted her, nearly 500 000, Macao citizens of Chinese race, the right of abode. After 1992 any, or all, of them could come and settle here under EEC legislation. But then the Portuguese have never been exactly hysterical over a person's skin colour.

Strangely enough, the thought that it may all be due to racism is preferable to the unbearable idea that, 156 years after Wilberforce, and the abolition of slavery, we have come to some secret deal with China to hand over some 3 000 000 highly qualified slaves along with the real estate!

If Britain ever has to stand at the Bar of the Court of World Public Opinion over her policy towards the British Hong Kong Chinese, as a result of awful events in the Hong Kong Autonomous Region, they must inevitably bring in a verdict of Guilty of racial discrimination.

Although the old men in Peking visibly have the blood of their own murdered people on their hands, their betrayal only differs, at present, from that of the British political consensus, in that, what the British are doing to their own Hong Kong people, is racism concealed in white kid gloves!

JOI GEEN!

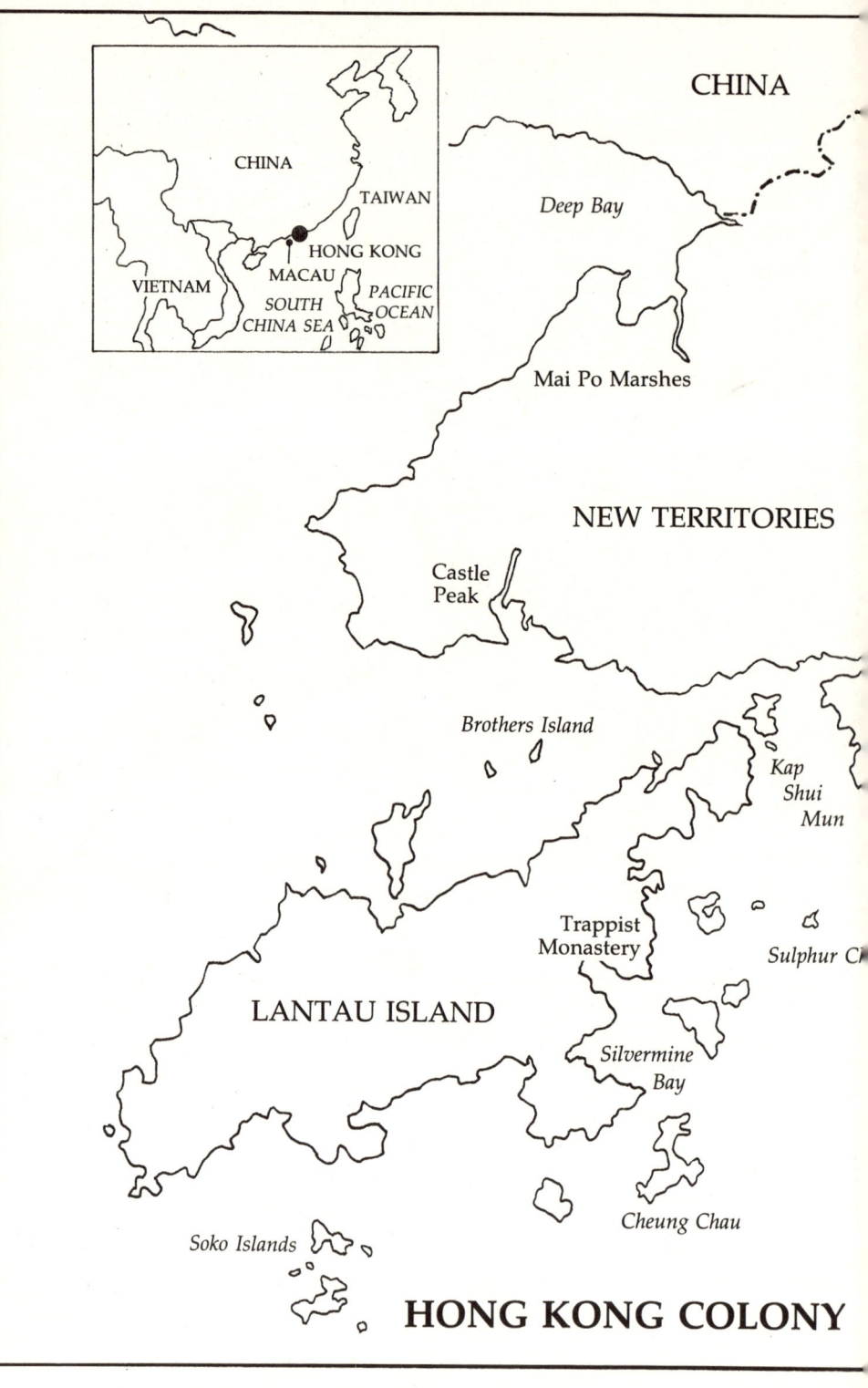

CHINA

Deep Bay

Mai Po Marshes

NEW TERRITORIES

Castle
Peak

Brothers Island

Kap
Shui
Mun

Trappist
Monastery

Sulphur C

LANTAU ISLAND

Silvermine
Bay

Cheung Chau

Soko Islands

HONG KONG COLONY

CHINA

TAIWAN

HONG KONG

MACAU

VIETNAM

SOUTH
CHINA SEA

PACIFIC
OCEAN